ABOUT THE
JOAN REVILL

Joan says:

I was fascinated by fortune-telling from as far back as I can remember and even 'descended' to Divination by Dice at one low point. However, when my progressed Sun reached Neptune, I discovered astrology. Up to then I hadn't realised it consisted of anything beyond knowing the zodiac signs. I don't think I thought about anything else for the next ten years. In those days, there were no astrology classes that I ever heard of, and the books available were pure slog and stodge - no doubt, deliberately guaranteed to put off any but the most determined. Still, my progressed Sun-Neptune would not be denied and I learned the hard way how to draw up a horoscope.

At the time I was trying to write and had a little success with a few humorous articles for magazines. I had seen <u>Prediction</u> and thought it would be a good idea to write a 'spoof' astrological profile and I picked on Sherlock Holmes. A book had just come out which, tongue-in-cheek, gave details of the great detective's private life, including birth data. No ordinary magazine editor would accept it - not surprisingly! - and I sent it to <u>Prediction</u> itself. After a while, dear old Harold Murton, the editor, sent me four guineas and said it would be wasted on his readers, but it had made him laugh and "how about writing some proper profiles?" He was deluged with them from then on. I still did the occasional fictitious character(s) - the Archers, the Forsytes etc., usually as light relief in the <u>Prediction Annual</u>. Some of these will be found in these pages. It all began - crikey! - thirty five years ago.

I had always read everything from Greek tragedy to sauce bottles, and squirrelled away fictitious birthdays, death days and events of any kind, hoping they would come in handy one day. And they have!

I have written three light 'Edwardian' novels as Jean Merrill, and a Young Adult book as Jean Revill. I have also co-authored with Jo Logan, editor of <u>Prediction</u>, <u>The Prediction Birthday Book</u>.

Joan Revill has the Sun in Cancer, the Moon in Leo and a Virgo ascendant.

First published in 2000 by Flare Publications.

A catalogue record for this book is available from the British Library.

ISBN 0-9530261-3-2

Design: Frank C. Clifford
Cover photo ©Bernd Ducke/Britstock-IFA (Tel: 0207 427 2300)

Editors: Fiona Graham, Frank C. Clifford
Astrological calculations produced by Esoteric Technologies' Solar Fire v4 -
www.esotech.com.au/

Printed by Biddles, Woodbridge Park Estate, Woodbridge Road,
Guildford, Surrey GU1 1DA

Every effort has been made to credit individuals whose words appear in this book. If we have accidentally omitted your name, please contact us and we'll update the source in the next edition.

The author's views are not necessarily those held by the Publisher. In addition, there may be mistakes, both typographical and in content, we would appreciate hearing from you if you discover any errors.

To Write to the Author:

To contact Joan Revill, please write
c/o Flare Publications, 29 Dolben Street, London SE1 0UQ, England

Visit our website at: **www.flareuk.com**

Flare Publications
P.O. Box 10126, London NW3 7WD, England (manuscripts)
Head Office: 29 Dolben Street, London SE1 0UQ, England (sales/written enquiries)

THE
SUN SIGN
READER

WHAT ASTROLOGY REVEALS ABOUT
AUTHORS, BOOKS AND FICTIONAL CHARACTERS

BY

JOAN REVILL

Flare Publications

Flare Astro-Profiles series
2000

THE SUN SIGN READER

We bookworm-astrologers have a field day when authors give one of their characters a birthday or a pertinent event an exact date. The most we can hope for and, indeed, are grateful for, is the resulting Sun sign but, occasionally, the year is also given. This enables a solar chart to be drawn up and real progressions and transits to be worked out with a fair degree of accuracy. Even more occasionally, a time is included which is treasure trove. Family sagas and soap operas are the best sources for these. Additionally, literary events are often dated. Again, these are of interest to the astrologer.

Why do authors select a particular day for a character to be born or for something to happen?

Do they know enough astrology to deliberately select a particular sign or configuration? Is the old subconscious working overtime? Is it all haphazard and meaningless?

Are the characters comfortable in the zodiac signs? Do the events in their fictitious lives coincide with the movements of the planets?

The Sun Sign Reader explores these questions and many more.

Here and there, along with the fiction, there are facts - dates of publications and birthdays of authors, for instance. There is also a space every day for your own notable dates, fact or fiction, to see how they rate.

First, to refresh memories and to get into the right mood, let's meet the characters and players found in the zodiac.

Happy reading!

Joan Revill

ARIES

ARIES the Ram is under the rulership of Mars. It's the first sign of the zodiac starting the astrological year on March 20/21 when the Sun enters it and day and night are of equal length all over the world. From this premier position it can be deduced easily that Ariens take the lead in everything as a matter of course. You will always find Ariens in the Top Ten. They are full of energy and enthusiasm which, if not used constructively, will be used destructively, so watch it! They are natural fighters. Should they be pacifists then they will be murderously militant pacifists, bopping the other side with their protest placards. They love speed and living dangerously. They are brave but wild, tactless and unbiddable. Basically kind but impatient and on a short fuse. It is the young man's sign with all the qualities and defects which go with that state. If not themselves capable of aggressiveness, their lives are likely to be violent and packed with crises. Healthwise they are prone to accidents or collapse through nervous exhaustion. Aries rules the head so migraines are another hazard. They have an Old Testament eye-for-an-eye philosophy and advocate strong government with no waffling. They are pioneers opening up new territories, high pressure sales persons, confident, uncomplicated and unaware of trodden-on-toes!

ARIEN KEYWORDS

- Number 1, first, beginning, new, pioneer, masculinity.
- Sunrise, birth, young man, first 30 years of life.
- Strong, brave, swashbuckling, military matters.
- Boss, leader, dictator, metal worker, butcher, soldier, surgeon, dentist, adventurer, revolutionary, crusader, fighter (hits back instantly), champion, hero, sport.
- Aggressive, ambitious, confident, optimistic, precocious, extrovert.
- Active, energetic, volatile, impatient, hyperactive.
- Simple, primitive, uncomplicated, savage.
- Head and face, prominent nose. Hair, hats and headgear.
- Wounds, rawness, burns, scalds, stings, blisters, headaches, neuralgia, blood, blood pressure, insomnia, stress through overwork.
- Disasters, explosions, accidents, operations, violence, speed, noise, anger, destruction.
- Heat, fire, fever.
- Razor, knife, sword, gun, battering ram, sharp instrument.
- Ram, mastiff, wolf, tiger, ant, rat.
- Ardent sex, lust, passion.
- Iron and steel, metal, engines, tools.
- England, Denmark, Germany, Poland, Japan.
- Thorns, thistles, broom, gorse, wormwood, nettles, cacti, chives, onions, peppers, highly-spiced foods, garlic, horseradish, mustard, absinthe.
- Red, ruby, bloodstone, diamond, bright primal colours.
- The small print!...Selfish, egoist, vain, greedy, coarse, overbearing, insensitive to others' feelings, demanding, rude, hot-tempered, fool-hardy, mad, fanatical, criminal, murderer.

~Introducing the Players ~

ARIES - KEY TYPES

✳ From a <u>Verray Parfit Gentil Knight</u> to <u>Noddy</u>

Leading the Arien Key Types must be Chaucer's VERRAY PARFIT GENTIL KNIGHT who was one of the pilgrims travelling to Canterbury. He espoused chivalry, truth and honour and had acquitted himself nobly in war. 'He wore a fustian tunic stained and dark/With smudges where his armour had left mark.' Also of his type is Sir Walter Scott's Crusader IVANHOE wearing the <u>Red</u> Cross of St. George, the lovely Rowena's champion in a trial by combat, and, from C.S. Lewis's Narnia, REEPICHEEP the chivalrous heroic mouse, a true knight whose outsize courage belied his small stature. His sword seemed never to be in its sheath and he wore a <u>red</u> feather in a circlet on his head. Then, every <u>Boys Own Paper</u> hero of G.A. Henty (<u>With Clive in India</u> etc.) and Baroness Orczy's Sir Percy Blakeney, the SCARLET PIMPERNEL. Fearless champions of the weak and Defenders of the Faith every one.

But even Aries can't keep up this standard and the Key Types too often degenerate into bad-tempered Angry Young Men whose energy spills over into anarchic political views like Kingsley Amis's LUCKY JIM's and professional blood-letters and military men like DR SLAMMER in <u>Pickwick Papers</u> who was a surgeon of the 97th. A choleric gentleman, very conscious of his honour, who challenged poor Mr. Winkle to a duel.

As for the ladies, before the new aggressive career woman came in to catalogue her own Key Type, they usually had to take out their energies in the home. Dickens had a perfect example in MRS. McSTINGER (<u>Dombey & Son</u>), a legendary springcleaner, off any one of whose floors an individual might have ate his dinner. She had appalling Great Cleaning Days when she was knocked up by the policeman on the beat at quarter to three in the morning and rarely succumbed before midnight, the object being that all the furniture had to be moved into the back garden at dawn and back again after dark. <u>Alice in Wonderland</u>'s QUEEN OF HEARTS, with her reiterated Arien cry of 'Off with his head', was a termagant whose gardeners had to paint the white roses red to escape decapitation. 'I picture to myself the Queen of Hearts as a sort of embodiment of ungovernable passion - a blind and aimless Fury' wrote Lewis Carroll. Not all Ariens go to such lengths but their favoured course <u>is</u> to chop through all difficulties.

Seriously immature Ariens join Enid Blyton's NODDY in his bright primary colours, driving his little car without anything like due care and attention, knocking down lamp posts and occasionally P.C. Plod. 'Well, they shouldn't get in my way' is Noddy's true-to-Key-Type defence.

~Introducing the Players ~

TAURUS

TAURUS the Bull is under the rulership of Venus. Strong, rock-like and enduring. Because they are so rational, sensible and down-to-earth, they are sometimes written off as slow, lazy and pig-headed in their obstinacy. The more primitive types may be, and all are regular in their habits leaving a well-worn rut behind them, but what does it matter as long as they're happy? And they are. Happy. And naturally good. Good-hearted, good-humoured. They are quiet, calm and charming with healing hands and voices until poked once too often when they become indomitable and implacable fighters. It is the sign most closely allied with money and materialism. Taureans are no luckier or greedier than anyone else but they have an enviable gift for handling and investing money wisely. Usually reckoned to be comfortably off through building up and conserving what they have. They are happiest in 'solid' occupations like agriculture, banking and building. At their best in the country growing radishes amongst their prize roses. Affectionate and loyal partners and parents. Perhaps surprisingly in such stolid folk there is a talent for the arts, particularly painting and writing. Their prose and poetry are so rich and textured that they appear to be painted too. They are musical. In fact, Taurus is one of the most likeable and worthy of all the signs.

TAUREAN KEYWORDS

- ⇨ Sign of Fixed Earth, earthy, immovable.
- ⇨ Solid, unflappable, slow, careful, sensible. May become lazy without stimulus.
- ⇨ Money, possessions. Treasurers, accountants, bankers, cashiers.
- ⇨ Food, larders, creature comforts, gourmands, pleasures of the table. Chefs, cooks, luxury, gracious living.
- ⇨ Agriculture, farmyard animals. Farmers, gardeners, greengrocers, florists, flowers. Country pursuits and sports. Conservationists.
- ⇨ Practical, arts and crafts, builders, architects, interior designers, feng shui experts. Manual workers, labourers.
- ⇨ Patient, enduring, don't accept defeat, reliable, industrious.
- ⇨ Throat and neck. Lovely voices. Singers.
- ⇨ Handsome. Girls have fairy tale princess looks, men are corpulent and strong.
- ⇨ Emerald, green.
- ⇨ Green countryside, particularly Ireland which traditionally comes under Taurus, but also rural England. John Bull who typifies old England is, by his very name, Taurean, a stout, down-to-earth character.
- ⇨ Soothing, calm, unexciting, contented, conservative, orthodox, conventional but, if moved, terrible in wrath.
- ⇨ Charm, strong sexual feelings, affectionate, faithful, tactile. Love to feel and touch and to be touched. Fabrics. Clay, stone, wood, all natural materials.
- ⇨ Dancers, musicians, artists, appreciation of the rich tapestry of words, good sense of colour, great sense of humour.
- ⇨ And then, despite all the above, comes the kink in the Bull's tail. Often, under the prosaic exterior the opposite sign of Scorpio casts a dark shadow over the sunlit meadow. A sinister, hidden world of faerie, magic, mystery and revenge is glimpsed momentarily.
- ⇨ The small print!...Gluttons, boring, dull stick-in-the-muds.

~Introducing the Players ~

TAURUS - KEY TYPES

✳ From <u>Ferdinand the Bull</u> to <u>Bill Sikes</u>

First must be FERDINAND the BULL from <u>The Story of Ferdinand</u> by Munro Leaf. He was of a dreamy peaceful nature, sitting under a cork tree enjoying nature thankful that he was too placid to ever be chosen for the bullring. Then he was stung by a bee and, instantly changing into a roused Taurean, went berserk, puffing and snorting and pawing the ground. This display landed him in the arena but the perfume of the flowers in the ladies' hair acted as a tranquilliser and he had to be returned to his cork tree to enjoy the beauty of the countryside again. MA and PA LARKIN from <u>The Darling Buds of May</u> by H.E. Bates also enjoyed an idyllic rural life style. Perfick! They also delighted in the pleasures of sex, for this sign is ruled by Venus in her negative or earthy guise. Chaucer's lusty WIFE of BATH actually was a Taurean as she told her fellow pilgrims. She boasted of being 'gap-toothed...it is the print of Venus and her seal.' She had had five husbands and was on the lookout for another. 'Alas, alas, that ever love was sin! I ever followed natural inclination/Under the power of my constellation.' Another key type of that illustrious company was the MILLER. The Wife of Bath was of a generous size and the Miller was a chap of 16 stone, a champion wrestler and a drinker with a store of tavern stories, filthy in the main! Taurus isn't mealy-mouthed and faces the Facts of Life with great humour and pulling no punches. He also played the bagpipes which satisfies Taurus's musical bent. MR. WALDO in Dylan Thomas's <u>Under Milk Wood</u> was 'seventeen snoring gentle stone'. Dickens' MRS. JARLEY in <u>The Old Curiosity Shop</u> was a Christian lady, stout and comfortable to look upon, who was the owner of a travelling waxworks, thus combining the gourmandising side of Taurus with the artistic. Taureans can become more than comfortable, they can become grossly overweight like the FAT BOY in <u>Pickwick Papers</u> and Frank Richards' BILLY BUNTER. They endear themselves by their delight in the pleasures of the table.

Another Key Type is JOHN WILLET the landlord of the Maypole Inn in Dickens' <u>Barnaby Rudge</u>. He was burly and renowned for his extreme obstinacy, slowness of apprehension and his dogged belief 'that what he said or did was right, and holding it was a thing quite settled and ordained...that anybody who said or did or thought otherwise must be inevitably and of necessity wrong.'

BULLDOG DRUMMOND the hefty, slogging-his-way-out-of-trouble, rather thick but intensely loyal hero of Sapper's thrillers is a Taurean Key Type and at rock bottom there's the brutal, bullying BILL SIKES in Dickens' <u>Oliver Twist</u>.

~Introducing the Players ~

GEMINI

GEMINI the Twins is under the rulership of Mercury. Jumping Geminis. The accent is on youth. They are attracted to young people and their current fads and consequently keep youthful in appearance and outlook themselves. Child prodigies, perpetual students. Versatile, witty, sophisticated, very intelligent but childishly mischievous and naughty. The 'primitives' are actively dishonest and live on their wits at others' expense. Fast talking, fast thinking. Must meet people, many ephemeral acquaintances. As this is the sign of the Twins - and they are no more likely to be or have twins than anyone else - it is nevertheless regarded as dualistic and two-faced. Life does seem to present them with two careers, two marriages, two children, two choices - two of everything. Communications of all kinds are highlighted - the Internet, E-mail, even the old-fashioned telephone and word processor. Writing is second nature to them, invariably clear and competent, factual rather than imaginative; humorous verse and parodies, juggling with words and rhymes. Crossword and Scrabble addicts. They have to be on the move and make good couriers and reporters. Slick and fashionable, fast and slap-dash. In looks true Geminis are tall and slender with long thin expressive hands and faces, rarely in repose. Athletic, dextrous but rather delicate and highly strung. Nervous complaints emanating from sensitivity such as allergies and asthma.

GEMINIAN KEYWORDS

⇨ Sign of the Twins. Not to be taken too literally but they often have a sibling who is very close or a friendship which seems karmic for good or ill. Are said to be two faced but they are so multi-faceted that they seem to lead double lives. Or treble. Or quadruple....

⇨ Extroverts, charmers, party-goers. Lovely smiles.

⇨ Light-hearted, slapdash, talkative, inquisitive, quick-witted, good at repartee, flippant.

⇨ Unsettled, impermanent, ceaseless comings and goings, meetings, mobility, quicksilver.

⇨ Cars, bicycles, journeys.

⇨ Crosswords, I.Q. tests, puzzles, labyrinths, trivial pursuits, words, names, pen-names.

⇨ Nerves, always on the go, hypochondria, psychiatrists.

⇨ Precocious, perpetual adolescents and students, young folk, flirts, gypsies.

⇨ Black coffee, stimulants, cigarettes, snack meals, vitamins, gadgets, toys.

⇨ Mischievous sense of humour, elves, 'little folk'.

⇨ Insects, birds, flying.

⇨ Letters, messages, telephone conversations, flying visits.

⇨ Lungs, bronchitis, asthma, allergies, delicate looking, tall and thin, lack stamina.

⇨ Hands, fingers, rings, gloves, bracelets, watches. Pianists.

⇨ Draughtsmen, cartoonists, caricaturists.

⇨ Tailors, needles, pinpricks.

⇨ Sharp, stinging, biting, satirists, guerrilla warfare.

⇨ Education, schools, playgroups, teachers, writers, enquiring minds,

⇨ The 1920s, art deco, glitter, sequins, glass, chrome, clarity.

⇨ U.S.A., London.

⇨ The small print!...Fibbers, conmen, childish, silly, shallow, light-fingered.

~Introducing the Players ~

GEMINI - KEY TYPES

* From <u>The Lordly Ones</u> to <u>Cut-Me-Own-Throat Dibbler</u>

'How beautiful they are the LORDLY ONES/Who dwell in the hills/In the hollow hills!' wrote William Sharp in <u>The Immortal Hour</u>. And it's up into airy Gemini's realm of Elves and Fairies, who were forces to be reckoned with in the Old Days. Shakespeare's ARIEL in <u>The Tempest</u> and J.R.R. Tolkien's LEGOLAS in <u>The Lord of the Rings</u> are the finest types. The sexless sprite Ariel could ride on 'the curl'd clouds'. Legolas the elf never aged or tired.

HARLEQUIN, once always a part of pantomime, bridges the gap between the ethereal and the earthly. He's a quick darting Mercurial figure, not scrupulously honest, a mischief maker, but so light and graceful, so clever and smart! Gemini has the gift of the gab and Congreve's heroine MILLAMANT in <u>The Way of the World</u> was a witty coquette with some brilliant dialogue. 'Let us be very strange and well-bred. Let us be as strange as if we had been married a great while; and as well-bred as if we were not married at all.' Alice, when <u>Through the Looking Glass</u>, got into metaphysical fisticuffs with those argumentative mirror-twins, TWEEDLEDUM and TWEEDLEDEE who explained logic to her. 'Contrariwise, if it was so, it might be; and if it were so, it would be; but as it isn't, it ain't.' And there's W.M. Praed's garrulous VICAR whose '...talk was like a stream which runs/With rapid change from rocks to roses;/It slipped from politics to puns,/It passed from Mahomet to Moses.' P.G. Woodhouse's BERTIE WOOSTER is a flippant Gemini type. 'Look at the tall thin one with the face like a motor mascot!' invited the Herald of the Red Dawn from his soapbox. 'Has he ever done an honest day's work in his life? No! He's a trifler!' (He's a Geminian!) MRS. BAYHAM BADGER in <u>Bleak House</u> painted a little, played the piano, harp and guitar a little, sang a little, read a little, wrote poetry a little, botanised a little and rouged a little. Another Dickensian dilettante in the same novel was HAROLD SKIMPOLE, 'a little bright creature...with a delicate face and a sweet voice - there was a perfect charm in him. All he said was so free from effort, spontaneous and with such a captivating gaiety that it was fascinating to hear him...'

In the remaindered drawer there's MR. FAIRLEIGH from Wilkie Collins' <u>The Woman in White</u>. He was the nervy type who must be protected from anything disagreeable at whatever cost to anyone else; in his case from signing over his niece's fortune to a rogue to his hysterical aversion to squeaky boots. Terry Pratchett's CUT-ME-OWN-THROAT DIBBLER resides in Discworld. He sells anything that can be sold hurriedly from an open suitcase in a busy street. A modern Harlequin.

~Introducing the Players ~

CANCER

CANCER the Crab comes under the rulership of the Moon. A feminine sign and most girls are at home here ending up as happy wives and mums, cooking and gossiping, reading romantic novels, rivetted to the 'soaps', home-making, keeping the family together. Shy with outsiders but kind, sympathetic and helpful. They crave well-stocked store cupboards and are good in hotels and large institutions ordering supplies on a grand scale. They squirrel away money and possessions and are fearful of <u>not having enough</u>! The men don't get off so well. They are often dominated by mother and lose, or are out of sympathy with, father. Cancerians are all conditioned by what happens to them in childhood and parents should remember this. A suffocating feminine influence makes them caring and charming but also hypersensitive which may warp their relationships when adult. Then they live solitary secluded lives, don't marry or marry late, often to a mother figure, an older woman-of-the-world, a widow. Some boys, especially the clever, imaginative ones escape into homosexuality. Others fight and go to the other extreme of bullying or ignoring women, living rough and indulging in macho behaviour. This type becomes the Empire building megalomaniac. Growing a protective shell is a common Cancerian trait for both sexes. Top heavy appearance. Should have a home by the sea.

CANCERIAN KEYWORDS

- ➭ Feminine principle. Mother, mothers and babies. Wife.
- ➭ The public, the hoi polloi.
- ➭ Seas, rivers, seashores, voyages, fishing, shells, armour, crustaceans, snails.
- ➭ Home-loving, domesticated. Catering trades.
- ➭ Passive, timid but fiercely possessive. Snappy if threatened.
- ➭ Nurturing, protective of self and others.
- ➭ Sensitive, easily hurt, haunted by suffering.
- ➭ Dreams, the occult and supernatural. Psychic. Mystics.
- ➭ Romantic, sentimental.
- ➭ Moods dependent on Moon's phases. Reflect others' emotions.
- ➭ Sympathetic, kind.
- ➭ Cautious, prudent, security-minded, savers, collectors.
- ➭ History, antiques, nostalgia. Edwardian era.
- ➭ Story-tellers, fantasy worlds, make-believe, imaginative, intuitive.
- ➭ Self-effacing, shy, brooding, inferiority complex.
- ➭ Charming, affectionate, harmless, humorous. Good memory.
- ➭ Business people. Entrepreneurs. Rovers.
- ➭ Breasts. Top-heavy appearance. Sideways progression. Emotional upsets, gastritis.
- ➭ Scotland, Africa, clan/tribal mentality. Belonging. Patriotic.
- ➭ Twilight, camellias, magnolias, water lilies, feminine fashions.
- ➭ Milk, cream, butter.
- ➭ Pearls, moonstones, silver, silk, white, cream, pale colours.
- ➭ The small print!...Mother fixations, prejudiced, zenophobic, childish sulks, clinging vines, morbid imaginations. Fat, lazy, sluttish. Hypochondriacs, neurotics. Boring.

~Introducing the Players ~

CANCER - KEY TYPES

✳ From <u>Moses</u> to <u>Polly Garter</u>

Books have been written theorising that the historical MOSES was mostly fictitious, a necessary legend borrowed from other cultures so, first and foremost, a literary Moses leading his people to the Promised Land with their flocks of sheep and goats illustrates the sign's protectiveness and homing instincts.

Lesser Key Types provide those whose instincts are still to defend family and possessions although not so heroically. SCARLET O'HARA in Margaret Mitchell's <u>Gone With The Wind</u> only really cared about her home, Tara. In the animal kingdom MOLE and BADGER in A.A. Milne's <u>Wind in the Willows</u>, have similar feelings for their own hearthstones. Mole, who had been living with Ratty, was suddenly and unexpectedly homesick. 'Shabby indeed, and small and poorly furnished, and yet his. And the home had been happy with him, too, evidently, and was missing him, and wanted him back and was telling him so...but with no bitterness or anger, only with plaintive reminder that it was there and wanted him.' Badger approved of Mole and showed him round his rambling domain because Mole understood what domestic architecture ought to be. In Professor Tolkien's Middle Earth, HOBBITS lived in warm, cosy, womb-like hobbit-holes with curved panelled sides, round windows and doors and well-stocked store-rooms. They were once a matriarchal society and had a passion for family history. Other types are manacled to the people rather than the place. They are fiercely possessive of their families like every JEWISH MOM who has ever been written about (loads!): MRS. MICAWBER (<u>David Copperfield</u>) who never would desert Mr. Micawber and who was rarely seen without one of the twins attached to her taking refreshment, and KANGA, in the A.A. Milne stories who kept baby Roo buttoned up in her pocket. Other Key Types are practically chained to their homes and worry constantly about them like Tove Jansson's obsessed housewife FILLYJONK in Moominland. 'It isn't fair. Nothing like this happens to anyone in my circle of acquaintances, only to me!'

David Copperfield was enchanted by DANIEL PEGGOTTY and his snug home which was a converted boat on Yarmouth beach. Dan was another Cancer type, the kindest of men who, although poor, took in lame ducks and only lost his temper and swore he would be 'Gormed!' if his generosity was ever mentioned. Terry Pratchett's SAMUEL VIMES, Captain of the City Watch, wasn't ambitious and worked his way sideways (the Crab's natural gait) rather than up. He was morose and cynical but like all true Cancer types, pink marshmallow inside. Pink marshmallow inside and out is POLLY GARTER, no-better-than-she-should-be, under the washing line in Dylan Thomas's <u>Under Milk Wood</u>, 'giving the breast to my bonny new baby. Nothing grows in our garden, only washing. And babies.'

~Introducing the Players ~

LEO

LEO the Lion is under the rulership of the Sun. By Divine Right Leos are the radiant ones of the zodiac! In looks the true ones are large and impressive with high complexions, broad faces and manes of hair. Men tend to be bearded and patriarchal, women glamorous and curvaceous. They are a mixture of arrogance and good nature, charm and ruthlessness. They like constant amusement and flattery. In fact, Leos are no grander or cleverer than anyone else but they manage to give the impression that they are! They want to be on the top table with the VIPs at some traditional 'do' where mere people aren't admitted, but the simple life also appeals, providing the mashed potatoes are superlatively cooked and served, the cutlery correctly placed and of antique silver. Leos can be cruel and insensitive to others' pain when the love of power gets twisted but, in ordinary circumstances, they are agreeable and benevolent enough, although they do like proper gratitude and appreciation. They attend the grand religious celebrations, splendidly dressed, and patronise the arts even if they have no talent of their own. They are good at heading a corporation as they can think big and delegate. In short, Leos are excellent at telling other people what to do. Leo rules the heart and this is said to be the weak spot, not helped by Leo's tendency to put on weight - they love their food and wine!

LEONINE KEYWORDS

⇨ Royal, famous, figurehead, front man, boss, hero, larger than life, imposing, imperial, dignified, noble, honourable, ladies and gentlemen, Society. Father, husband.
⇨ Uncomplicated, sunny temper, warm loving nature, radiant, striking, good manners.
⇨ Heart, centre, robust health, strong, fine head of hair, commanding, authoritative, stout, broad, handsome, upper part heavily built then tapers away.
⇨ Grand scale, king size, big ideas, ambition.
⇨ Religious, divine inspiration, spiritual, myth and legends.
⇨ Extravagant, generous, Stock Exchange, inherited wealth.
⇨ Bright colours, jewels, massive displays, gold, amber, topaz, ceremonial dress, expensive clothes, cosmetics.
⇨ Citrus fruits, plants which follow the sun.
⇨ France, Italy, Rome, Bath.
⇨ Misplaced trust, easily deceived.
⇨ Fidelity, loyalty.
⇨ Love of children.
⇨ Creative, actors, musicians, writers.
⇨ Classics, classic architecture, cars etc.
⇨ Courageous, confident, successful, desire for glory and admiration. Want to be loved.
⇨ Conscious of social position, hierarchy, family pride, caste, tradition.
⇨ Comfort loving, hedonist, connoisseur of food and wine, luxury, warmth, cats.
⇨ Delegates, the broad canvas.
⇨ Historic buildings, castles, palaces, mansions, country houses, grand gardens, parks and pleasure grounds, conservatories.
⇨ The small print!...arrogant, toady to superiors and browbeat inferiors, show-offs, snobbish, vain, greedy, selfish, social climbers, self-important.

~Introducing the Players ~

LEO - KEY TYPES

✳ From <u>Sons of the Morning</u> to <u>Humpty Dumpty</u>

The grandest Leo Key Types are radiant like Wordworth's '...happy few, who dwell on earth yet breathe empyreal air - SONS OF THE MORNING', (<u>The Excursion</u>). In C.S. Lewis's Narnia books there's a splendid royal lion, ASLAN, who fits the bill and, in fact, symbolises Christ.

The next best Key Types are regal, the arbiters of their own little circles. HYACINTH BUCKET - sorry Bouquet - for example, giving her renowned candlelit suppers in <u>Keeping Up Appearances</u>. And she looks the part - large, well-dressed, brimming with confidence. EMMELINE LUCAS in the E.F. Benson <u>Lucia</u> novels is the Queen of Riseholme Society and an arch-snob. She is more Up Market than Hyacinth being able to drop into Italian and having servants. She patronises the arts and plays pianoforte duets. A.A. Milne's CHRISTOPHER ROBIN is regarded as a god by his nursery animal friends and wears his authority easily.

The EARL of CLINCHAM in Daisy Ashford's <u>The Young Visiters</u> led a merry life in his 'compartments' at the Crystale Pallace and was not averse to getting Mr. Salteena into High Society - for a price (£42.). He dressed for the Prince of Wales's 'levie' in satin knickerbockers with diamond clasps, to say nothing of a splendid cocked hat, while ETHEL MONTACUE was a hoity-toity miss, always out for a good time, who took to life at the Gaierty Hotel like a duck to water. Dickens produced the aptly-named MRS. LEO HUNTER. She collected celebrities - head-hunted them, as her name implies. Mr. Pickwick was caught in her version of a candlelit supper - a fancy dress breakfast, a feast of reason and a flow of soul. She wrote the celebrated <u>Ode to an Expiring Frog</u>.

Two dictators, both stout and with overweening opinions of themselves are NAPOLEON the pig in George Orwell's <u>Animal Farm</u>, who became corrupted by power, and A.A. Milne's TOAD of Toad Hall. Toad lived in a mansion and had been left well-off by his father. He just had to keep in front of the Joneses with first a caravan and then a powerful motor car. Good-hearted but a complete egomaniac.

Finally HUMPTY DUMPTY, portly and imposing, who is on such excellent terms with royalty. In <u>Through the Looking Glass</u> he insists that he is not proud and shakes hands with Alice to prove it, but he is obviously a most superior egg. Even words, awkward and fretful for most of us, know their place with Humpty and understand that they have to mean what he wants them to mean. Which is to be Master - that's all. With typical Leonian magnanimity he paid them overtime for doing extra work.

~Introducing the Players ~

VIRGO

VIRGO is under the rulership of Mercury. Reserved, unassuming, matter-of-fact, plain dealers, practical, common-sensible. Traditionally regarded as modest but, in fact, they have an excellent opinion of themselves and a pretty poor one of everyone else. Irritatingly critical. However, they set themselves impossibly high standards, even higher than those they set for others. They must <u>not</u> be wrong! They are the powers behind the throne, super-efficient public servants who are unknown to the public - which suits aloof Virgo. Discreet, discriminating, good judges of quality and workmanship as they are so meticulous themselves. Pessimists, realists, cynics, prone to melancholia and nervous breakdowns. They see everything in black or white and are considered harsh. True they aren't sympathetic but will help those genuinely in need although they can't resist throwing in a moral lecture. They don't attract much notice or get much help but prefer to rise by their own efforts. They work hard and are good at examinations. They are teachers, librarians, researchers and do-ers of detailed, fiddly, precision work. Useless at showing emotion and often remain celibate. Their homes are simple and uncluttered. They are picky vegetarian, non-smoking teetotallers, easily scared by the latest health alarms. Hypochondriacs despite being determined keep-fitters and calorie counters.

VIRGOAN KEYWORDS

⇨ Clever, industrious, perfectionist, self-critical, conscientious.
⇨ Teachers, librarians, secretaries, PAs.
⇨ Purity, spotless, immaculate, celibate, moral, prudish, young girls, virgins.
⇨ Medical types, physical fitness, clinical, hygiene.
⇨ Worriers, 'nerves', stress, ulcers, digestive disorders, asthma, eczema, lame.
⇨ Health foods, food fads, alternative medicines, vegetarians, environmentalists.
⇨ Handsome, girls particularly have classical beauty. Tall, slender. Small well-formed hands and feet. Good with hands, skilled worker, craftsmen, practical.
⇨ Neat and tidy, well-dressed and groomed, elegant, fashion plates, dressmakers.
⇨ Cool, stand-offish, efficient, quiet, discriminating, logical, rational.
⇨ Witty, wry sense of humour, sharp tongue.
⇨ Switzerland, Paris.
⇨ Readers, writers, scholars, students, offices, books, newspapers, facts.
⇨ Budgets, figures, accuracy, careful with money.
⇨ Nonconformist, cynical, unemotional, pessimists, tied to routine.
⇨ Gardeners. Herbs, shrubby plants, cereals, cornfields, small bright bedding plants, municipal gardens, lilly-of-the-valley, lavender, nut trees.
⇨ Quicksilver, agate, black and white. Intricate, complicated patterns.
⇨ Fastidious, minutely analytical, details, dextrous.
⇨ Shy, reserved, no 'side', working class, small businesses, unpretentious.
⇨ Miniatures, watches, musical boxes, mechanical toys.
⇨ Service to others, public service, humble, household drudges, hard toil with little reward, cleaners, servitude. Subordinate, power behind the throne.
⇨ Socialists. Education, self-improvement.
⇨ The small print!...old maidish, fussy, complaining, hypochondriacs, hidebound.

VIRGO - KEY TYPES

* From <u>Maud</u> to <u>Mr. Woodhouse</u>

For the top grade Key Types look for purity and perfection as exemplified by Lord Tennyson's MAUD '...faultily faultless. Icily regular... dead perfection.' Coming down to earth, Virgo is the workers' sign ranging from the valued upper servant downwards. P.G. Woodhouse's omnipotent JEEVES must lead the way. MALVOLIO in <u>Twelfth Night</u> was steward to Olivia who used him with 'exalted respect' but unfortunately his holier-than-thou attitude - a common Virgo fault - led to his downfall. Lewis Carroll's WHITE RABBIT in <u>Alice</u> was a Court official, timid, perpetually worried and overworked. He, of course, lived in a neat little house with W. RABBIT on a well polished brass plate and wore spotless white kid gloves. There is a finish about Virgo work, whether technical or artistic. <u>He</u> always has the little slots in the screws at the same angle, <u>her</u> stitchery is minute and precise. They excel at detailed work and fiddly occupations. Dickens' JENNY WREN (<u>Our Mutual Friend</u>) and MISS LA CREEVY (<u>Nicholas Nickleby</u>) must have been Virgos. Tiny Jenny Wren made dolls' clothes for a living and Miss La Creevy ('a mincing young lady of fifty') painted miniatures. Jenny, moreover, was lame, a common Virgo affliction, and had a very sharp tongue.

No one would dare pity a true Virgo, however apparently poor and unlucky. They are often solitaries like the CAT in Kipling's <u>Just So Stories</u> who 'walked by himself and all places were alike to him.' They are not the marrying sort. Many are celibate or marry late. MISS RACHEL WARDLE 'the Spinster Aunt' in <u>Pickwick Papers</u> had a touch-me-not-ishness in her very walk. In Dylan Thomas's <u>Under Milk Wood</u> MISS MYFANWY PRICE and the draper MR. MOG EDWARDS were apparently madly in love yet neither had the slightest intention of giving up their single bliss. Another Key Type to awaken on that famous morning in <u>Under Milk Wood</u> was MRS. OGMORE PRITCHARD in her 'iceberg-white, holily laundered crinoline nightgown.' She took the sign's sanitised image to its ultimate. Although advertising for paying guests she refused all bookings as she objected to persons in her nice clean rooms breathing all over her chairs. Virgos wage war on dust and disorder and nasty germs which accounts for their fascinated perusal of their <u>Family Doctor</u> (unpteenth edition).

Some take up medicine as a career but more are likely to turn into hypochondriacs like dear, nervous MR. WOODHOUSE in Jane Austen's <u>Emma</u>, ('An egg boiled very soft is not unwholesome.') On the lowest grade are the drudges and skivvies like THE MARCHONESS in Dickens' <u>Old Curiosity Shop</u>. They are the do-ers of all the dirty jobs, unsung and unthanked, but without them civilisation would collapse. Virgos like to congratulate themselves on that!

~Introducing the Players ~

LIBRA

LIBRA the Scales is under the rulership of Venus. They just have to be charming and delightful to qualify! Eager to please and to be pleased, polite, civilised, sociable. Rather sentimental, perhaps shallow, all-on-the-surface people. They side-step trouble or try to patch things up and negotiate between warring factions. Artistic work and the luxury trades attract, so do <u>feng shui</u>, interior decorating, flower arranging, collecting <u>objets d'art</u> and antiques. Their homes are marvels of space and light. Valuable vases contain one perfect spray of flowers; oriental pictures painted on silk adorn the walls. They live for love; must have a partner even if they quarrel. The most flirtatious, tender and loving sign of the zodiac. Not much interested in children unless they are very pretty and cute. High-flyers at fashion. Exotic foreign dishes are provided for their classy dinner parties. Having said all that there is a darker side. Some Librans take to a military career and are anything but peace loving. This may be a reflection of their opposite sign Aries or the outcome of the strong Libran wish to achieve a balance and harmony. In some cases, to do this it is necessary to employ strong arm tactics and knock heads together. Similarly the mimic warfare of the law courts leads others into the legal profession. It is the sign of Justice after all.

LIBRAN KEYWORDS

- ⇨ Sweetness and light. Charm, beauty, peace, happiness, pleasure-loving, social graces, dreamy, fantasy-loving.
- ⇨ Rather 'precious'.
- ⇨ Collectors of antiques, ornamentation, good taste, elegance, fashionable, dancers, entertainers.
- ⇨ Plump, dimpled, clear skin. Young girls.
- ⇨ Well-liked, gentle, accomplished, amiable, ladies and gentlemen, nice manners.
- ⇨ Partnership, marriage, harmony. Flirtatious, affectionate.
- ⇨ Connoisseurs, lovely homes. Polished, civilised, delicate, refined.
- ⇨ Perfumes, luxuries.
- ⇨ Balance, even keel, calm, soothing.
- ⇨ Indecision, sitting on the fence, seeing both sides.
- ⇨ Justice, law and order, legal practitioners, arbitrators, diplomats, fair play, urbane, aristocratic.
- ⇨ Pastel shades.
- ⇨ Roses, vines, apricots, rose quartz, copper, tinsel, spangles, coral, confectionery, sweet light wines, sugar and spice.
- ⇨ Far East, Japan, North China, Tibet, Vienna.
- ⇨ Kidneys, lumbago.
- ⇨ Doves.
- ⇨ BUT if the scales are upset Librans become belligerent and warlike presumably because of the urge to keep stability. If things seem to be going too much one way, then Libra will use violence if necessary to keep the balance steady.
- ⇨ The small print!...They back away from suffering or unpleasantness. Lazy. Weak-willed. Can't say No.

~Introducing the Players ~

LIBRA - KEY TYPES

* From <u>Kai Lung</u> to <u>The Vicar of Bray</u>

Bertrand Russell considered the Chinese national temperament delightful and commended the leisurely calm of their cultured classes. An artist nation he called them, with the virtues and vices ('a certain callousness') to be expected of the artist. Libra is a very Eastern sort of sign, its delicacy and politeness captured beautifully by Ernest Bramah's hilarious tales of KAI LUNG, the itinerant story teller. These narratives are 'permeated with the odour of joss sticks and honourable high mindedness.'

Perhaps more importantly though, Libra is the sign of Justice and who better to typify that than clever PORTIA in her disguise as a judge in <u>The Merchant of Venice</u>. 'A Daniel come to judgment', as the unsuspecting Shylock hailed her. Another judge is Lewis Carroll's KING of HEARTS. He presided at the trial of the Knave of Hearts in <u>Alice</u> and also enshrines the soothing ability of the sign to pour oil on troubled waters - in his case after their stirring up by his Arien Queen. He was as gentle and forgiving as she was belligerent. A bulging Key Type drawer contains all those sugary little heroines who litter literature. Dickens has them in droves. DORA COPPERFIELD nee Spenlow ('She had the most delightful little voice, the gayest little laugh...'), DOLLY VARDEN ('dimpled and fresh'), LUCIE MANNETTE ('slight and pretty') are just a few. An older faded type is JULIA WITITTERLY in <u>Nicholas Nickleby</u>. She 'had an air of sweet insipidity...She was reclining on a sofa in such a very unstudied attitude that she might have been taken for an actress all ready for the first scene in a ballet.' Her proud husband described her as 'very delicate, very fragile, a hothouse plant, an exotic.' She was, he said, an ornament to the fashionable world but her complaint was Soul (too much of). AMY MARCH, the youngest and prettiest, sometimes spiteful, vainest and most artistic of the <u>Little Women</u> (Louisa M. Alcott) personifies another sub-type. Her garden contained a Venusian bower, small and earwiggy but pretty with honeysuckles and morning glories, tall white lilies, delicate ferns and as many brilliant picturesque plants as would consent to blossom there. On the masculine side, Chaucer's SQUIRE was 'embroidered like a meadow bright/And full of freshest flowers, red and white./Singing he was, or fluting all the day;/He was as fresh as is the month of May./He could make songs and poems and recite,/Knew how to joust and dance, to draw and write./He loved so hotly that till dawn grew pale/He slept as little as a nightingale.'

And for the well-known dithering Libran Key Type let's drop into song too with that arch sitter-on-the ecclesiastical-fence the VICAR of BRAY for - Whatsoever King shall reign, Still I'll be the Vicar of Bray, Sir!

~Introducing the Players ~

SCORPIO

SCORPIO the Scorpion is under the rulership of Pluto. Capable of the greatest feats of endurance and acts of the worst infamy. They can be saints or sinners, killers or victims and they can change tack convulsively. The change is convulsive because this is a 'fixed' sign and stubborn past belief. Scorpions really can cut off their noses to spite their faces! They will go to the stake for their beliefs and indulge in voluntary self-denial for no discernible reason. It's the sign most connected with death and, phoenix-like, rebirth after death, hence a (sneaking) belief in reincarnation. Fate certainly works in strange ways in their lives. They are not always lucky in their parents who are uncongenial or lost to them early in life. They are themselves passionate jealous spouses, whose marriages are heaven or hell. Stern parents themselves. They do not have the best of health but, being Scorpios, fight tooth and nail to overcome disabilities and weaknesses. Their work leads them into dark dangerous places. They are to be found in the police, the river police, the prison service, on oil rigs, in hospitals, laboratories and mortuaries. They are social workers and public health officers. In their scanty leisure hours they go sailing, pot-holing, walk alone at night and - practice black magic!

SCORPIO KEYWORDS

⇨ Secretive, solitary, implacable, reserved, intense hidden feelings, icy, personal magnetism, powerful, deep, exacting, implacable, strong and silent, inner strength, sacrifice, abrasive, proud, heroes or... (see end)
⇨ Investigatory, research, crime, police, violence, undercover agents, lawyers, psychologists, analysts, penetrating, corrosive, demolition workers, destruction, soldiers, archaeologists, miners, disagreeable filthy jobs, sinks, drains, WCs, waste products. The dead, graveyards, death wish.
⇨ Financial matters, accountants, advisers and trustees, wealth, treasure trove.
⇨ Surgeons, medical matters, undertakers, prison officers, chemists, herbalists,
⇨ Freemasons.
⇨ Disasters, brute force, ordeals. Disappearance. Volcanoes, hot springs.
⇨ Psychics, occultists, witches and wizards, healers. Fate, enigmas, Karma, dark shadows.
⇨ Passion, love at first sight, rape, fierce lover, sex, erotic, possessive.
⇨ Vitality, energy, courage, dominant, hard, self-disciplined, ruthless, self-denial, riding roughshod, stamina.
⇨ The sea, water sports, dark lakes, still water, underwater filming, divers. Petrol, oil, minerals, orchids, blackthorn, dark red flowers, cypress. Black pearls. Eagles, rats.
⇨ Darkly handsome, thickset, strong features, deep set eyes, heavy brows, prominent nose, thin lips.
⇨ Satirical humour.
⇨ Tenacious hold on life, prone to infection and allergies. Ear, nose, throat.
⇨ Sexually related diseases. Bladder. Ulcers, boils, abscesses.
⇨ Algeria, Syria, Liverpool, New Orleans, Washington D.C.
⇨ The small print!...or villains. Cruel, treacherous, dangerous, fanatics. Pollution. Corruption. Grudges. Vendettas.

~Introducing the Players ~

SCORPIO - KEY TYPES

✳ From <u>Dr. Jekyll</u> to <u>Mr. Hyde</u>

George Bernard Shaw said there was nothing so good or so bad that you couldn't find an Englishman doing it. Substitute 'Scorpio' for 'Englishman' and you have the measure of the sign. Scorpio can go either way or, as in <u>The Strange Case of Dr. Jekyll and Mr. Hyde</u> by Robert Louis Stevenson - both. DR. JEKYLL, a chemist, had a dual personality. He discovered a drug which enabled his lower nature to absorb his finer instincts and, while the effect lasted, to indulge in depravity, even murder. This sub-personality, MR. HYDE - gradually took over and grew too powerful to be dismissed. Medical men are a Scorpion Key Type. Chaucer had a DOCTOR riding to Canterbury who was well grounded in astronomy, natural magic, the humours and all the ancient medical and astrological authorities. He was careful in his diet, 'only digestives, nutritives and such.' On the distaff side, Terry Pratchett's GRANNY WETHERWAX was the greatest witch in Discworld. She mixed her potions and brews in a scullery in her cottage. <u>Not</u> a white witch. A tongue and a temper, secretiveness and occult powers. Dickens weighs in with a medical student - BOB SAWYER - in <u>Pickwick Papers</u>. His cheerfully callous nature - 'Nothing like dissecting to give one an appetite' - is almost as terrifying as the others. Non-medical Key Types, but sexy, magnetic, unforgettable, ruthless characters are portrayed in Emily Bronte's HEATHCLIFF, Charlotte Bronte's EDWARD ROCHESTER and George Bernard Shaw's PROFESSOR HIGGINS in <u>Wuthering Heights</u>, <u>Jane Eyre</u> and <u>Pygmalion</u> respectively.

The ladies have the supremely ambitious Scorpion Key Type of the murdering LADY MACBETH ('Infirm of purpose! Give me the daggers!'). Bertie Wooster's terrifying AUNT AGATHA makes a worthy henchwoman for her. P.G. Woodhouse described her as having a face like a well-bred vulture and she could turn Bertie inside out with a glance. Two Rebeccas - Daphne du Maurier's REBECCA de WINTER and W.M. Thackeray's BECKY SHARP from <u>Vanity Fair</u>, adventuresses, beautiful, selfish <u>femmes fatales</u> the pair of them.

Dickens' MISS HAVISHAM in <u>Great Expectations</u> was jilted on her wedding day and years later still wore her bridal attire and brooded in her derelict mansion. Her passionate love had turned to implacable hatred and she schooled the adopted ESTELLE to hardness and bitter pride leading men on to love her and then to break their hearts. A very dark Scorpio type.

JACK BLACK the cobbler in Dylan Thomas's <u>Under Milk Wood</u> was a religious fanatic who roamed the village at night in his religious trousers 'their flies sewn up with cobbler's thread' searching for the naughty couples. 'Off to Gomorrah!' Finally Lewis Carroll's JABBERWOCK with eyes of flames that whiffled through the tulgey wood and its slayer the BEAMISH BOY are both Scorpio types - victim and killer, fiend and hero - Jekyll and Hyde.

~Introducing the Players ~

SAGITTARIUS

SAGITTARIUS the Archer is under the rulership of Jupiter. Sunny bracing people! In looks they should be tall and athletic with long equine faces. This is a lucky sign and such faults as Sagittarius has are 'easily forgiven'. These faults stem from being larger than life. Frank and open themselves they are often tactless and insensitive to more fragile signs' feelings. They love fun but their practical jokes can be clumsy and hurtful. That apart they are popular, enthusiastic, optimistic and cheerfully philosophical. Hail-fellow-well-met is their motto. They are cosmopolitan with wide-ranging minds and many interests. They are adventurous and if they can't go out physically in search of excitement, they read and travel in thought. Best education is in a progressive school. Sagittarians demand to be on equal terms with their teachers and to be able to argue and discuss freely. Older students get on very well indeed. Traditionally they enter the Church, the Law or the theatrical profession. They're all for the outdoor life, especially horse riding, racing and camping but are happy party-going and pub-crawling. They enjoy sexual freedom, particularly for women. They enter unconventional unions and their own children are given unlimited freedom. Generous, animal loving, happy-go-lucky types, always looking for the far horizon.

SAGITTARIAN KEYWORDS

- ➪ Optimism, enthusiasm, tumbling headlong, joie de vivre, high spirits, jolly good sorts, favourite uncles. Great sense of humour. Clowns and comics.
- ➪ Landed gentry, huntin', shootin' and fishin', large country houses, large families, dogs, horses, and outdoor life.
- ➪ The Church, the Law and the Stage - but the upper echelons.
- ➪ Orthodox religion, barristers and judges, actor-managers.
- ➪ Provision merchants, big business, success.
- ➪ Philosophers, sages, wise men, tutors, professors, visionaries.
- ➪ Disseminating news, publishing, broadcasting, international communications, writers, public speaking, the media.
- ➪ Explorers, travellers, immigrants.
- ➪ Democratic, matey.
- ➪ Physical and intellectual freedom, frank, open, popular, easy-going.
- ➪ Careless of danger.
- ➪ Handsome, tall, athletic, long legged. High forehead, baldness. Long nose. High complexion.
- ➪ Fortunate, philanthropic, thinks big, luxury goods, comfort. Generous.
- ➪ Liver, hips and thighs, suffers from over-indulgence, dominant first finger, hearty handshake.
- ➪ Australia, Spain, Arabia.
- ➪ Parades and shows, restaurants. Pool rooms, racetracks, lotteries. Archery.
- ➪ Oak trees. Ash and mulberry trees. Sapphires. Topaz. Purple, rich colours. Ceremonial robes.
- ➪ Eagles, elephants.
- ➪ The small print!...Pompous, boasters. Wasters, gamblers. Loud, vulgar, rough.

~Introducing the Players ~

SAGITTARIUS - KEY TYPES

✳ From <u>Chiron</u> to <u>Pollyanna</u>

The original Sagittarius or Archer was the legendary CHIRON, wisest of the Centaurs, who was placed among the stars as a reward for his noble character by Zeus. He taught Achilles and other Greek heroes and, being half man, half horse, was a renowned hunter. So too was the 'unting grocer JORROCKS of Robert Smith Surtees' <u>Jorrocks's Jaunts & Jollities</u> whose lot in life had cast him behind a counter instead of on a horse, a defect which he remedied as soon as he could afford to. There was a combination of fun and good humour in his looks that pleased at first sight. "By 'eaven, it's sublime!" he exclaimed watching the hounds streaming off. " 'ow the old wood re-echoes their melody." At the top of the greenwood tree is ROBIN HOOD a notable archer and cheerful outlaw with, like Chiron, his devoted band of followers or pupils. It was believed that he had aristocratic lineage and was the Earl of Huntingdon. Chaucer had a YEOMAN in his little band who had peacock-feathered arrows and a mighty bow. 'His head was like a nut, his face was brown,/He knew the whole of woodcraft up and down.' These are all outdoor Key Types.

Others are great travellers. PEREGRINE PICKLE was a swashbuckling scamp and Tobias Smollett's novel described his peregrinations and adventures. Eleanor Farjeon's MARTIN PIPPIN was a troubadour, a wandering singer and an enchanting story teller.

Centaurs were said to be shape-shifters and Sagittarians are certainly versatile. Another of Chaucer's pilgrims was a PARSON 'rich in holy thought and work...a learned man'. There never was a better priest. 'Christ and His twelve Apostles and their love/He taught, but followed it himself before.'

There are legal Key Types like John Mortimer's RUMPOLE of the Bailey, that defender of the completely worthless and provoker of the pompous; untidy, wig askew, tolerant of the world's foibles.

The ladies tend to be athletic like John Betjeman's tennis-ball-thwacking JOAN HUNTER DUNN and Arthur Ransome's hearty NANCY BLACKETT master of the <u>Amazon</u>, and terror of the seas (<u>Swallows and Amazons</u>). JOSEPHINE in Dickens' <u>Hard Times</u> was a celebrated equestrienne, daughter of Sleary a circus proprietor. She didn't baulk at showing her legs! It was a happy little company. They rode anything, danced on rolling casks, slackwires, tightropes and bare-backed steeds. 'They all assumed to be mighty rakish and knowing, they were not very tidy in their private dresses, they were not at all orderly in their domestic arrangements...yet there was a remarkable gentleness about them.' Finally, optimistic Key Types - Dickens' MR. MICAWBER who lived in hourly expectation of something turning up, and Eleanor Porter's POLLYANNA who, whatever disaster befell, found the silver lining and was glad, <u>glad</u>, GLAD!

~Introducing the Players ~

CAPRICORN

CAPRICORN the Goat is under the rulership of Saturn. The lucky ones make it to the corridors of power, to state administration centres where your status is known by the size of your square of carpet. The unlucky ones are stuck into dull monotonous routine where hard work and loyalty go unnoticed. Whichever rung of the ladder they are on they try to make it higher but this is a slow process for most Capricorns. Success and their heart's desire come late for them. They are plain, hard, cautious but very ambitious folk; loners however surrounded by others and acquainted with the Dark Night of the Soul. The really unhappy and unfortunate degenerate into killjoys and sourpusses and they have to take hold of themselves to prevent this. They like everyone in their proper place. India, with its caste system, is ruled by Capricorn. As might be expected, their early years are often fraught through no fault of their own. Father may be to blame; they lose him or suffer through him. They have few or no children of their own and, if they do, are strict or at odds with them. They marry late or for advantage. They are faithful and devoted but it's hard for them to show affection. They have excellent qualities of the homespun variety - duty, responsibility, reliability and solid worth.

CAPRICORNIAN KEYWORDS

⇨ Cold, concentrated, hard, old age, responsibility, caution, seriousness, pessimism, tradition, authority, practical, ambitious, industrious, conventional, duty. Worldly success but delayed. Honest, prudent, maturity. Frustration.

⇨ Plodding, melancholy, introvert, conserved energy, solitary, prosaic, shy, inarticulate. Rules and regulations.

⇨ Limits, boundaries, gates and doors, obstacles, bondage.

⇨ City life.

⇨ Poverty, unhappy child, orphanage.

⇨ Conservative, materialistic, faithful.

⇨ Osteopaths, politicians, jailers, managers, bricklayers, sculptors.

⇨ Long thin faces, lantern-jawed, large bones, deepset eyes.

⇨ Premature ageing, old men, servants, humble folk.

⇨ Skeleton and skin, skin troubles, rheumatism (knees especially), dental trouble, longevity, colds, cramps.

⇨ Fate.

⇨ Goats.

⇨ Mountaineering.

⇨ Crystal, jet, onyx, rubies, coal, iron. Dark stones. Monkshood, hemlock, moss, ivy, pine, elm, yew. Black.

⇨ India, Albania, Mexico, Afghanistan, Oxford, Brussels.

⇨ BUT the Goat has a fishy tail and, despite the Grim Reaper's rulership, this sign can occasionally kick over the traces and indulge in outbursts of wild humour and nonsense.

⇨ The small print!... Discontent, dreary, morbid, narrow outlook, miserly, stupid, servile. Snobbish, social climber.

CAPRICORN - KEY TYPES

✳ From <u>Duke Orsino</u> to <u>EEYORE</u>

The grandest Capricorn Key Types are high in their professions or in the social pecking order. Shakepeare's DUKE ORSINO starts <u>Twelfth Night</u> with 'If music be the food of love, play on,' and is a melancholy gentleman with a taste for sad songs. POLONIUS in <u>Hamlet</u> is the King of Denmark's Lord Chamberlain, full of wise precepts which he passes on to his son - 'Neither a borrower nor a lender be, For loan oft loses both itself and friend, And borrowing dulls the edge of husbandry.' Unfortunately he was a meddler and got stabbed behind the arras. MRS. PROUDIE, wife of the Bishop of Barchester in Anthony Trollope's <u>Barsetshire Novels</u>, was another highly-placed dignitary - not that she had an official position but she usurped her husband's and ran the diocese for him. She was a good woman in her way and meant well but was feared and disliked. MISS ABBEY POTTERSON, landlady of <u>The Six Jolly Fellowship Porters</u> in Dickens' <u>Our Mutual Friend</u>, was another who ran her little kingdom with a rod of iron. Again, a good woman, but not to be trifled with. 'A man must have drunk himself mad drunk indeed if he thought he could contest a point with her.' Some boozy regulars harboured muddled notions that, because of her dignity and firmness, she was in some way related to the Abbey at Westminster. Dickens went in for Capricorn Key Types in a big way; the harsh gloomy MURDSTONES in <u>David Copperfield</u>, the hard-headed facts-facts-facts THOMAS GRADGRIND in <u>Hard Times</u> ('his voice was inflexible, dry and dictatorial') and EBENEZER SCROOGE in <u>A Christmas Carol</u> whose name has become synonymous with miserliness.

On the credit side he had David Copperfield's great-aunt BETSEY TROTWOOD who, although granite-like in appearance and manner, turned up trumps and took him in when he was destitute. She was still walking six miles at a stretch in winter weather when fourscore years and more, Capricorn being as tough as old boots once over its early years. <u>Her</u> Capricornian advice to David was to be a fine firm fellow with a will of his own. With resolution. With determination. With strength of character.

Two of S.G. Hulme Beaman's Toytown characters are Key Types for the sign - ERNEST the Policeman, a real old-fashioned bobby-on-the-beat who took everyone's name and address without fear or favour ('I hope I knows me duty') and that forerunner of VICTOR MELDREW (<u>One Foot in the Grave</u>), MR. GROWSER ('This is disgraceful! You ought to be ashamed! It ought not to be allowed!')

A.A. Milne's EEYORE the donkey had a happily miserable life of it standing in a corner of the forest thinking sadly, 'Why?' and, sometimes, 'Wherefore?' and, occasionally, 'Inasmuch as which? How Like Them. Pathetic. Nobody minds, nobody cares!'

~Introducing the Players ~

AQUARIUS

AQUARIUS the Water Carrier is under the rulership of Uranus. They are aristocratic looking in the long, thin, bony style. Long, narrow hands and feet. Beautiful faraway eyes, clear cool voices. Sometimes they are marred by, for example, a speech impediment, physical defect, freakish height or gross overweight. In these cases Uranus is prominent in the horoscope and badly aspected. Friendly, charming, civilised, if somewhat unemotional and detached. Fascinating, witty cynics. Clever, farseeing, experimental, independent. Not conventionally religious but liable to get caught up with some pseudo-scientific movement. Political animals but despite their upper class mannerisms they are intellectually left wing with the humiliating realisation that, honestly, they do not like the working classes. They prefer their own U-types. Domesticity means little, they prefer club and hotel life. Marriage is on shaky ground unless they are allowed to go their own way. If there are children they never seem to actually <u>belong</u> to them. Illnesses are sudden and not like other peoples'. Aquarians always have to be different! Advanced, unconventional treatments are hopeful. As the New Age sign they are fascinated by new techniques, by science fiction projects, abstract art, experimental literature and....astrology! They are bureaucrats, Eurocrats, very well-meaning people whose excellent ideas aren't always grounded in fact. They plan Utopia but forget the drains. They range from geniuses to mental misfits and the two extremes often meet, which is disconcerting for the rest of the zodiac!

AQUARIAN KEYWORDS

- ⇨ Genius, intellectuals, the elite.
- ⇨ Truth, idealism, democracy, Socialism.
- ⇨ Eccentric, erratic, bizarre, original, unconventional, unpredictable. Light and airy.
- ⇨ Artistic, gifted. Magical.
- ⇨ The unexpected and inexplicable. X-files. Sudden shattering events.
- ⇨ Reforms, revolutions, freethinkers, agnostics, atheists, opposition in politics.
- ⇨ Detached, urbane, unbiased, dispassionate, independent, free, strange. Bohemian.
- ⇨ Aeronautics, astrology, radar, rays, light, science, inventors, electricity, statistics, politics, sociology, computer technology. Antiquities. Space Age.
- ⇨ Clubs, societies.
- ⇨ Humane, friendly, kind, ladies and gentlemen, the public good, cool, calm, unaffected, unimpressed by show.
- ⇨ Good looking, fine eyes, light distinctive voices, unusual, looks/dress.
- ⇨ Ankles, circulation, nervous system.
- ⇨ Divorce.
- ⇨ Birds, dinosaurs, griffins.
- ⇨ Uranium.
- ⇨ Wild nature, orchids. Violet.
- ⇨ Russia, Sweden, Moscow, Brighton.
- ⇨ The small print!...Aquarius taken alone is a clever affable sign but the position and aspects of Uranus can turn its good qualities topsy-turvy to give extreme mad ludicrous opinions. Destructiveness. Fanatical pervert. Cruel and callous.

~Introducing the Players ~

AQUARIUS - KEY TYPES

* From <u>Captain Nemo</u> to <u>Mrs. Jellyby</u>

CAPTAIN NEMO, scientist, inventor, musician and master of the submarine <u>Nautilus</u> comes first. He was a Jules Verne creation in <u>Twenty Thousand Leagues Under The Sea</u> and perfect Aquarian Key Type. Enigmatic, coldly assured, a man of civilised taste who had renounced the world to live in and off the sea. 'There only is independence! There I am free!' He was tall and handsome with remarkable eyes and fine tapered hands indicative of a highly nervous temperament. CAVOR invented Cavorite, an anti-gravity substance which created a cyclone and took the roof off his house, followed by the furniture and then the cavorite itself. This type rates scientific research above such annoyances. He's from <u>The First Men in the Moon</u> by H.G. Wells. Dickens' SCIENTIFIC GENTLEMAN mistook Mr. Pickwick's flashing lantern for an undiscovered phenomenon and committed to paper 'the date, day, hour, minute and precise second at which they were visible; all of which were to form the data of a voluminous treatise of great research and deep learning.' DOCTOR DOLITTLE, brainchild of Hugh Lofting, was an eccentric country physician, more interested in natural history and scientific research than in his patients. Uniquely he could communicate with animals and undertook worldwide expeditions. He was a conservationist and humanitarian who hated hunting, caging animals and any form of tyranny. Terry Pratchett's Discworld's technological genius is LEONARD of QUIRM, the gentlest and most harmless of creatures who spends his time inventing explosive and other lethal devices.

George Bernard Shaw's JACK TANNER in <u>Man and Superman</u> was the author of the <u>Revolutionist's Handbook</u> and a political theorist of immense wit who expounded Shaw's Fabian philosophy in dazzling coruscations of words - 'prodigiously fluent of speech, restless, excitable, possibly a little mad.' MISS JEAN BRODIE in <u>The Prime of Miss Jean Brodie</u> by Muriel Spark, was an eccentric teacher who dominated and fascinated 'her' girls and became sympathetic to Hitler and Nazism. MADELINE, Ludwig Bemelman's heroine, a convent school-girl in Paris, was completely 'different' from the other little girls, an enchanting individualist. FLORA POSTE (<u>Cold Comfort Farm</u> by Stella Gibbons) was the deliciously cool, detached, reforming Aquarian type.

Dickens' MRS JELLYBY in <u>Bleak House</u> expressed some beautiful sentiments on The Brotherhood of Humanity while sitting in a nest of waste paper in a dirty room in a filthy house with her children neglected and her bankrupt husband preparing to throw himself from the window. 'He is a little out of spirits,' she remarked in the calmest manner. She was sweet and pretty with lovely eyes which didn't seem to focus on anything nearer than Africa. All her time was given up to crackpot humanitarian projects and Women's Rights. 'Never have a mission my dear child,' is <u>Mr.</u> Jellyby's only recorded utterance.

~Introducing the Players ~

PISCES

PISCES the Fishes is under the rulership of Neptune. Changeable. Fishes are fickle and light are their vows. They are amiable, sympathetic (not to say gullible), easily duped, defrauded and involved in secrets, scandals and mysteries. Romantics. Incurable optimists and humorists yet easily affected to tears. Somewhat timid, they try to keep well away from trouble, which gets them even deeper in the mire. They are the arch-escapers of the zodiac and the escape can be reprehensible through drugs or drink or very advantageous to them. For instance, they excel at acting as they can assume another persona or mask. As authors they specialise in biography where they can enter another's world. The supernatural attracts and they are psychic. They are not hard workers and fall for shady pursuits which seem to promise easy money. It's the most fertile sign and traditionally produces the largest families. They like being part of some involved and complicated domestic relationship. Good cooks and wine connoisseurs. Can't be trusted with money, they're improvident, careless, too open-handed. They are not particularly robust, lungs are a weak spot. The girls are lovely but put on weight. They live in worlds of fantasy and aren't always scrupulously honest because they can't face reality. If forced to they are in a pitiable state. In the meantime, they enjoy life and can find delight in the simplest things.

PISCEAN KEYWORDS

⇨ Dual nature, self-deception, escapism, unreality, fantasy, dreams, sleep, hallucinations, imagination, superstition.
⇨ Astronomers, poets, mystics, mediums.
⇨ Mysterious, glamorous, exotica.
⇨ Anaesthetics. Clouds, fog, gas, floods, veils, masks, shape changers.
⇨ Easy-osy, adaptable, gregarious, talkative, indiscreet, placid, kind, good-natured, generous, charitable, versatile, affable, credulous, easily deceived, compassionate, sweet, sentimental, easily hurt, gentle, an easy touch, vague, forgetful.
⇨ Artists, actors, musicians, film stars.
⇨ Trades connected with cloth, wool, footwear, hotels. Welfare/charity workers.
⇨ Food and drink, parties, entertainments.
⇨ Mazes.
⇨ Religion, Christianity.
⇨ Sorrow, self-sacrifice. Refuges, prisons, hospitals.
⇨ Tender, longing for love, fickle, secret affairs, scandals.
⇨ Fertility, sensual, hedonistic.
⇨ Lungs, feet, sensitive to cold and heat, catarrhal, delicate, morbid fears.
⇨ Dancers, footballers.
⇨ Plump, pale, strange eyes. Spiritual appearance. Romantic dress.
⇨ Ships, sailing, fish. Trees near water, lakes. Exploration. Large animals, dolphins.
⇨ Rock crystal, white sapphire, aquamarine, mauve, plastic, rubber.
⇨ Portugal, Normandy, Alexandria.
⇨ The small print!...Sloppy, muddly, unreliable, dependent, lazy, con-men, fraudsters, self-indulgent, crafty, drifters, weak, addicts.

~Introducing the Players ~

PISCES - KEY TYPES

* From <u>Prospero</u> to <u>Mrs. Gamp</u>

PROSPERO raised the Tempest in Shakespeare's play of that name by his magical arts and was a very high-up Piscean indeed. He was the rightful Duke of Milan but 'being rapt in secret studies, neglected worldly ends', and was betrayed by his brother and cast adrift with his baby daughter in an open boat. That's the sort of thing that happens to other-worldly Piscean types, although not on such a grand scale usually. More normal but still occult Key Types are Noel Coward's hearty medium MADAME ARCATI in <u>Blithe Spirit</u>, Dylan Thomas's sexy slovenly gypsy fortune-teller MRS DAI BREAD TWO in her revealing red silk dress, and Terry Prachett's witch MAGRAT GARLICK a relentless doer-of-good works in Discworld, particularly prone to rescuing baby birds and crying bitterly when they die. She has a watery-eyed expression of hopeless goodwill and collects occult jewellery. <u>She</u> wears a startling green silk dress.

There is a plethora of watery tearful females - Hans Christian Andersen's LITTLE MERMAID, Shakespeare's OPHELIA who, rejected by Hamlet, drowned herself, Dickens' MRS. GUMMIDGE, a fisherman's widow, living on Yarmouth beach in a converted boat, 'a lone lorn creetur and everthink goes contrairy with me', and George Moore's ESTHER WATERS a religious girl who reels from homelessness through seduction and poverty to humiliation in the lying-in hospital and the workhouse. As a Key Type this must be the most miserable. Much happier types are Tove Jansson's MOOMINS, gentle billowy creatures who drift about in Moominland. MOOMINMAMMA especially is a perfect love, as calming and soothing as an eiderdown.

The daydreaming Piscean Key Type is exemplified by James Thurber's WALTER MITTY who, while his wife was having her hair done, became Commander Mitty piloting a hydroplane through a terrible storm (or Tempest), Dr. Mitty, a top-flight surgeon, Mitty the crack shot and Captain Mitty bomber pilot. Finally taking a last drag at his cigarette, he faced the firing squad with a faint fleeting smile playing about his lips. 'To hell with the handkerchief!' said Walter Mitty the Undefeated.

Idle Piscean Key Types can be found in Jane Austen's amiable LADY BERTRAM in <u>Mansfield Park</u> who put herself out for nobody and Dylan Thomas's NOGOOD BOYO who either fished all day or didn't fish all day in <u>Under Milk Wood</u>. Hypocritical Fish have their own Key Type in Dickens' REV'D MR. STIGGINS (<u>Pickwick</u>), the drunken Shepherd of the Brick Lane Temperance meetings.

Two garrulous NURSES, centuries apart, are Juliet's in <u>Romeo and Juliet</u> and Dickens' MRS. GAMP (<u>Martin Chuzzlewit</u>). 'Ah, what a wale of grief!' cried Mrs. Gamp possessing herself of the bottle and the glass. Thanks to her, large unwieldy umbrellas became known as 'gamps' - just the thing in a Tempest!

~Introducing the Players ~

QUICK GUIDE TO THE PLANETS

The SUN and MOON, of course, aren't planets. Without the Sun there wouldn't be any planets or, come to that, any us. All that can be said in this context is that, as the very heart and being of our solar system, the Sun's place in the zodiac when viewed from the earth 'sets' the horoscope. The sign it occupies is energised and decides our basic temperament. The strength of other bodies may be sufficient to modify this or to distort our personal circumstances so that the normal meaning is warped, but the Sun remains paramount. Rules Leo. The Moon, unless ruling the horoscope or otherwise being strongly placed, cannot be said to have much influence on character. Its usefulness is in timing progressions and events. For a woman it may have strong bearing on her health. For a man it has a distinct correlation with his mother and any other significant woman in his life. In a wider sense, for both sexes, it shows the attitude of the public towards him or her. Rules Cancer.

MERCURY is the invisible planet, swallowed up in the Sun's radiance. It is usually in the Sun's sign but can never get further away than one of the adjoining signs. Like the Moon, unless it rules the chart, it has little effect on its own. It is popularly supposed to signify the intelligence - good relationships with other planets help, poor relationships hinder. It often shares these with the Sun anyway so nothing new is found. It also rules Gemini and, in the absence of any other contender, Virgo.

VENUS is allowed to stray a little further from the Sun's apron strings and manages to get as far as two signs away if so inclined. Invariably consulted in matters of the heart, its placing and aspects (relationships with other planets) give an indication of the love life. It is also one of the money rulers and financial as well as sexual affairs come under its patronage, which complicates the astrologer's life. Rules Libra and, in the absence of any other contender, Taurus.

MARS is straightforward. Second only to the Sun in symbolising energy, it takes two years to circle the zodiac. Well placed and configured with helpful planets it's all vim and vigour, an active, lively presence. Conversely, aggressive and intimidating or, if the rest of the chart is weak, it denotes the victim of violence, accidents, operations and sheer malevolence. Rules Aries.

JUPITER, the largest planet, takes twelve years for its circuit. It has always been regarded as benevolent. Involved in the worst of bad-star days, its presence offers Divine Protection. Good luck, success, health, wealth and happiness are

~Introducing the Players ~

promised by Jupiter. Sad experience can't always bear this out. Jupiter exaggerates whatever is there. If it's involved with amiable signs and planets - fine. If with darker forces - not so fine. Rules Sagittarius.

SATURN was the most distant planet the ancient stargazers could see. It dragged along on its thirty year round, bringing plague and pestilence they thought. It was, in those days, the final outpost of the solar system, and spelt the end of life. All gloom and misery were attributed to it and the Saturnine temperament was a sad one indeed. However, as Jupiter isn't always as wonderful as hoped, so Saturn isn't always as bad. It has all the homespun virtues and its children reap steady, enduring rewards for hard work. Then too occasionally, just occasionally, Saturn kicks up its heels with the best! Rules Capricorn.

URANUS was first definitely identified in 1781 thanks to the telescope. The three last discovered planets have taken time to settle down, to get themselves the right names and to show what they are capable of. Uranus personifies the eccentric, the unconventional, the temperamental, the genius and the crank. It throws life into disorder which may be good for those whose Sun sign it is traversing (it takes about seven years to get through each sign). Or not. An invigorating, refreshing influence if you can stand up to it. Thoroughly impossible if you can't.

NEPTUNE is a seriously strange planet, given to occult studies and mysteries, myths and legends. Unworldly, untidy. Caught up in webs of fantasy, films and glamour which may be completely beneficial or may cause the Neptunian to drift and degenerate into very dangerous waters. Fog, mist, deep water, silence. Illusion, disillusion, confusion. Escape, either physical or mental. Neptune is a tricky planet. It moves so slowly - about fourteen years to traverse one sign - that it probably affects whole generations rather than individuals but ruling, strongly placed or allied with Sun, Moon or fast-moving planets, its subtle influence can be memorable. Even more exaggerative than Jupiter. Rules Pisces.

PLUTO may or may not be a real planet. So far astrologers have taken it as one. A mere pinpoint in the sky, it takes about 240 years to complete its tour of the zodiac. Has even less individual influence than Neptune. Whole generations have it on the same degree. Even so, when stirred into life by close proximity or aspect to one of the fast-moving bodies, it can cause devastation. Vicious attacks, the underworld, gang warfare, disappearances, destruction of property, epidemics, catastrophes are all grist to Pluto's mill.

1930/1931, Fenchurch St. Paul, East Anglia
Ringing in the New
(from <u>The Nine Tailors</u> by Dorothy L. Sayers)

There were eight bells all with their names with which they had probably been baptised. Gaude, Sabaoth, John, Jericho, Jubilee, Dimity, Batty Thomas and the great Tailor Paul himself. All had their characteristics and they gave tongue with a will, rioting and exulting high up above the ringers in the dark bell-tower. 'Tin tan din dan bim bam bom bo...every bell in her place striking tuneably, hunting up, hunting down, dodging, snapping, laying her blows behind, making her thirds and fourths, working down to lead the dance again.' Outside the cold, flooded fen country stretched away; in the ringing chamber the men's shadows went up and down upon the walls and in the bell chamber itself <u>murder</u> was being done! You tamper with church bells at your peril. They have a long and honourable history giving thanks and giving warning and figure prominently in folklore and legend. Their sonorous iron gravity and authority must come under Saturn and Capricorn. The maximum number of changes which can be rung on eight bells is 40,320. It's called 'accomplishing the extent' and takes eighteen hours. For more about bells and their ringers read Ronald Blythe's <u>Akenfield</u>. They have a great tradition of it in Suffolk and East Anglia generally.

1948, Baltimore County
Birth of **IAN BEDLOE**
(from <u>Saint Maybe</u> by Anne Tyler)

On his 19th birthday in 1967, Ian found himself bringing up his year old niece and her older stepbrother and stepsister because he believed he had driven their father (his brother Danny) to suicide and so, indirectly, been the cause of the death of their mother also. An exaggerated sense of Capricorn duty caused him to give up his life to caring for them and he didn't marry until he was 41 and they were off his hands. In short, he was a saint. This guilt complex drove him to the Church of the Second Chance which he was to serve faithfully but his bitter experience still made it impossible for him to forgive himself. The daily grind of caring for the children made him feel that

~ Capricorn ~

he was on a treadmill.

> "I've been atoning and sometimes lately I've
> hated God for taking so long to forgive me. Some
> days I feel I'm speaking into a dead telephone.
> My words are knocking into a blank wall."

He apprenticed himself to a cabinet maker and got much satisfaction
from the craft. The Clutter-Cleaner, who eventually married him,
noted that his personal needs were so simple and plain that she had
nothing to do. He owned six books on how to be a better person and
his clothes smelled of nutmeg. She also liked him for his fine face, all
straight lines, and all Capricorn too! Anne Tyler made a good choice
of birthday for him.

JANUARY 3

1825, England
Birth of **CHRISTABEL MADELEINE LA MOTTE**
(from <u>Possession</u> by A.S. Byatt)

Another 4-star Author's Choice for a birthday. Christabel was
unmistakably Capricorn. Every observation convicts her! She adored
her father, an historian. Capricorns are often dominated by that
gentleman or he is engaged on very serious work. She wrote
children's stories and religious poetry. A young cousin thought she
resembled a governess - a Jane Eyre - 'so powerful, so passionate, so
observant beneath her sober exterior.' She was considered cold by
many although she was passionate enough when she fell in love with
Randolph Ash, a married man. A child resulted but Duty led to her
parting with Ash and giving their child to her sister to pass off as her
own. An added bitterness was that the child didn't like her, she was
happier with her adoptive mother. In many ways a sad life. A woman
friend with whom she lived committed suicide when Ash came along
and Christabel was guilt ridden for the rest of her life. She ended up
'like an old witch in a tower' with no intimate friend. 'I have no
graces. I live circumscribed and self-communing.' And, again, 'My
Solitude is my Treasure, the best thing I have. I hesitate to go out. If
you opened the little gate I would not hop out.' Her epitaph read,
'After mortal trouble, let me lie still.'

~ Capricorn ~

JANUARY 4

1888, London
Promotion!
(from <u>The Diary of a Nobody</u> by George and Weedon Grossmith)

As the result of 21 years industry and strict attention to the interests of his superiors in office, Mr. Pooter was rewarded with promotion to the position of senior clerk and a salary increase Of £100.00 p.a. Capricorn Triumphant. (It must be admitted that some of the shine was taken off by his son Lupin, who had been working for a stockbroker for only a few weeks and who had not paid particular attention to the interests of his superior, but who had, nevertheless, been put on to 'a good thing' which had netted him £200.00 in a day!)

JANUARY 5

1890s, Berkshire
Twelfth Night
(from <u>The Golden Age</u> by Kenneth Grahame)

This is the Twelfth Day of Christmas when the lady's (or gentleman's) true love sent all those lords a-leaping and swans a-swimming as a grand climax to the festivities. Originally this season was the Roman Saturnalia - the office party with grapes and colonnades. Christian celebrations were grafted on to a much older cult. Tonight the mummers made their rounds and put on the age-old ritual show.

> 'They came striding into the kitchen, powdering
> the red brick floor with snow from their barbaric
> bedizenments and stamping and crossing and
> declaiming till all was whirl and riot and shout.'

Young Harold was scared and took refuge with Cook but older Edward 'feigned a manly superiority to illusion, and greeted these awful apparitions familiarly as Dick and Harry and Joe.' The children watched enthralled the mock battle with wooden swords involving the traditional characters of St. George, the Dragon, the Doctor, the Princess and, of course, the 'Obby 'Oss. Kenneth Grahame didn't intend it, but in ancient lore the reign of Saturn was known as the <u>Golden Age</u>.

~ Capricorn ~

1854, early hours, Yorkshire
Birth of SHERLOCK HOLMES
(from <u>Sherlock Holmes</u> by William Baring-Gould)

There are whole societies out there devoting themselves to researching the life of the great detective and Mr. Baring-Gould is an undisputed authority. The Capricornian physical characteristics of height, lean-ness and long, thin face, certainly back up his assertion as far as astrology is concerned. The Sun, probably in the 3rd house of the mentality, conjoined Jupiter which makes that towering intellect even more so and denotes his involvement with the mighty of this world. The King of Bohemia, Royal Families of Europe, Prime Ministers, American billionaires, Illustrious Clients and Noble Bachelors all tugged at the bellpull of 221b Baker Street. Capricorn, even without Jupiter, is a quietly socially-aspiring influence, determined to climb the status ladder and to excel in the career. But, still in Saturnian mode, Holmes was introspective and not a party-going animal. "I was never a sociable fellow," he remarked. An unemotional, cold nature, an insistence upon facts, are all Holmesian trademarks. He evidently matured well and retired in old age to Sussex to keep bees.

Early 1900s, Germany
Patience Rewarded
(from <u>Fraulein Schmidt and Mr. Anstruther</u> by Elizabeth von Arnim)

Rose-Marie Schmidt today sent off her papa's book on Goethe to an English publisher. She had translated it from German into English and, without the dear old professor knowing, had pruned and omitted and re-written and, in fact, done a very free translation indeed. Well, she was desperate. It had already been rejected in its original state by every publisher in Germany and she decided it was high time she took a hand. Luckily her papa spoke little English and didn't notice. A few days later an acceptance arrived! Papa was over the moon and most complimentary about the English who knew a good thing when they saw it.

Today, in 1930s London, the <u>Provincial Lady</u> (E.M. Delafield) was taken to a Literary Club dinner and sat next to a best-selling author who told her, in the kindest way, how to evade paying super-tax. Surely a top-flight literary Capricorn. But who? Certainly not zoologist **GERALD DURRELL**. He was born today in 1925 and wouldn't have been old enough. He wrote the celebrated <u>My Family and Other Animals</u>.

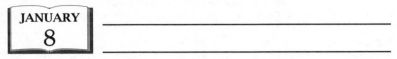

JANUARY
8

1950s/1960s, Belfast
Birth of **JANE REID**
(from <u>In a Blue Velvet Dress</u> by Catherine Sefton)

Jane was a bookworm. Not a Bookworm Astrologer which would have been nice for us but a Bookworm Capricorn which means that she was a rather serious little eleven year old. In this story she stayed with a completely bookless family while her parents were away and her own case containing 29 favourite volumes goes astray. A little ghost - in a blue velvet dress - did her best and brought her a book every night from a long-ago library. They were all old but none the worse for that and many of them feature in these pages - Dickens, Maria Edgeworth, R.D. Blackmore, Frances Hodgson Burnett... Jane devoured them all, even <u>Eric</u>, or <u>Little by Little</u> with the boring bits left out. E. Nesbit's Psammead and Phoenix books were her favourites but the true bookworm can, as Jane did, read the <u>Telephone Directory</u>, <u>The Radio Times</u>, <u>How a Young Hostess Should Behave</u> and <u>A History of Great Temperance Reforms</u> and get <u>something</u> out of them!

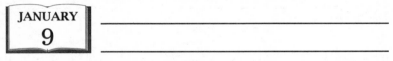

JANUARY
9

1807, New Style, Moscow
A Mazurka
(from <u>War and Peace</u> by Leo Tolstoy)

Despite its reputation for gloom Capricorn the Goat can, on occasion, kick up its hooves with the best. This evening at a ball Denisov, a noted dancer of the mazurka, with Natasha as his partner, treated the company to a dazzling performance. 'At the right beat of the music he looked sideways at his partner with a merry and triumphant air, suddenly stamped with one foot, bounded from the floor like a ball, and flew round the room taking his partner with him.'

You wouldn't catch **SIMONE de BEAUVOIR** or **KAREL CAPEK**

~ Capricorn ~

joining in! They were born today in 1908 (4.00 a.m., Paris) and 1890 (Bohemia) respectively and were unadulterated Capricornians. She was a pessimistic prophetess of doom and unremitting feminist, author of <u>The Second Sex</u>. <u>And</u> a leading existentialist, a philosophy which only other existentialists, like Jean Paul Sartre, understand, and even to them it's pretty depressing and Capricornian. Capek wrote the chilling play <u>R.U.R.</u> (Rossum's Universal Robots) forecasting a world taken over by automatons (which is coming true). He coined the word 'robot' from the Czech 'robota' meaning forced labour. A Saturnian principle if ever there was.

JANUARY
10

1890, New York
Birth of **JOE BELL**
(from <u>Breakfast at Tiffany's</u> by Truman Capote)

He owned and ran a bar on Lexington Avenue, and was a good friend of Holly Golightly's (Audrey Hepburn if you're a film goer). In fact, he was in love with her, but hopelessly. He admitted that he hadn't got an easy nature and said it was because he was unmarried and had a sour stomach. 'Anyone who knows him will tell you he's a hard man to talk to. Impossible if you don't share his fixations, of which Holly is one. Some others are ice hockey, Wiemaraner dogs, <u>Our Gal Sunday</u> (a soap serial he has listened to for fifteen years) and Gilbert and Sullivan.' He ran a quiet bar, no neon lights or TV. He had a froggy voice (a harsh, discordant voice is another Capricorn trait), and was small with a bony, sloping face suitable for somebody taller. He sucked digestive tablets and liked to walk the New York streets alone at all hours. Clincher - he was kind under a gruff exterior.

JANUARY
11

1930s(?), England
They also Serve who Only Stand and Wait
(from <u>Towards Zero</u> by Agatha Christie)

Angus MacWhirter tried to commit suicide today but it didn't come off and he landed up in hospital where he was given a good talking to by his young nurse. He had done wrong, she said.

"God may need you. It may be just by <u>being</u> somewhere - not doing anything - just by being at

~ Capricorn ~

a certain place at a certain time...you might just
- just walk along a street some day and just by
doing that accomplish something terribly
important - perhaps even without knowing what
it was."

She had the second sight and was proved to be right. Saturn,
Capricorn's ruler, is the planet of Fate. MacWhirter's birthday is not
known but it wouldn't be surprising if he turned out to be a Capricorn.
A former employer called him a 'damned pig-headed Scot' and both the
trait and the nation 'come under' Capricorn. He was later hired by an
eccentric peer who respected his grit and honesty. The appointment
was indeed 'terribly important' as he was the one to discover the vital
evidence which cleared an innocent woman of murder.

JANUARY 12

1920s, England
Birth of **ELSIE CONNOLLY**
(from <u>Oxford Blood</u> by Antonia Fraser)

She was one of those outwardly pathetic 'other-peoples'-babies'
Nannies, hired to live in before and after the birth of Society women's
children, to be their mother during their earliest and most formative
weeks and then to be sent on their way with grateful thanks and a fat
cheque. They invariably picked up dirty linen, in more senses then
one. Nurse Elsie was no exception. She had a secret which she
wanted to share with someone, a guilty secret which was weighing on
her mind. It had burdened her for years. When she was dying she
wanted to off-load it on someone, which was where Jemima Shore,
Investigator, came in.

1997, Illinois, U.S.A.
HAL 9000 Computer, Production No. 3, became operational
(from <u>2001: A Space Odyssey</u> by Arthur C. Clarke)

Programmed to run the spaceship <u>Discovery</u> independently, if
necessary, of its human crew, HAL, like Nurse Elsie, knew a secret. As
for her, guilt caused a breakdown. Capricorn, like the other earth
signs, human or technical, takes responsibility very seriously - too
seriously. Those born today must have over-developed consciences.
Read the book and watch the film to know what happened!

~ Capricorn ~

3019 Third Age, Middle Earth
Cold & Fear
(from <u>The Lord of the Rings</u> by J.R.R. Tolkien)

This was a terrifying day for the Company of the Ring-bearer on its way to Moira. In the coldest hour of pre-dawn their camp was attacked by wolves and they were only saved by Gandalf's wizardry for these were no ordinary wolves. Dawn revealed no trace of their corpses. They set off again and trudged across a barren Capricorn landscape of stones, along a broken decayed path, bleak and waterless which wound between ruined walls and paving stones of an ancient high road. The stream which had formerly run across the region had been dammed and turned into a black still lake. Beyond it, vast impassable cliffs reared up. They managed to skirt the lake and to find the Elven Door in the grey face of the rock but it took hours to find the password which would open it. Then, before they could climb the stone stairs beyond, a Thing came out of the lake and - everyone's nightmare - slimy tentacles tried to drag them down. It got Bill the pony before the Door closed. They were in the Mines of Moira. They climbed 200 broad shallow steps to an arched passage and went on, lit only by Gandalf's staff. They glimpsed stairs and arches, passages and tunnels, fissures and chasms - Saturn would have loved it!

1930s, England
Coughs & Sneezes Spread Diseases
(from <u>Diary of a Provincial Lady</u> by E.M. Delafield)

Capricorn and Saturn are a cold sign and a cold planet and are prone to catch all the bronchial and rheumatic ailments. Today the Provincial Lady found she had a cold.

> "I have occasion to observe, not for the first time,
> how extraordinarily plain a cold can make one
> look, affecting hair, complexion and features
> generally, beside nose and upper lip."

Yes, yes, all Capricorn and Saturn. She ran out of hankies. Cook, not-one-to-make-a-fuss, and the children also displayed disquieting signs.

~ Capricorn ~

3019 Third Age, Middle Earth
Death & Destruction
(from <u>The Lord of the Rings</u> by J.R.R. Tolkien)

And now the Company of the Ring-bearer hit rock bottom. They had to cross the Bridge of Khazad-dum but were sorely pressed by Orcs, black Uruks of Mordor, cave-trolls and an unknown Evil which Gandalf hadn't met before which nearly did for him and all his magic powers. They fled along archways and huge halls where mighty carved pillars held up the roof high above. Then the floor fell away into a black chasm. A slender stone bridge spanned it with one curving spring of 50ft. Before they could get across their enemies caught up with them and in their midst was the worst horror of all - the <u>Balrog</u>! Gandalf held the bridge to allow the rest to escape but was obliged to destroy it, taking himself and Balrog down with it. "Fly you fools!" he cried, and was gone. The party was left stunned and leaderless but Aragorn took command and they managed to escape from the dreadful place and get into the sunlight where, at last, their grief wholly overcame them. Aragorn urged them on. "We must do without hope," he said, which is a typically Capricorn sentiment.

1874, Lancashire
Birth of **ROBERT SERVICE**

A man's poet! 'The Canadian Kipling.' His style was distinctive, easily parodied and, at one time, his <u>Bar Room Ballads</u> were so popular that they could be quoted (in the authorised or unauthorised versions) in any low dive or honky-tonk in the world.

> 'Back of the bar, in a solo game,
> sat Dangerous Dan McGrew,
> And watching his luck was his light o' love,
> the lady that's known as Lou...'

He emigrated to Canada when he was twenty and lived for many years in the Yukon and the Alaskan Klondike, getting an education 'in the school of hard knocks.' That's Capricorn.

~ Capricorn ~

A Sombre Day

A tinge of sadness about today's authors' birthdays. **ANNE BRONTE** (b. 1820, Yorkshire) was the youngest of the sisters, quiet, shy and delicate. She suffered from religious melancholia but was sent out as a governess. She drew on her experiences to write her novel Agnes Grey but her best-known work was probably The Tenant of Wildfell Hall. She died of TB when only 29. **RONALD FIRBANK** (b. 1886, Wales) came from a rich, titled, manufacturing family but he too had some sort of nervous illness which made speaking and eating difficult. He died when 39. His novels like Valmouth (made into a musical which would have tickled him pink) were too way out for his day and he got no encouragement or recognition. He lived a strange, lonely life, always on the outside. **NEVIL SHUTE** (b. 1899, Lancashire of Australian parents) despaired more and more of the human race the older he grew. On the Beach, when the world ends on the heels of an atomic disaster, is representative of his later books. His best known is probably A Town Like Alice.

1981, London
A Suicide-Birth
(from Spring Sonata by Bernice Rubens)

This is seriously weird. Bernice Rubens gives a conception time for Buster Rosen - 10 a.m. BST, September 22, 1977. That's the Jewish Day of Atonement, Yom Kippur. A Saturnian day of mourning. The birth was due on June 29, 1978 but Buster refused to be born. We know it's true because Dr. Brown, a NHS consultant, says so. He was today conducting a post-mortem on a vastly pregnant woman, in the course of which he retrieved his notebook from her womb containing the whole fantastic story. From the moment of conception Buster was a sentient being who eavesdropped on the world into which he was to be born. He didn't like it. In a previous life he had been a child prodigy killed in a road accident and had been sent back to continue his career. He was now a violin-playing foetal phenomenon. His mother was a talented pianist, his father just nasty, his grandma an all-Jewish dominant Mom. Mother had a Caesarean section but Buster not only dodged the knife but snatched in the notebook and pencil and a violin and bow (the violin was to be played to herald his birth). Mother got huge and was confined to a wheelchair. She and Buster played duets secretly but were discovered by father who arranged for them to give a concert. Sickened, Buster sawed through the umbilical cord with his bow killing his mother and himself. A melancholy end/beginning. Saturn is the patron planet of pagans and Jews according to the old wizard, Michael Scott. The author was a Booker prize winner in 1970.

JANUARY 19

1917, England
Birth of **EUNICE PARCHMAN**
(from <u>A Judgement in Stone</u> by Ruth Rendell)

Eunice was the live-in 'help' at the Coverdale's. She had a birthday today but told no one. She never did. It was years since anyone had sent her a card or given her a present. She was alone in the house. The telephone rang but she didn't answer it. She didn't like telephones, they alarmed her. However, it kept on and very reluctantly she picked it up. Oh dear! All the later deaths resulted from this simple action, although probably they were only postponed. It was Mr. Coverdale who asked her to look for some papers on his desk. She put the telephone down and hid but the Coverdales were getting near to the truth and were to die for it. The slab-like, unresponsive Eunice could neither read nor write and was prepared to murder to cover up. Yes, Eunice was right on Capricorn's bottom rung. 'A stone that breathed,' her author called her. Her horoscope shows Sun and Mercury exactly conjoined in Capricorn opposed by Saturn, Capricorn's ruler. Mercury is the planet of communication and getting about. Saturn in opposition impedes this. It suggests Eunice's illiteracy and her later imprisonment. It all hangs together and Eunice was very lucky not to have hanged with them.

JANUARY 20

1898, London
Birth of **MOGENS WESTERBY**
(from <u>Asta's Book</u> by Barbara Vine)

He was destined to be killed on the Somme and there was nothing else much to say of him. He was just one of the ordinary ones of the earth. His mother, Asta, recorded that he wasn't clever but he was a nice

~ Capricorn ~ Aquarius ~

kind boy. She wondered where he got if from - not from anyone in her family, it must have been from his father's family of 'brutish peasants'.

JOY ADAMSON, lion-tamer, author of <u>Born Free</u> was born today in 1910 and wouldn't have thought much of being lumped together with Mogens. She was a somewhat autocratic lady by all accounts. Oddly enough though, she too was destined to be shot dead. It was at her home in Kenya on January 3, 1980.

JANUARY 21

St. Agnes

The Eve of St. Agnes on January 20 was renowned for its rites with mirrors, pins, garters, dumb cakes etc., indulged in by young ladies anxious to learn the names of their future bridegrooms. Or as John Keats put it in his poem, <u>The Eve of St. Agnes</u>:

> 'They told her how, upon St. Agnes Eve,
> Young virgins might have visions of delight,
> And soft adorings from their loves receive
> Upon the honey'd middle of the night,
> If ceremonies due they did aright.'

Madeline faithfully carried out the rituals but young Porphyro, à la Romeo and Juliet, had persuaded an old servant to let him into Madeline's bedchamber. Keats then paints in words a luscious picture of the room, Madeline, Madeline's dress and a profusion of fruit which, for no apparent reason, Porphyro heaped up beside the bed. Madeline awoke believing Porphyro to be the promised vision of delight but he convinced her he was real and they stole away through the drunken guests into the storm, <u>aye, ages long ago</u>. Edith Sitwell's commentary in her <u>Atlantic Book of British and American Poetry</u> on 'this miracle of poetry' gets technical. Long, high vowel sounds and dark vowel sounds give a texture of calm moonlight and menacing shadows, of 'delicate arabesques of dim sparkles' (produced by sharp 't' sounds) and 'glittering cold airs dying away again'. Glitter, sparkle and delicate arabesques sound airily Aquarian all right but enjoy!

> 'St. Agnes Eve! Ah, bitter chill it was!
> The owl, for all his feathers, was a-cold...'

~ Capricorn ~ Aquarius ~

1901, Isle of Wight
Death of Queen Victoria
(from <u>The Houses in Between</u> by Howard Spring)

Sarah Undridge nee Rainborough had an eventful day. She visited her nephew's new art gallery in Brook Street, she heard that her son had been wounded and his batman killed in the war in South Africa, and Queen Victoria died.

> 'The new century came, and the Queen lived through the first three weeks. It was a strange day - that January day when we read of her death. Well, this was the end of it for her; a bloody and desolate end enough, but now it was over. We passed from one century into another, from the "Victorian golden evening" into the Edwardian dawn.'

And, astrologically, from Capricornian rigidity and sobriety into untrammelled and revolutionary Aquarius. It was indeed 'a strange day'.

1918, 8.00 a.m., Bracket Towers, Bracket Basing, nr. Romney Marsh, Kent
Birth of **DAME HILDA BRACKET**
(from <u>Memories of One Little Maid</u> by Dame Hilda)

She has both Sun and ascendant in Aquarius and ruling Uranus also in Aquarius. All of which explains why Britain's premier prima donna is in a class of her own. For all her pearls and bouffant hair-do's, Dame Hilda comes over as a 'Mod'. Flamboyant, unconventional, eccentric, sliding into the downright odd. A very odd woman indeed. In fact, one sometimes wonders if she's a woman at all! She is the descendant of a terribly aristocratic family and shines in both blue-blooded and Bohemian circles. Dame Hilda has not married, probably a wise decision. A dominant Uranian influence contains the seeds of discord and divorce, the Aquarian nature not being one to take kindly to the trammels of domesticity or of being 'tied'. Her life has been one of unbridled excitement, her war work especially - but that remains

~ Aquarius ~

an official secret. Her partner in musical and domestic life is Dr. Evadne Hinge. As Hinge and Bracket they were for many years preeminent in their duets of well-loved favourites... Ivor Novello medleys and selections from Gilbert and Sullivan bringing repeated demands for encores. In retirement the strains of We'll Gather Lilacs and A Reg'lar Royal Queen still permeate the grateful Sussex air.

JANUARY 24

1862, New York
Birth of **EDITH WHARTON**, novelist

She was an Aquarian free-spirit, an energetic, whirling, cosmopolitan socialite, a keen observer of social mores and a vivid, satirical writer. She drove a huge, powerful Packard furiously. She had a wide circle of equally witty, literary friends but her sexual relationships were not very satisfactory. She divorced her husband who was said to have gone mad but this may have been an exaggeration on her part - she suffered from 'nerves' herself. In World War I her Aquarian social conscience came to the fore and she worked with Belgian refugees, took charge of an orphanage of 60 children, ran a workshop for unemployed women and 'charity' restaurants. A formidable woman but fundamentally kind. Her novels include The House of Mirth.

JANUARY 25

1759, Ayrshire
Birth of **ROBERT BURNS**

1874, Paris
Birth of **SOMERSET MAUGHAM**

1882, shortly after Noon, Kensington, London
Birth of **VIRGINIA WOOLF**

Aquarian writers crowd in today, every one of them - unusual. Burns, of course, is Scotland's national poet, as well known for his boozing and womanising as his haunting love poems. He was very radical in his views and had scant regard for the Church. Tonight is Burns' Night, so they'll certainly be singing his Auld Lang Syne. Maugham looked like a Chinese idol and had a dreadful stammer. He gave up a medical career to become a playwright with great success. He later turned to writing novels - The Moon and Sixpence - and short stories

~ Aquarius ~

- Rain - and his reminiscences - <u>A Writer's Notebook</u>. He married but it was a transient affair as he was homosexual and lived with his young secretary Gerald Haxton. He was accused of cynicism but retorted, Aquarian-like, that he merely told the Truth. Virginia Woolf had a beautiful, aristocratic, mask-like face. She was one of the great innovative novelists - <u>To the Lighthouse</u> and <u>Mrs Dalloway</u> - using experimental techniques such as the so-called stream-of-consciousness. She was an excellent critic and essayist, malicious but brilliant. She suffered from mental disturbance and drowned herself in 1941.

Finally, today in 1954, the public had its first chance to hear that dazzling word juggling which is <u>Under Milk Wood</u> by Dylan Thomas who, maddeningly, was a Scorpio! It was recognised immediately as innovative. Thomas's cast of eccentric, completely individual characters ear-mark it for the Aquarian file instantly.

JANUARY 26

1931, Antarctica
Scientific Research in Terra Terrabilis
(from <u>At the Mountains of Madness</u> by H.P. Lovecraft)

A search party from the Miskatonic University Expedition, formed to drill for deep level specimens of rock and soil from the Antarctic, found the remains of the camp which had been set up a few days earlier to begin the experimental drilling. The men and dogs had been savaged beyond belief in circumstances of unimaginable horror. Prior to the attack they had been sending back astonishing reports of skeletal fragments of saurian and mammal life so, before starting the return journey, scientific zeal drove the narrator and a companion, Danforth, to fly further on over a strange mountain range. They got back sixteen hours later with Danforth having a nervous breakdown and a joint determination to keep their discoveries secret. They had seen from the air a 'Cyclopean maze of squared, curved and angled blocks', a massive and frightful stone city. With the craziness of all scientific researchers, they landed and explored, carefully photographing and recording. They calculated the age of edifices hewn from solid rock as 50 million years yet linked with these signs of preterrestrial life were carved designs and diagrams reminiscent of the latest findings in mathematics and astrophysics. They deduced from the sculptures and carvings the coming of alien, star-headed, winged beings from outer space, who fought their battles with some now-unknown form of energy. They created scientific knowledge ...but H.P. Lovecraft was the master of cumulative horror and must be swallowed whole not taken in driblets.

~ Aquarius ~

JANUARY 27

1890s, Shores of the Baltic
A 'Different' Picnic
(from <u>Elizabeth and Her German Garden</u> by Elizabeth von Arnim)

By way of a change today Elizabeth went for a picnic on the desolate, ice-bound shores of the Baltic. Deep snow, a hard frost, no wind and a cloudless sky - what could be better? No people, no mosquitoes. She had the sleigh brought out, wrapped up everyone in furs and off they went in the highest of spirits. Dry, bright, intense cold is healthy, she believed, and it's better to go out and enjoy it rather than skulk indoors.

JANUARY 28

1873, 10.00 p.m., St. Sauveur-en-Puisaye
Birth of **COLETTE**, author

A sharply distinctive Gallic writer. After an enchanted childhood she married Willy, a journalist, who plunged her into the Parisian demi-monde and slave-drove her into writing books which he passed off as his own. They divorced in 1906, which was unheard of at the time, and she went on the music halls, an equally unheard of act of Aquarian defiance. She lived with a transvestite <u>marquise</u>, re-married, re-divorced, re-re-married and kept on writing. She became admired, honoured and fêted. Her best loved book is, of course, <u>Gigi</u> which was made into a film and seen by everyone. The theme of a young girl being groomed by her two elderly respectable aunts to become a courtesan was equally unheard of.

JANUARY 29

1854, Manchester
Madness!
(from <u>The Rag Nymph</u> by Catherine Cookson)

Young Millie Forester had been sent to a Catholic convent for her own safety but it was a nightmare and one of the nuns, Sister Mary, hated her from the start and treated her cruelly. Millie's long golden hair, in

~ Aquarius ~

particular, inflamed her and she became obsessed by the notion that it had to be cut off. Today she cracked completely and went mad in the cloakroom, attacking Millie with the scissors and screaming that she was Evil! Evil! Mother Superior slapped her face hard, which brought her to what few senses she had left, and she was taken back to her cell, still frothing at the mouth. However, Millie had to leave.

JANUARY 30

1946, London
Birth of **JOHN BIRD**, editor

He is the founder of The Big Issue, a street paper and radical enough for Aquarius. So is he. He was born in a slum and brought up in an orphanage. He drifted into crime and politics (what's the difference?) and was a continual irritant to the worthy social workers. Finally, an approved school sorted him out and he became a mature student. And now he's got the MBE! He's lived on the streets himself and knows all about the homeless. His philosophy is that we have to help ourselves - we mustn't give our lives over to politicians.

1983, England
Scandalous News-sheets
(from The Growing Pains of Adrian Mole by Sue Townsend)

Adrian spent his Sunday afternoon reading The News of the World and marvelling at the number of vicars who were running away with attractive divorcees. That's Aquarian life, Adrian!

JANUARY 31

1960s, England
Transformation!
(from Charlie and the Chocolate Factory by Roald Dahl)

Today Charlie Bucket found the fifth and final Golden Ticket in a bar of chocolate and his and his family's grim existence was turned topsy-turvy and dusted with magic. Mr. Willy Wonka, surely an Aquarian, owned the chocolate factory in the town where the Buckets lived and had an international reputation as the maker of the most delicious confectionery ever. Nobody was allowed into the factory because of spies, it was staffed by tiny Oompa-Loompas, but one day, to universal excitement, Mr. Wonka launched a competition. Five Golden Tickets would be planted at random in his chocolate bars and the five finders would be given a day at the factory and a lifetime's supply of sweets. (The one who survived the course would get the <u>real</u> prize, but none of them knew about that). Poor little Charlie only got one bar of chocolate a year on his birthday but there was no Golden Ticket in his Wonka's Whipple-Scrumptious Fudgemallow Delight and that was that. However, today he found a fifty pence piece in the gutter and was so hungry (they lived on cabbage soup) that he couldn't resist taking it to the nearest shop and buying two Wonka Fudgemallow Delights, and the second one contained A GOLDEN TICKET!!! Into Aquarian time now so today could be your Golden Ticket day too.

FEBRUARY
1

1950s, England
Birth of **BERNARD 'BOUNDER' CARTWRIGHT**
(from <u>Araminta's Wedding</u> by Jilly Cooper)

Jilly Cooper, who knows about such things, quite properly made Bounder Cartwright an Aquarian. Aquarians are handsome, aristocratic, elegant, amusing, but not cut out for lasting, intimate relationships. The lives of your true, blue-blooded Aquarians are akin to being on a roller-coaster. Bounder turned up in London in the 1980s. No one was richer, smarter or more glamorous. He was an excellent polo player. He was 'sex on Lamborghini wheels'. He had long, narrow, aristocratic feet and rarely paid for his perfectly tailored suits. But in the '90s the Stock Market, the property market and Lloyds collapsed and yuppies like Bounder had everything repossessed, even Bounder's dog's beanbag went. It meant a rich wife and Bounder lit on the junoesque (i.e. fat) only daughter of the Earl of Atherstone, Araminta, who would inherit twenty million and half Lincolnshire. Bounder's creditors cried off, wedding plans went ahead. Bounder's parents' arrived from the U.S. - Sybil a painted Wicked Fairy and Josslyn a jolly decent sort in a tweed skirt. They were lesbians who had adopted Bounder. The roller-coaster nosedived when Araminta's mother unexpectedly produced a son and heir, thereby impoverishing Araminta. Nigel Dempster reeled. Then Bounder's real parents came to light and he became the richest man in England. Would he marry Araminta? Yes! He settled for the quiet life and the occasional bit on the side. The bridegroom having three mothers at the ceremony was unusual but Happy Birthday, Bounder!

~ Aquarius ~

1882, Dublin
Birth of **JAMES JOYCE**, author

Literary anarchist, author of <u>Ulysses</u> (once incomprehensible now comprehensible and allowed to be a masterpiece) and still incomprehensible <u>Finnegan's Wake</u>, for which he devised his own language. Through the thicket of obscurity, obscenity peeped and both books were banned for many years. Some reviews: <u>The most colossal legpull in history</u>; <u>The foulest book that has ever found its way into print</u>; <u>Enough to make a Hottentot sick</u>. (The last from <u>The Sporting Times</u>!) Nevertheless, Joyce's work struggled into the world and kicked down the existing literary partitions. The psychoanalyst Jung was fascinated by Joyce and no wonder for Joyce was the strangest man. He was obsessed by religion but repudiated Catholicism very early in life. He was full of fears and phobias. He wouldn't live in the country because God was less likely to strike him dead by (Uranian) lightning if he was with a lot of innocent people. He was terrified of thunderstorms. He had, all told, a miserable life - 'every moanday, tearsday, wailsday, thumpday, frightday, shatterday' of it. He and his girl friend lived on the continent always on the move in self-imposed exile and poverty. He didn't marry his Nora until 1931 and only then because of some legal requirement. Aquarians like the illusion of being unfettered. He died of peritonitis, delirious. What brand of delirium served as delirium for James Joyce is hard to fathom, but there you are. He was an excellent singer and pianist.

1901, England
Birth of **ROSAMOND LEHMANN**, author

True to Aquarius her novels were considered quite shocking and so, for a different reason, was <u>The Swan in the Evening</u>. This is a scrupulous record of the mystical experiences she underwent following the sudden death of her daughter from polio. It shows her as 'a sceptic, born into an agnostic family...marrying one atheist and remarrying another' (her first marriage was dissolved), falling over backwards to <u>prove</u> survival after death. Aquarius has to make certain. 'In another 50/100 years it may well be <u>proved</u> that survival of death is a scientific fact,' she wrote. She was scathing about 'the silliness, sensationalism, vulgarity and credulity that muddies and clogs up the lower reaches of spiritualism, fortune-telling, astrology and the like.' Luckily she found the books of Geraldine Cummins and made discoveries which thrilled and astounded her. She became convinced that unimpeachable evidential records were available and the 'greatest of the world's great minds had always known... that we are souls travelling in eternity; the Tibetan and the Egyptian Books of the Dead say it; the Upanishads, the Bible, Socrates, Plato, Plotinus, Dante, Blake, Wordsworth, Shakespeare, Emily Bronte... and Teilhard de Chardin.' Whether Miss Lehmann convinces or not, The Swan in the Evening, like all her books, is beautifully written. She is considered one of the most beautiful women of her time too.

FEBRUARY 4

2021, Southwold, Suffolk
A Bleak Future
(from The Children of Men by P. D. James)

A glimpse into another author's idea of what's in store for us. This despairing book of society's future is a one-off from the popular crime novelist P. D. James. It's an infertile world where children are no longer born and where old people are disposed of in mass suicide ceremonies given the name 'Quietus'. Today Dr. Theo Faron witnessed an all-female one. They changed into white night-dresses in the former jolly beach chalets and with a band playing old time favourites like Bye-bye Blackbird they filed into two small barges which were decorated with flowers. Two soldiers in each boat shackled their ankles and to the singing of Abide With Me the boats cast off, accompanied by a motor boat to bring the soldiers back to land once the barges were nicely sinking. It seemed quiet and orderly enough, but it wasn't suicide as Theo discovered when one of the old ladies tried to break away. It was state murder.

FEBRUARY 5

1914, 7.40 a.m., St. Louis, Missouri, U.S.A
Birth of **WILLIAM BURROUGHS**, 'Beat' novelist

A grandson of the adding machine Burroughs. Although one of the élite, he was attracted by New York low life and became a junkie. He's another Aquarian writer whose style opened up new vistas but the black humour, obscenity and sadism thereby displayed didn't please

~ Aquarius ~

all. Norman Mailer (another Aquarian) believed him to be the only living American novelist to conceivably be possessed by genius. His aim was to dispense with words, 'an ox-cart way of doing things', and to substitute images.

> 'They will be laid aside eventually, probably sooner than we think. This is something that will happen in the space age.'

He shot to horrified fame with <u>The Naked Lunch</u>. Interested in Sci-Fi, Zen, Scientology and Dr. Reich's Orgone Theories, Burroughs had five planets in eclectic Aquarius. He said it's common-sense evolution that mankind will have to undergo biological alterations as we penetrate further into space. If we wish to survive we must use our intelligence to plan mutations not allow them to occur at random. His writing is experimental and the most advanced techniques of painting, music and film are applied to it. Like Norman Mailer, he had wife trouble. He shot his second by accident in a bit of William Tell horseplay. Their son died young of drink and drug abuse. Mary McCarthy called him 'A soured Utopian'.

FEBRUARY 6

1935, London
Inexplicable!
(from <u>The Hollow Man</u> by John Dickson Carr)

Dr. Grimaud and his friends met regularly in the back parlour of the <u>Warwick Tavern</u> in Museum Street. Tonight they were discussing vampires when a stranger entered and produced a grubby calling card announcing that he was Pierre Fley, Illusionist, and the fun started. This is one of John Dickson Carr's famous 'locked room' mysteries. Two persons were to be killed. The murderer of the first literally disappeared into thin air. The second victim was done in in the middle of an empty street with watchers at each end, yet not a soul saw the murderer and no footprints appeared in the snow. Superintendent Hadley did not believe in goblins or wizards but several people began to wonder whether the figure which stalked through the case might not be a hollow shell. If you removed the cap and coat and the child's false face you might reveal - nothing, like the man in a certain famous romance by Mr. H.G. Wells.

1812, Portsmouth
Birth of **CHARLES DICKENS**

The genius of the day, the month, the year, the decade, the age, and all innocent of the Aquarian urge to experiment. He just wrote rich, satisfying masterpieces. However, he was certainly an Aquarian social reformer. Thanks to him the infamous Dotheboys Halls vanished, the debtors' prisons, the Bumbles and Poor Law Guardians took a knock from which they never really recovered. His contempt for religious hypocrites finished off the Chadbands and Pecksniffs. Politics? He declined two invitations to stand for Parliament as a Whig but he had connections with that august institution having been a Parliamentary reporter in his youth. The Eatonswill by-election ("The eyes of the world are on Eatonswill") can still be read with profit, let alone relish. He founded the <u>Daily News</u> in 1846 'to strike a blow for the poor' and went to the U.S. with the highest of hopes expecting to find an Aquarian Utopia. What he did find was 'slavery and corruption upheld and defended' and a Congress worse than our own Parliament. Another Aquarian dream shattered. His home life was peculiar. He had an enormous family for whose existence he apparently blamed his wife solely and in the end separated from her. Even Dickens didn't dare try to divorce her, not in Victorian London, but intention was there. Pretty young actresses were more to his taste. He had Aquarian stage fever and the dramatic readings of his own works were said to have shortened his life which was caused by a quick, unexpected stroke.

1828, 12.00 p.m. (Noon), Nantes
Birth of **JULES VERNE**

Genius pervades this bit of the zodiac. Here's another. A scientific, and therefore even more Aquarian, genius. His science-fiction seemed the wildest flight of fancy when it first appeared but all has come amazingly true, even down to the actual locale of the Moon probe launchings. In <u>Round the Moon</u> his adventurers were fired off from a gigantic cannon only a few miles from what is now Cape Canaveral. The Compleat Aquarian he was always up to the minute with the latest scientific discoveries and possibilities and was clever enough to see even further developments ahead, so much so that professional scientists looked forward to his books and queued up with the rest for A Journey to the Centre of the Earth, Twenty Thousand Leagues under the Sea, Around the World in Eighty Days and the rest, which you will find used lavishly through these pages. The Bookworm Astrologer thinks the world of him as he was as generous with his dates as he was with his scientific information. As for his private life, he married a widow but catastrophe struck in 1886 when he was shot and crippled for the rest of his life by an insane nephew.

FEBRUARY 9

1890s, England
An Eccentric
(from The Invisible Man by H.G. Wells)

John Dickson Carr's Hollow Man was still proceeding - today Dr. Gideon Fell took a hand - but, of more moment, the Invisible Man, who was mentioned on February 6, arrived on the scene. Muffled up from head to foot and with a soft felt hat pulled right down over his face, he came walking through the biting wind and driving snow to the Coach & Horses inn and flung down his portmanteau. "A fire!" he cried. "In the name of human charity! A room and a fire!" But even when the fire was burning briskly he refused to take off his hat and coat or his gloves. Next day his luggage arrived - all books and bottles - and the carrier's dog went mad and bit him. Obviously a mad Aquarian scientist.

FEBRUARY 10

1898, 4.30 a.m., Augsburg, Germany
Birth of **BERTOLT BRECHT**, dramatist

He found fame in 1928 with The Threepenny Opera. A Marxist and eccentric, he first studied science but got caught up with politics to such an extent that he was exiled from his native Germany when the Nazis took over. In 1949 he went to East Berlin where he built up a fine dramatic company which performed his modern, left-wing, propaganda plays like Mother Courage and The Caucasian Chalk Circle. He has been called the most original dramatist and producer of the century. He was never interested in artistic effect, only in how to slam home his message to the audience to force them to think and to participate. He kept to his early scientific training and Aquarian

~ Aquarius ~

stars by stating the problem coolly and clearly and by observing the behaviour of the human guinea pigs involved. Although a devout Communist he was fettered to Aquarius and his relations with the Russians (e.g. Authority) were not all that they might have been. Aquarians find left-wing creeds very pleasing in theory and when applied to others, but don't bargain on fitting into them themselves.

FEBRUARY 11

1963, London
Suicide of SYLVIA PLATH, poet and novelist

Sylvia Plath was a Scorpio born October 27, 1932. She married our late Poet Laureate **TED HUGHES** but they separated in 1962. The last straw must have come today (when Mercury approached her natal Saturn in Capricorn, a terribly depressing influence) and she committed suicide. In 1998 Ted Hughes published a book of poetry addressed to her called Birthday Letters. From the astrologer's point of view the most interesting piece is St. Botolph's which described their first meeting at a party in Cambridge in February 1956. He evidently had a good working knowledge of astrology and was able to predict that the evening would entail disastrous expense. It was 'a planetary certainty, according to Prospero's book.' Jupiter conjunct the Moon in Leo and Venus in the opposite sign of Aquarius is pretty lush by anybody's book. The conjunction fell on his natal Sun (he was born August 17, 1930) and on her natal ruling Mars. Then it gets puzzling and there are astrological references which don't 'jell'. However, he left it, he said, for serious astrologers to worry over. If you don't want to, enjoy the poems anyway, they're a moving and lasting memorial.

FEBRUARY 12

A Supersonic Day

In New York 1940 at 5.15 p.m., **SUPERMAN** was first broadcast, although he had made a tentative appearance in Action Comics No. 1 in June 1938 (see June 1). However, this is counted as his 'birthday'. Faster than a bullet, more powerful than a locomotive, he came from another planet and Aquarius is the only possible zodiac sign for him. His dress is weird too - underpants on top of everything else - only an Aquarian could get away with it. On the birthday, Mars and Saturn were exactly conjoined in Aries which means personal danger, violence

~ Aquarius ~

and injury and tests of strength. Well, Superman could never be accused of taking it easy. We are given to understand from a certain Cheese Lovers' magazine that this is also the birthday of **GROMIT**, the gadget-minded, well-read pooch of Wallace and Gromit fame. He too is an astronaut and thinks nothing of going to the Moon for Wallace's supper cheese.

FEBRUARY 13

1907, England
Birth of **GEORGE COVERDALE**
(from <u>A Judgement in Stone</u> by Ruth Rendell)

A gentleman-Aquarian, very civilised, kind, well-bred and handsome, a successful business and family man, but his 58th birthday in 1965 was to be his last. His only mistake in life was to employ Eunice Parchman as a live-in help and on St. Valentine's Day she was going to slaughter him and his entire family. At that time a nasty little conjunction of Uranus and Pluto was moving through Virgo and had come into opposition with George's natal Saturn. Given the nature of the three planets, it presages collapse of the old order. He was the first that Eunice shot dead. **RUTH RENDELL** was born on February 17, 1930. She has a conjunction of Mercury and Mars in Aquarius which is excellent for a writer, especially of crime novels.

FEBRUARY 14

St. Valentine's Day

Plenty of literary Valentines flying about today amongst our old friends. Bathsheba sent Farmer Boldwood one (<u>Far from the Madding Crowd</u> by Thomas Hardy) and Joan Smith sent Eunice Parchman one which, as Eunice was illiterate, was a waste of money (<u>A Judgement in Stone</u> by Ruth Rendell). The 14-year old John Ridd climbed up Bagworthy Water, met Lorna Doone again and fell in love (<u>Lorna Doone</u> by R.D. Blackmore). On the other side of the Valentine heart, the memorable trial of Bardell v. Pickwick was heard today at the Guildhall in London. Sam Weller noticed the irony. "Walentine's day - reg'lar good day for a breach o' promise trial." Not that the Bardell/Pickwick relationship had ever been anything other than landlady and lodger but Mrs. Bardell fell into the hands of the wily Dodson & Fogg, solicitors, who retained Serjeant Buzfuz as their Counsel. 'Serjeant Buzfuz began by saying that never, in the whole course of his professional experience - never, from the very first moment of his applying himself to the study and practice of the law - had he approached a case with feelings of such deep emotion.' W.S. Gilbert was later to draw upon this in his breach-of-promise case in Trial by Jury. "With a sense of deep emotion I approach this painful case/For I never had a notion that a man could be so base!"

FEBRUARY 15

c. 1910, U.S.A.
The New Broom
(from Dear Enemy by Jean Webster)

This was Sally McBride's first day at The John Grier Home for Orphans. She was a pretty, lively socialite who had been manoeuvred, much against her will, by her friend Judy Abbott (the Daddy-Long-Legs girl) to run the Home and improve it. She began today in Aquarian time which presaged well for revolutionary treatment. She was awakened at 6.00 a.m. by a gong and lay for a time listening to the 25 little girls having face-washes in the lavatory overhead, then she introduced herself to them at breakfast in the dining room.

> 'Horror piled on horror - those bare drab walls, oil-cloth-covered tables with tin cups and plates and wooden benches, and, by way of decoration, that one illuminated text, THE LORD WILL PROVIDE! The trustee who added that last touch must possess a grim sense of humour...I never knew there was any spot in the world so entirely ugly; and when I saw those rows and rows of pale, listless, blue-uniformed children, the whole dismal business suddenly struck me with such a shock that I almost collapsed.'

FEBRUARY 16

Late 18th century, Curtain Wells
Aquarian Revolt
(from The Passionate Elopement by Compton Mackenzie)

There was a rebellion at Curtain Wells famed, like Bath, for its chalybeate springs. It was pouring with rain when the gentry came out of church and they refused to walk to the Pump Room to drink the

~ Aquarius ~

waters, they said there was enough of the stuff coming down outside. This backsliding so appalled General Sir Jeremy Dummer that he had an apoplectic fit and died. The unrepentant were more inclined to blame the fatality on to the Public Breakfast which Curtain Wells had accorded Sir Jeremy the previous day to commemorate his 21st consecutive winter at the spa and at which he consumed two plates of turtle soup, the better part of a codfish, the wing of a capon, the wing of a duck, the breast of a pullet, a hot buttered apple dumpling and two or three slices of ham which he hadn't noticed before, washed down by two tankards of old ale, one bottle of Maderia and two of port.

FEBRUARY 17

3019, Third Age, Middle Earth
Aquarian Aerial Rescue
(from The Lord of the Rings by J.R.R. Tolkien)

On January 15 Gandalf the Wizard fell from the Bridge of Kazad-dûm with the Balrog. They fell together for days, still fighting in the midst of fire, then plunged into deep water, cold and black as death. They reached the bottom where Balrog fled into tunnels as old as time gnawed out by nameless things. Gandalf had to follow the Balrog which knew the way up the Endless Stair to the peak of Zirak-zigil. There the Balrog was recharged with fire and they had another furious fight until the Balrog was at last conquered and broke the mountainside in its dying. Gandalf lay forgotten and alone while the stars wheeled overhead and each day was as long as an earthly life age. It was here today that the great eagle Gwaihir the Windlord found him and bore him away to Lothlorien for healing. He was as light as a swan's feather and the sun shone through him.

FEBRUARY 18

1983, England
Student Revolt
(from The Growing Pains of Adrian Mole by Sue Townsend)

Adrian was excluded from school for a week for writing a revolutionary poem on the toilet wall. 'What future is there for the young?/What songs are waiting to be sung?...' Jupiter and Uranus were in exact conjunction in Sagittarius which no doubt aroused these dramatic stirrings of individuality in Adrian and his beatings against the bars of conventionality, and the Sun in Aquarius of course.

~ Aquarius ~ Pisces ~

1928, New York
Birth of **CHARLIE GORDON**
(from <u>Flowers for Algernon</u> by Daniel Keyes)

When Charlie Gordon wrote his first 'progris riport' on 'March 5 1965' he said that he had turned 37 two weeks before so today seems a likely bet for the date. Anyway, 'cusp' birthdays are always tricky. On 19/20 February 1928 not only did the Sun move from Aquarius to Pisces but the Moon, close behind, moved from Capricorn to Aquarius. Neptune, an exaggerating influence, opposed the Sun whichever sign it was in so Charlie was going to dither between the two. His 'progris riport' verified this as it unfolded. He began as a Piscean, an engaging moron, sweet, innocent, liked by everyone in the building where he worked as a janitor and in the evening class he attended under his adored Miss Kinnian. He was superstitious and had a rabbit's foot and a lucky penny to protect him. They didn't. Two psychologists began tests on him and Algernon, a laboratory rat. Algernon beat Charlie hollow in the intelligence tests until the doctors operated on Charlie's brain and turned him into a genius (exaggerated Aquarius). He became much clever than they, so clever that he realised that he and Algernon had learned too much, too fast, and their brains would disintegrate. Algernon died and Charlie reverted to his earlier Piscean state, happy enough although he had dim memories of what it felt like to be an Aquarian genius.

1868, Early hours, bottom of the Atlantic
Neptune's Kingdom
(from <u>Twenty Thousand Leagues Under the Sea</u> by Jules Verne)

A perfect Pisces/Neptune day. Captain Nemo of the 'Nautilus' took Professor Aronnax on a walk beneath the ocean waves. They donned heavy diving suits and, following his leader, the Professor soon found himself walking along rough roads and through thickets of dead trees, fish swimming among their petrified branches. Among submarine wonders, the Captain led the way up the slopes of a volcano still vomiting torrents of red-hot lava which lit up the unbelievable scene below - the ruins of a submerged city. 'Its roofs were sunken, its temples demolished, its arches in pieces, its columns on the ground,

~ Aquarius ~ Pisces ~

but its proportions were clearly outlined, reminding me of the stately architecture of Tuscany. There were the remains of a gigantic aqueduct; here the encrusted remains of an Acropolis; vestiges of an ancient port on the shore of a vanished sea which had given shelter to merchant ships and craft of war; the outlines of crumbled walls and long lines of wide deserted streets, an ancient Pompeii buried beneath the sea! Where was I? I felt I must speak and tried to take off the globe of brass that imprisoned my head. But Captain Nemo stopped me with a gesture. Then picking up a piece of clayey stone, he went up to a black basaltic rock and traced on it the single word - ATLANTIS!'

FEBRUARY 21

1862, Westminster Bridge, London
Exploration by Sea and Air
(from Five Weeks in a Balloon by Jules Verne)

At 5.00 a.m., with Mars rising in the east, three explorers boarded the Resolute on the first stage of a journey which was to take them by sea to Zanzibar where they were to embark in a balloon which would travel across Africa. Five weeks? Well, with winds of 240 m.p.h. they could cross Africa in twelve hours but Dr. Fergusson, who had initiated and led the expedition, intended to land at intervals and explore. He particularly wished to find the source of the Nile. The project was extremely hazardous. Dozens had died of fever or at the hands of murderous tribes in similar attempts. Even in a balloon it wasn't going to be a picnic but, as Dr. Fergusson said, "The man born to be hanged will never drown." Not much comfort in the face of dangers which would make Richard Branson's hair stand on end. The expedition was financed by the Royal Geographical Society at the cost of £2,500.00. They made it on May 24 and received the Society's gold medal for the most noteworthy exploration work of 1862.

FEBRUARY 22

1920s/1930s, Canada
Piscean Fantasy
(from Emily's Quest by L.M. Montgomery)

Emily, a poetical, aspiring authoress, went for a walk by herself this evening in a creamy, misty sunset which was followed by bright moonlight. It was a fairy world of glamour, a white moon-world. 'I

~ Pisces ~

went through the orchard where the black shadows of the trees fell over the snow; I went up to the gleaming white hill with the stars over it; I lurked along fir copses dim with mystery, and along still wood aisles where the night hid from the moonshine; I loitered across a dreamland field of ebon and ivory... And every breath was a lyric and every thought an ecstasy; and I've come back with a soul washed white and clean in the great crystal bath of the night. But Aunt Elizabeth said people would think me crazy if they saw me roaming around alone at this time of the night. And Aunt Laura made me take a drink of hot black currant decoction lest I might have taken a cold.' (Emily is from the same pen as <u>Anne of Green Gables</u>, not so well-known but much the same in character.)

FEBRUARY 23

1928 (?) a leap year anyway, U.S.A.
Birth of **SUZY**
(from <u>Sweet Thursday</u> by John Steinbeck)

Suzy arrived in Cannery Row out of the blue and was taken on as a hustler in the local hook house. The proprietress, Fauna, was a dab hand at the stars and specialised in startling revelations. She soon got Suzy's birthday, although the year was suspect. "You're fish," she said. "I don't even like fish," said Suzy. "Why, hell, I break out if I look at a fish." "If you ain't lied about your birthday, you're a fish. Now, let's see - fish is to Jupiter...carry two...and three left over in the House of Venus..." From this unorthodox procedure, Fauna deduced that Suzy would marry a Cancer, e.g., someone who worked with crabs, which could only be Doc who collected and sold various marine creatures. Fauna, who also fancied herself as a matchmaker, challenged Doc who plucked out of the air the first date he could think of which <u>wasn't</u> his birthday - July 4. "Holy apples! He's a gone goose," shrieked Fauna. And he was. Suzy had had a sad life, been ditched in her teens when pregnant, lost the baby, done time for vagrancy and was penniless. She was useless as a hustler as she kept falling in love with her clients. She was pretty, her prettiness varying with her moods. She was Pisces. If she was born in 1928, she had Sun <u>and</u> Moon in the sign.

~ Pisces ~

1957, New Jersey
Birth of **GARY MURPHY** aka GARY SONEJI
(from <u>Along Came A Spider</u> by James Patterson)

A villainous Piscean, a piranha cruising amongst the minnows. A child kidnapper and serial killer in a big way - he claimed hundreds of victims. He lived in a fishy fantasy world, unable to separate dreams from reality. At the age of twelve he had convinced himself that he was the Lindbergh baby kidnapper and murderer in 1932. In his defence there was a sob-story childhood of being shut up in the basement by a cruel stepmother and sexually abused by father, but whether there was any truth in all this was another matter. Anyway, it was no excuse for his violent treatment of others. Brutality isn't a Piscean trait but his other characteristics certainly were. He was a good subject for hypnosis. He was a brilliant mimic, actor and master of disguise; he could play any part he needed. He was a sociopath who, right up to the last page, when he had been caught and tried, could manipulate and fool most people. He claimed to have a multi-personality. Good Gary Murphy just didn't know what bad Gary Soneji was up to. Best-selling author Patterson chose Gary's birthday well.

1917, England
Birth of **THOMAS JERICHO**
(from <u>Enigma</u> by Robert Harris)

Even the title is Piscean! Thomas lived a secret life. He was an only child and his mathematical genius kept him apart from others and made him a solitary. Apparently colourless and insignificant-looking, Mars conjoined his Sun which gave him plenty of energy when directed into the fishy Piscean world of official secrets, chess problems and code-breaking. When war came he was drafted into Intelligence and in 1943 sent to the famous Bletchley Park to work on breaking the U-boat code. There he worked himself into a breakdown from nervous exhaustion which wasn't helped by his strange romance with the lovely, mysterious Claire who disappeared leaving him teetering on the edge of madness. It turned out that she herself was a government spy using a false identity...

~ Pisces ~

1991, New York
Dancing Feet
(from <u>Loves Music, Loves to Dance</u> by Mary Higgins Clark)

Funeral day of Erin Kelley, latest victim of a serial killer with a shoe fetish. Erin had been answering personal advertisements for a TV research project. One which took her eye began, 'loves music, loves to dance...'. She had made a fatal mistake in answering it. Her body was found on February 19 with the murderer's trade mark - her own shoe on one foot and a new dancing shoe on the other. This evening 'Charley' as he called himself in his insane moments, went through his stack of shoe boxes each labelled with a girl's name and each containing her missing shoe and the mate of the pair he had provided for her to dance with him before strangling her. A scuffed Nike and a black satin sequinned slipper in one; a white sandal and a gold slipper in another; a leather boot and a pink and silver stiletto... feet and shoes come under Pisces, so does dancing, but rarely in such bizarre circumstances.

1996, Oxford
Emergency Ward
(from <u>Death Is Now My Neighbour</u> by Colin Dexter)

Chief Inspector Morse was diagnosed as having diabetes. The doctor at the Health Centre said it was serious and wouldn't let him drive himself home. He was taken by ambulance to the Radcliffe Infirmary despite being in the middle of a murder enquiry. His pancreas had completely packed up and his blood sugar level was off the end of the chart. "God knows what damage to your eyes and your kidneys," said the doctor. Morse was told he would be on daily insulin injections for the rest of his life - his boozing had caught up with him. Drink and medicine both come under Pisces.

~ Pisces ~

1980, Logopolis, Earth
Birth of the **5th Dr. WHO**

In the first episode of this adventure, Dr. Who foiled the Master's plan to dominate the Universe but, today, was thrown from the gantry of a radio telescope and 'died' which meant that the 4th Dr. Who (Tom Baker, Aquarius) regenerated into the 5th Dr. Who (Peter Davidson, Aries) so this must be his 'birthday'. He had the Piscean charm, naive enthusiasm and vulnerability. He was all innocent curiosity and made mistakes. He didn't stop to consider the risks he was taking. An affinity with cricket and dressed the part too. Pisces rules sports where you play with your feet - chiefly football of course. In <u>Warriors of the Deep</u> he showed he was a strong swimmer, at home in his own element. Finally, he had the Piscean saintly characteristic of self-sacrifice. In <u>The Caves of Androzani</u>, he gave the only dose of the only antidote to <u>spectrox toxaemia</u> to Peri and 'died' himself - only to come up again, this time as Dr. Who No. 6 in the person of Colin Baker (Gemini).

1856, Penzance
Birth of **FREDERICK**
(from <u>The Pirates of Penzance</u> by W.S. Gilbert and Arthur Sullivan)

Oh! Poor Wandering One! As pretty Mabel warbled and if ever a child was born into a pretty kettle of Fish that someone was Frederick, the 'prentice Pirate of Penzance. But what a finned wonder the boy was. Not only was the Sun in Pisces but Jupiter and Neptune too. A triple conjunction within eight degrees. Jupiter and Neptune are co-rulers of Pisces which leaves the Comic Opera Astrologer fairly gobsmacked! Frederick's profession and Frederick's should-have-been profession were both maritime. Due to his nursemaid being hard of hearing he was apprenticed to a pirate instead of a pilot. His nature was warm and sympathetic, some would say gullible, receptive and impressionable. He was prey to sorrow and despondency and could easily dissolve into tears. The confusion and muddle which dog the Piscean-born, spared no effort to dog Frederick. On his 21st birthday, when the pirates were knocking back the pirate sherry in celebration of Frederick now being a fully-paid up pirate, Frederick announced his

~ Pisces ~

intention of leaving them and joining the Penzance police. The Pirate King countered with a paradox. As Frederick's birthday was on February 29 he was only five and a bit and would have to wait until 1940 (1944 actually because he forgot there was no leap year in 1900) before finishing his indentures or being able to marry Mabel. Mabel said she would wait.

MARCH 1

Future, England
Births of **DR. WREN**, Archbishop of Lincoln
and **MRS. CHURT**, Cook
(from The Cockatrice Boys by Joan Aiken)

An apparently ill-assorted pair but they strike up a friendship when they find they share the same birthday - as one does. They meet aboard the Cockatrice Belle, an armoured train run on wind power and manned by the Cockatrice Corps. 'Cockatrices' are what people call the plague of basilisks, snarks, flying hammerheads, kelpies and other impossible monsters which get though the hole in the ozone layer and devastate the English countryside. Everyone lives underground and subsists on thistledown tea and dandelion root porridge. Being Pisceans these two are very nice people. Dr. Wren, who is also a physician, is well up in the best ways of dealing with the forces of evil and Mrs. Churt is a worthy second in addition to providing unlimited blackberry tea and words of comfort.

Joan Aiken favours this birthday as she gave it to **DIDO TWITE** (Dido and Pa), although not so appropriately. Dido is a sharp, streetwise little Cockney. Neither does it fit Jane Austen's pompous snob **SIR WALTER ELLIOT** (Persuasion). Professor Tolkien did better with **ARAGORN** in The Lord of the Rings. Although of the noblest lineage he went under many guises and names but the hobbits, whom he escorted on their perilous quest, knew him as 'Strider'.

~ Pisces ~

c.1950, California
Peril on the Lake
(from <u>The List of Adrian Messenger</u> by Philip MacDonald)

Today 'Benjamin J. Knight' attempted to drown the 12-year old boy who stood between him and the title of Marquis of Gleneyre. He had already polished off the lad's grandfather, the 18th Marquis, to say nothing of Adrian Messenger and the ten ex-soldiers on his 'List'. Any one of them could have convicted him of his treacherous behaviour and betrayal of them during the second world war, which wouldn't have helped George Brougham (his real name) in his bid to join the English aristocracy. His father had been the black sheep of the family and had emigrated to Canada but he was legitimately in line for the title. Of course, this final murderous design was foiled and George met his own end at the bottom of Jackman's Gorge. Dangerous waters, betrayal, false identities - it was a Piscean day. <u>The List of Adrian Messenger</u> is one of the Golden Age classics of crime literature. John Huston successfully filmed it with Kirk Douglas as the master-of-disguise Brougham - although it was said that Huston did it because he wanted the chance to ride to hounds on location in Ireland.

1911, Rocky Mountains
Black Gold
(from <u>Campbell's Kingdom</u> by Hammond Innes)

Old Stuart Campbell, a prospector for oil, was involved in a disaster at the goldmining community of Come Lucky. It had been snowing heavily for a week and the chinook which then started to blow, set off a series of avalanches which engulfed the mine workings and spread for a mile across Thunder Creek. Nearly a hundred people lost their lives. However, it unleashed a river of oil.... Oil, petrol, gas, fog and snow are all ruled by Neptune through its sign of Pisces.

1900, London
Birth of **ALBERT EDWARD LADYSMITH STEPTOE**
(from TV series <u>Steptoe & Son</u> by Ray Galton and Alan Simpson)

(Ladysmith was Relieved the previous month which led to many
lewd music hall jokes!)

Another birthday for Albert has been put forward - September 26, 1899. We strongly refute this. <u>Ladysmith</u> hadn't been heard of then. Anyway, he's Pisces! Smelly old Steptoe bleating away in his junkyard lets down the Piscean side something rotten but the rough has to be taken with the smooth. Pisces can be sluttish beyond belief but there was always an air of pathos about Albert, ghastly though he was. He and his son, Harold Albert Kitchener Steptoe, lived at The Mews Cottage, Oil Drum Lane, Shepherd's Bush, which is now practically foreign territory but Albert knew all the kids by name. Pisceans are tolerant and can get on with anyone regardless of class, colour or creed. The constellation of Pisces shows two fish tied together yet swimming in opposite directions, which illustrates the relationship between the Steptoes: Harold yearning to be upwardly mobile and socially acceptable, Albert content with squalor. It was a love/hate relationship. Albert swam easily with the more common Fish! He was not keen on activity and was always looking for the easy way out. He lived a fantasy life building up his supposed heroics in WWI, while allowing his real life to degenerate into undisciplined chaos. He was selfishly determined to keep Harold with him and scotched every hope poor Harold had of marrying a nice girl or bettering himself. Albert was resilient, as cunning as a cartload of monkeys, and as slippery as a pretty kettleful of Fish!

c.1890, Germany
Birth of **ROSE-MARIE SCHMIDT**
(from <u>Fraulein Schmidt and Mr. Anstruther</u> by Elizabeth von Arnim)

Today she wrote to Mr. Anstruther in London thanking him for his birthday wishes. She was a punctilious correspondent so her birthday was probably today. Even if a day earlier she still came under Pisces and her self-assessment proved it.

~ Pisces ~

'Of course I am full of contradictions...I do not pretend to think quite the same even two days running; if I did I would be stagnant, and the very essence of life is to be fluid... My attitude towards life is one of open-mouthed wonder and delight.'

She was to have married Mr. Anstruther. They were <u>secretly!</u> engaged but he jilted her in favour of a richer lady. It broke her heart but when he wrote to her again after his romance fell apart she was generous enough to reply and sympathise, but not to take him back. She had been very ill after their parting. A cold had settled on her lungs (of course!) but it was over and she was clinging to the present and keeping cheerful. Death had once sat beside her for quite a long while but had gone away and she was walking out in the sun every day and listening to the chaffinches. Rose-Marie was lovely and funny and sweet and Mr. Anstruther was an idiot to have ditched her.

MARCH 6

1859, Audley Court, Essex
Confession!
(from <u>Lady Audley's Secret</u> by Mary E. Braddon)

Today a scene of high Victorian melodrama to widen Piscean eyes. Pisces lives on sensationalism, other peoples' emotions will do if there aren't enough of their own. Lady Audley's secret was revealed when she confessed to the murder of her first husband, George Talboys, by pushing him down the well at Audley Court when he threatened her with exposure to the man she had married bigamously, Sir Michael Audley. "It was then that I was mad. It was then that I drew the loose iron spindle from the shrunken wood and saw my first husband sink with one horrible cry into the black mouth of the well. There is a legend of its enormous depth. I do not know how deep it is. It is dry, I suppose; for I heard no splash; only a dull thud. I looked down and I saw nothing but black emptiness. I knelt down and listened, but the cry was not repeated, though I waited for nearly a quarter of an hour - God knows how long it seemed to me - by the mouth of the well." Such a best-seller that Mrs. Braddon's publisher was able to build a new house which he called 'Audley Lodge'.

~ Pisces ~

1946, Dartmoor
Piracy!
(from Maddon's Rock by Hammond Innes)

Today, in his prison cell, Jim Vardy was slipped the previous day's newspaper and was jerked out of his mood of despair. The headline read: FIRST POST-WAR UNDERWATER TREASURE HUNT: Trikkala's Master to Salvage Bullion. There followed an interview with the master, a Captain Halsey, who said it was exactly a year since his ship, the Trikkala had sunk carrying a cargo of silver bullion, which he now intended to recover. Vardy knew all about the Trikkala. He had been on her when she sank and, like the rest of the crew, would have met a watery death in the unseaworthy lifeboats if he hadn't mutinied and boarded a raft instead. As a result he was doing a stretch in Dartmoor. Now, Halsey's evil plot became clear and he made up his mind to escape and to get his revenge. It's all Piscean piracy and mutiny on the high seas, imprisonment on false evidence and the terrifying Maddon's Rock itself set in raging arctic seas. Hammond Innes is a seafaring type, experienced in ocean racing and cruising as might be expected from his books. He is not a Fish but, second best, a Crab born July 15, 1913.

1928, Providence, U.S.A.
Confusion
(from The Case of Charles Dexter Ward by H.P. Lovecraft)

The antiquarian researches of young Charles Dexter Ward, particularly into the life of an evil ancestor called Joseph Curwen, had driven him into madness. He had stumbled upon secrets he should never have known and horror beyond all human conception. He wrote to the family doctor, Dr. Willett, of a monstrous abnormality and ranted wildly of all civilisation, perhaps even the fate of the universe, hanging in the balance. Today Dr. Willett, three alienists and Charles's father paid him a momentous call, determined to remove him to a private nursing hospital. He was agitated and reeked of strange and noxious laboratory odours but admitted that his mind had suffered as a result of his abstruse studies. It was his archaic style of speech, his altered appearance, his replacement of modern by

~ Pisces ~

ancient ideas and his tendency to pause as though listening for very faint instructions before answering them, which marked him out as 'removed from the normal'. However, he accompanied them willingly almost as if his removal was the merest incident which would speedily be resolved. In fact they were not speaking to Charles Dexter Ward who was dead but to his killer, the wicked sorcerer Joseph Curwen who had taken over Charles's body.

MARCH 9

1971, Los Angeles
Hospital
(from The Terminal Man by Michael Crichton)

At 3.30 p.m. Harry Benson was admitted to a Neuropsychiatric Research Unit in handcuffs and with a police escort. He was a brilliant computer scientist specialising in artificial life and machine intelligence. Two years previously he had been in a car accident and later began to suffer blackouts during the course of which he must have been fighting but remembered nothing of it. He gradually lost touch with reality, retreated into Piscean fantasy and became convinced that machines were taking over the world. Acute Disinhibitory Lesion Syndrome was diagnosed - e.g., he lost all inhibitions against violent acts. He was resistant to drugs and, as he was becoming increasingly aggressive, surgery seemed the only solution. It was decided to implant electrodes deep in his brain to send out soothing and pleasant impulses. Not all the staff were happy - and with reason. Benson discovered how to stimulate his pleasure zones, escaped and went on the rampage. This is from the Scorpionic author of Jurassic Park and is on-the-edge-of-the-seat reading. The astrologer sees that during the duration of Benson's hospital stay the Sun and Mercury in Pisces were closing up their opposition to Pluto and their square to Mars to form two distinctly nasty T-squares.

MARCH 10

1883, England
A Piscean Puzzle
(from The Five Orange Pips by A. Conan Doyle)

A letter with a foreign stamp lay upon the table in front of Colonel Openshaw's plate. It was not a common thing for him to receive

~ Pisces ~

letters, for he had no friends of any sort. "From India!" he said as he took it up. "Pondicherry postmark! What can this be?" Opening it hurriedly, out there jumped five little dried up orange pips, which pattered down upon his plate. His nephew, who was present, laughed but the laugh was struck from his lips at the sight of the Colonel's face. His lip had fallen, his eyes were protruding, his skin the colour of putty as he glared at the envelope which he still held in his trembling hand. "K.K.K!" he shrieked and then, "My God, my God, my sins have overtaken me!" "What is it, uncle?" gasped the nephew. "Death," said he.

MARCH 11

Early 1930s, England
Haunted House
(from When Last I Died by Gladys Mitchell)

According to her diary, Bella Foxley was worried about her cousin Tom who was staying alone in a haunted house in the village and, just after midnight, she left the inn where she was staying and went to check on him. She threw gravel up at his window until he came and said he was all right and the house was quieter than usual. He told her to go back to the inn before his wife, Muriel, missed her and had one of her nervous attacks. Bella thought she saw someone standing behind him and called out, "The headless coachman is just behind you!" He laughed and the figure disappeared. Next morning the milkboy found him. He must have tumbled out of the window after she left and was hurt. Muriel was prostrate. She said the ghosts wanted the house for themselves. Did they? This is one of the intrepid Mrs. Bradley cases. Not only are there headless coachmen and poltergeists but an ancient well and crypt and secret passages to say nothing of murderous subterfuges and all the usual Piscean tricks. Oh, and Bella never wrote the diary at all.

MARCH 12

1913, Columbus, Ohio
The Day the Dam Broke
(from My Life and Hard Times by James Thurber)

'The Columbus, Ohio, broken-dam rumour began about noon of 12 March 1913. Suddenly on High Street, somebody began to run.' Nobody knew why but somebody else too broke into a trot, then

~ Pisces ~

somebody else. Within ten minutes everybody on East Side was running. 'A loud mumble gradually crystalized into the dread word "Dam" "The dam has broke!"' Two thousand people started running east away from the river. "Go east! Go east!" went up the cry. The Thurber family performed their usual mad carnival. Mother took with her a dozen eggs and two loaves of bread. Grandfather thought that the townsfolk were fleeing from Nathan Bedford Forrest's cavalry, refused to leave and had to be laid out with the ironing board and carried which slowed them down. Aunt Edith Taylor got to Grant Avenue where she was caught up by Dr. Mallory, whom she'd already passed, who was screaming, "It's got us!" It wasn't until they collapsed, expecting to feel the icy waters, that a boy on roller skates swished past and they realised that they had mistaken the sound for that of rushing water. Some people got twelve miles away before giving up and trudging home. The dam hadn't broken and if it had not even a trickle of water would have reached East Side where the panic started. But that's Pisces - rumours, rumours....

MARCH 13

Year Unknown
Deep Waters
(from Lesson VIII of The First Reader by Gertrude Stein)

> 'The thirteenth of March was a day when it was
> dangerous to play. The Moon was full that is to
> say the Moon was full of Moon. The water tide
> came in and out and everywhere all about it was
> dangerous to go in and out....'

Wealthy, cosmopolitan Gertrude Stein was an Aquarian (February 3, 1874). At the time she seemed downright peculiar but is accepted as a genius now. She also wrote: 'A rose is a rose' and 'Pigeons in the grass Alas' and was called a Cubist writer, a writer who pushed abstraction to its furthest limits. Even fellow Aquarian **SINCLAIR LEWIS** (February 7, 1885) couldn't decide whether she was crazy, joking or contributing new rhythms to an outworn English style. But this is meant to be Pisces not Aquarius (and Stein did have a Pisces ascendant). The Lesson continues with a little boy who had a name defying the elements and going out in the rain and he got drowned, which is the sort of thing which happens on the thirteenth of March - 'no little boy should say when then.'

~ Pisces ~

1906, Coombe Bluff, West of England
Shipwreck!
(from <u>A Horseman Riding By</u> by R.F. Delderfield)

This afternoon Tamer Potter clambered down from the cliff top to the tiny bay which he thought of as Flotsam Cove to see if the Almighty had sent him any sort of bonus. He began a methodical search of the boulder-strewn margin between high and low tide. Caught up in the rocks he found a park bench which had blown off some esplanade and worked to free it. The weather was wet and muggy with a gale force wind blowing itself out and a particularly thick sea fog rolling in and obliterating everything. He freed the bench and then heard confused and subdued shouting which seemed to come from all points of the compass but he pinpointed its centre as a sandstone pinnacle about a cable's length from the beach. 'It was an eerie sound, a combination of human and metallic noises, a steady grinding and crashing with overtones of voices raised in fear and punctuated by hoarse shouts and just once a long and piercing scream.' Sea, dense fog, shipwreck and beachcombing - just another Piscean day.

The Ides of March

They are notorious because of the soothsayer's warning which <u>Julius Caesar</u> did not heed before his assassination. The account is first found in Plutarch's Julius Caesar which is where Shakespeare found and used it in his play of the same name. 'What is still more extraordinary, many report that a certain soothsayer forewarned him of a great danger which threatened him on the ides of March, and that when the day was come, as he was going to the senate-house, he called to the soothsayer, and said, laughing, "The ides of March are come"; to which he answered, softly, "Yes, but they are not gone."' That translation was by Langhorne. Shakespeare too would have used a 'crib'. College girl Judy Abbott (<u>Daddy-Long-Legs</u> by Jean Webster) wouldn't have needed to. She was studying Latin prose composition and today she wrote, 'I have been studying it. I shall be studying it. I shall be about to have been studying it. My re-examination comes the seventh hour next Tuesday and I am going to pass or BUST!' Soothsayer's and gypsy's warnings come under Pisces. It is

~ Pisces ~

infuriating that Geoffrey Chaucer, whose <u>Canterbury Tales</u> are crammed with astrology, gave no hint of his own (unknown) birthday. Unless... could it have been today? Apparently for no reason in the unfinished <u>Squire's Tale</u>, the Ides of March was the nativity of a noble Tartar king who received a magical, mystical, brass horse as a birthday present. (Sounds Piscean.)

MARCH 16

1911, England
Birth of **VIOLET NIGHTINGALE**
(from <u>Ulverton</u> by Adam Thorpe)

On her 42nd birthday in 1953 it was cold and sleety and she had spam for lunch.   She was the cartoonist, Herbert Bradman's, live-in secretary/assistant.   She kept a diary but, to be unkind, she was a rather ordinary lady, one of the masses, disappointed in love.   She spent the day typing - Herbert was writing his LIFE - and went to the cinema alone on the bus to see <u>It Always Rains on Sundays</u>. She sat next to someone with a horrible cough.   For her birthday she had a bottle of Cherry Heering, which had leaked, stockings, cigarettes, an Aertex corset, bathcubes and an Ivor Novello gramophone record (she had nothing to play it on).   She went to bed at midnight with the Cherry Heering and entered up her diary.   'Feel like giggling.   Old times.   Whirling about.   Too much Cherry Heering. Cheery Heering. Herry Cheering. Bappy Hirthday Violet! O, golly.' (Pisces and drink, unfortunately, go together!)   Violet's diary is only one episode in the story of Ulverton which spans three centuries.   Its publication in 1992 was greeted as a masterpiece.

MARCH 17

Late 1940s, Cladda, Western Highlands of Scotland
The Sea! The Sea!
(from <u>The Singing Sands</u> by Josephine Tey)

Josephine Tey's sleuth, Alan Grant, today saw the Singing Sands of Cladda for the first time.   He was walking across a great waste of wet green grass which looked as if it would go on for ever so it was a shock to find the Atlantic Ocean bang slap in front of him... 'and if it was not beautiful it was, nevertheless, impressive in its sweep and simplicity. To right and left, as far as the eye could see, were the long lines of breaking water and the pale sands.' Endless miles of pure white sand.

~ Pisces ~

Some said that they did indeed 'sing' as the fine surface sand was swept along by the wind, others said they simply squeaked when trodden on. All the same, looking out over the Atlantic with nothing between the observer and America it wasn't surprising that the Hebrideans had thought it was the gateway to TIR NAN OG, the Gaelic heaven, the Land of Eternal Youth. It did Grant (who was convalescing) a power of good. He felt the uncanny sensation of unlimited space. He was happy.

MARCH 18

1879, night, on the Delaware River, U.S.A.
Stargazing
(from Specimen Days in America by Walt Whitman)

'One of the calm, pleasantly cool, exquisitely clear and cloudless early spring nights - the atmosphere again that rare vitreous blue-black, welcom'd by astronomers. Just at eight, evening, the scene overhead of certainly solemnest beauty, never surpassed. Venus nearly down in the west, of a size and lustre as if trying to out show herself, before departing. Teeming maternal orb - I take you again to myself... Arcturus is now risen, just north of east. In calm glory all the stars of Orion hold the place of honour, in meridian, to the south - with the Dog-star a little to the left. And now, just rising, Spica, late, low and slightly veil'd. Castor, Regulus and the rest, all shining unusually clear.'

MARCH 19

1775, The Maypole, Chigwell
A Ghostly Tale
(from Barnaby Rudge by Charles Dickens)

On this wild and stormy night, a stranger came into the Inn and asked questions about a nearby great house called The Warren and its owner. The parish clerk, Solomon Daisy, repeated the story he had told many times before. Twenty-two years ago, on just such a night, he had been sent for to toll the passing bell. He had just laid hold of the bell rope when he heard another bell ring once. Just once. He was terrified and raced home. Next morning he heard that the owner of The Warren had been murdered in his bed, still holding a piece of cord attached to the alarm bell which had been cut by the killer. The steward, Mr. Rudge, and a gardener were missing together with a

~ Pisces ~

cash bcx but Mr. Rudge was found later, also murdered.

> "Everybody now knew that the gardener must be the murderer, and though he has never been heard of from that time to this, he will be, mark my words. The crime was committed this day two-and-twenty years - on the nineteenth of March, one thousand seven hundred and fifty-three. On the nineteenth of March in some year - no matter when - I know it, I am sure of it, for we have always, in some strange way or other, been brought back to the subject on that day ever since - on the nineteenth of March in some year, sooner or later, that man will be discovered".

Shock horror! The stranger <u>was</u> the murderer! And he wasn't the gardener, he was ... Read it!

MARCH 20

1990s, England
The Day before the Birthday of **BRIDGET JONES**
(from <u>Bridget Jones's Diary</u> by Helen Fielding)

On the eve of her 30-something birthday in 1990-something, Bridget decided that to give a party for nineteen and planned to serve Shepherd's Pie with Chargrilled Belgian Endive Salad, Roquefort Lardons and Frizzled Chorzio followed by Grand Marnier soufflé. She spent the evening looking forward to tomorrow when she expected to be acclaimed as a brilliant cook and hostess. Seasoned readers of her diary would be very doubtful and with reason. Bridget Jones is disarmingly human and has most of the weaknesses of the human frame, particularly the Piscean human frame. This is the last day of the zodiac year and 1990's best-selling diarist, Bridget Jones, joins up with the first day of the zodiac year and 1930's best-selling diarist, Lorelei Lee. Both have birthdays on March 21. 'On the cusp' of Pisces and Aries. Lorelei is pure clear-cut, diamond-hard Aries but Bridget still retains her softer, more complicated, Piscean heritage, with her up-and-down moods and her confused ramblings which are both comical and touching. The usual astrological bleat goes up - if only we knew the <u>years</u> they were born, and the <u>times</u>, and the <u>places</u>! If only!

~ Pisces ~ Aries ~

c. 1905, Little Rock, Arkansas, U.S.A.
Birth of MABEL MINNOW aka **LORELEI LEE**
(from <u>Gentlemen Prefer Blondes</u> by Anita Loos)

Aries is the No. 1 sign of the zodiac and, at heart, an egoist. Under a glossy veneer, about 1mm thick, is Lorelei Lee. "Being Aries you must come first - it's primeval," wrote actress Bette Davis who also graced the sign. Ariens can expect some violence in their lives, if they don't dish it out first, it's dished out to them. Mabel wasted no time. She shot her first lover but was acquitted by a kindly judge who changed her name and sent her to Hollywood. There she met Gus Eisman, the Button King, who sent her to New York and then to Europe to complete her education. He also told her to keep a diary - hence the book. Four breathless months of excitement such as Ariens love. "I have to begin to realise that I am one of the kind of girls that things happen to." And they did. She married a plutocrat and became a film star, so her optimistic outlook was justified. "I always say everything always works out for the best." 'Diamonds Are A Girl's Best Friend' is Lorelei's theme song and diamonds are one of Aries birth stones. Rubies are too, because of their colour. To be truly authentic, Lorelei should have been a redhead, but we can't have everything. In Europe, Lorelei was taken to meet Dr Sigmund Freud who, after "an intreeging conversation" said all she needed was to cultivate a few inhibitions. He then stumbled off on the arm of his "assistance", shattered by the experience of meeting a red-blooded Arien who always did exactly what she wanted and was not in the least repressed or frustrated. Anita Loos was a Taurean, but she certainly knew her Ariens.

1933, Balham, London, England
Birth of **MARGARET GODFREY**
(from <u>Doon with Death</u> by Ruth Rendell. This acclaimed first novel created a stir in 1978 as lesbians were then a taboo subject.)

Now the passive Arien woman. Margaret is a shadowy figure. Brought up by an aunt, she married an equally shadowy man and lived in near poverty. She was pretty in an old fashioned way, didn't smoke or wear make-up. Her only outings were to church socials. She was an ordinary housewife, ex-teacher, her interests limited to the church, cooking and knitting. In order to compensate, her short life ran externally along Arien lines. Both parents were killed by enemy

~ Aries ~

action in 1942; she was the victim of a strong character's violent passion, and she was brutally murdered in the summer of 1963. The key to her character lies in her Venus in Pisces opposed by Jupiter, which conjuncts Neptune. The latter huge planets have the effect of blowing up and exaggerating whatever they touch. Were the birth time known, Venus must have been either chart ruler or on the ascendant. Venus in Pisces is shadowy and a natural victim. It signifies tragic, self-sacrificing love. Her marriage brought no material advantage while the love of another for her led to her death. Neptune rules Pisces so Margaret was doubly doomed. A Venus/Neptune/Pisces connection points to secrets and deceit, practised by or against the native. In a way, Margaret did deceive her husband. She met up with her old school friend Fabia (the Doon of the title) who was rich, clever, beautiful, and passionately attracted to mousy Margaret. Doon wrote Margaret 134 love letters and sent her expensive books which Margaret didn't read. One day Doon persuaded Margaret out to lunch but afterwards Margaret committed the sin of falling asleep while Doon was quoting love poetry to her and pouring out her heart. Doon murdered her.

Why did **RUTH RENDELL** (February 17, 1930, 9.00 a.m., South Woodford, England) choose that birth date for Margaret? The strange thing is that although she herself has Sun in Aquarius, she has Venus in Pisces opposite Neptune too. A Venus, moreover, in the Neptunian/Piscean 12th house. Our horoscopes are complicated things containing a number of people in different guises. Margaret Godfrey is present in her creator's chart and, perhaps, has had to be written out. Midsummer 1963 saw bloodthirsty Mars very active in Margaret's chart. Her progressed Sun and Venus were coming up to a trine aspect with progressed Mars - raw passion. Uranus was transiting natal Mars. In June and July - Margaret was murdered at some unspecified date then - Mars transited Virgo and conjoined its own natal place, the transiting Moon, Uranus and, most ominously, Pluto.

| MARCH |
| 22 |

Sometime in the 24th Century, Planet Earth,
Official Stardate unknown
Birth of **CAPTAIN JAMES T. KIRK** of Starship Enterprise
(from Star Trek by Gene Roddenberry)

Bit of cheating here! Captain Kirk's alter ego is William Shatner born March 22, 1931 in Montreal, Canada at 4.00 a.m. However, in the minds of millions, William Shatner is Captain Kirk and so they must

~ Aries ~

share the same birthday, although centuries divide them. Captain Kirk is the tuppence-coloured, <u>Boys' Own</u> type hero whose response to any hostile situation is a quick punch on the jaw. An uncomplicated character. William Shatner, according to his fellow crewmembers, is a full-blown Arien who docked their lines in order to enhance his own. Poor old Scotty for one wouldn't speak to him off the set let alone beam him up. Leonard Nimoy held his own but he, too, is an Arien. His character, Mr Spock, being born on Vulcan, is completely outside our starscope. William Shatner, a very active and go-getting man with, it is said, a cruel sense of humour, breeds Dobermans. What else?

MARCH 23

1862, London, England
Birth of **MIRIAM CROMER**, murderess
(from <u>Waxwork</u> by Peter Lovesey)

Sgt Cribb saw in her eyes an implacable force and strength of will. She was guilty of two murders and had planned for her husband to hang for them. She was an astonishing woman, entirely in command of herself. Her servants considered her to be iron-willed. Police questions didn't shake her but her weakness was her over-confidence. Some Arien quotes:

> "My actions were determined by impulse alone. Why do you suppose I married Howard? It was a whim. Howard was there and I wanted him."

She admitted that she sought only self-gratification. In other circumstances Sgt Cribb felt she might have been a social crusader for she refused to acknowledge defeat. Her trial provided a challenge for her strength of purpose and she came within an ace of cheating the hangman.

The most interesting astrological point is the conjunction of Sun and Neptune in Aries in her horoscope. Neptune has the power to exaggerate whatever it touches. Far from softening the Arien Sun, it increased the sense of personal omnipotence. It also shows the Neptunian scandal, deceit and deviousness which were part and parcel of Miriam's make-up. Throughout her life progressed Neptune was getting ever closer to the natal Sun. Her trial and conviction took place in June 1888 when her progressed Mars was in dangerous aspect to Pluto. In her birth chart, the feminine Moon was in cold Capricorn, and in that sign conjunct natal Mars on the morning of her execution, June 25, 1888.

~ Aries ~

1812, England
'orrible Murder!
(from <u>Ghost Stories of an Antiquary</u> by M. R. James)

Stephen Elliott (12) was an orphan adopted by his sinister relation, Mr Abney, who lived in an appropriately Gothic setting. Today had been windy and noisy. Stephen felt the presence of an endless procession of unseen people sweeping past, borne on, resistlessly and aimlessly, vainly striving to catch at something that might arrest their flight. In the evening he received a message to go to Mr Abney's study at 11 p.m. He was delighted to have the opportunity to stay up late but should have been warned when, looking in at the door earlier, he saw Mr Abney sprinkling some incense onto a brazier and an old silver cup filled with red wine, while a glance at his ephemeris would have shown the Sun in Aries, and Uranus, planet of sudden, outrageous events, rising in Mars' negative sign of Scorpio. Luckily for the heedless lad, two of his dead predecessors hadn't swept past but had swept in and done their vengeful work. Mr Abney was in his chair, '..his head thrown back, his face stamped with an expression of rage, fright and mortal pain.' In his left side was a terrible, lacerated wound, exposing the heart. A savage wild cat might have inflicted the injuries, the coroner decided.

1960s, 6.00 a.m., Virginia Water, England
Birth of **PEREGRINE RODERICK CLYDE-BROWN**
(from <u>Vintage Stuff</u> by Tom Sharpe)

Mr Sharpe gave the time and day but not Peregrine's year of birth. The time must surely have been 6.00 a.m. <u>GMT</u> not BST which would give an Arien ascendant and a double dose of the sign. Treble if the year was 1964 or 1969 as in those years Mars conjoined the Sun on March 25. In any case, Peregrine was an out-and-out Arien of a certain breed. He didn't know the meaning of fear and carried out orders quite literally. The aptitude expert unhesitatingly recommended a military career, which the astrologer could have done and much cheaper! Peregrine was sent to an army school whose War Memorial honoured the 938 Old Boys who had fallen in both World Wars. At 15 Peregrine was 6ft tall, weighed 11 stone and was

~ Aries ~

immensely strong, doing 100 press-ups every morning. He was not bullied. He ate assault courses, was a good shot and brought a violence to boxing that alarmed his instructors and terrified opponents. As No 960401 in South Armagh he notched up 5 IRA, 2 poachers, an off-duty RU constable, a sheep and a Landrover. The local Protestants joined with the IRA in declaring his 16 square miles a No Go area.

TOM SHARPE, born March 30, 1929, is himself a Sun-Arien with Uranus conjunct the Sun, a disruptive, unpredictable trait, both being close enough to Peregrine's Sun to be interesting. His Mars in Cancer is square to all of them and very inflammatory it is. Mr Sharpe could obviously empathise with his terrifying creation.

1967, mid afternoon, Baltimore, U.S.A.
Birth of **GINA MEREDITH**
(from <u>Morgan's Passing</u> by Anne Tyler)

The horoscope's ascendant could have been in Leo or Virgo. In either case a clutch of planets, Pluto, Uranus and the Moon, would have been rising in Virgo. Tad Mann's interesting theory has it that planets close to the ascendant show the actual circumstances attending the birth - the people present and so forth. Certainly Gina's arrival was dramatic enough to satisfy a Pluto/Uranus conjunction. Her parents were puppeteers working out of sight in a dark booth (very Plutonian) and she disrupted the performance of Cinderella before an audience of children at the Presbyterian Church. Amongst them was Morgan who passed himself off as a doctor and delivered the baby in the back of the car. Morgan spent his life taking on different, more exciting personae at the drop of a hat - or hats. He had a vast collection and wore whichever best fitted his role. He later became Gina's stepfather. (Her real father had a violent Arien temper.) The Moon in Virgo personifies Gina's mother, Emily. Emily was very quiet, neat austere and withdrawn with a strong dash of Quaker. She was orderly and very good with her hands and worked for Crafts Unlimited.

Gina, of course, is a Sun-Arien. If the ascendant was in Leo then the Sun, as life ruler, was doubly strong. She kept her parents continually occupied and teetering on the verge of exhaustion. Even as a toddler she was aggressively sociable, a noisy, enthusiastic insomniac. She hated solitude and was bung full of fierce energy and good nature but given to hysterical outbursts if upset. All classic symptoms of Aries. We never get past Gina being 12 years old. Perhaps as well. Saturn in close conjunction with the Sun suggests the Arien high spirits are destined to be dampened down somehow, sometime...

~ Aries ~

**'On the 26th March (1816) the Lady of Lieutenant-Colonel
Crawley of the Life Guards Green, of a son and heir.'**
(Galignani's Journal)
(from <u>Vanity Fair</u> by William Makepeace Thackeray)

The 'Lady' in question was the notorious Becky Sharp. (Another
Sharp - a most Arien name!) The Crawleys were on the continent in
1815/1816 at the time of Waterloo when 'all the world was at Paris
during the famous winter.' Rawdon Crawley junior grew up 'rosy and
dirty, shouting lustily, and happy in the making of mud pies.' 'A fine,
open-faced boy...sturdy in limb... fondly attaching himself to any who
were good to him.' This did not include his mother who at first ignored
him and then actively hated him as he interfered with her <u>affaires</u>.
Once she struck him and that finished the relationship. Luckily, he
and his father were great pals. "He's the finest boy in England,"
declared the Lieutenant-Colonel. "He's a regular trump!"
'Rawdon...was fonder of the society of men than of women and never
wearied of accompanying his sire to the stables.' He went pheasant-
shooting, rat-hunting in the barn and fox hunting. He was happy at
school despite fagging and beating. He succeeded to the title on the
death of his baronet uncle and lived happily in the country, huntin'
and shootin'.

1921, Pankot, India
Birth of **SARAH LAYTON**
(from <u>The Raj Quartet</u> by Paul Scott)

Sarah was a quiet Arien. She came from a military family with a
history of service in India. Her father was a Lieutenant-Colonel
(another!) in the Pankot Rifles. She served as a corporal in the
Women's Auxiliary Corps during WW2. She had a mother and sister
but she was the one they leaned on and she had to take responsibility
when her father was a PoW in Japan. Her critics said it made her
domineering. She was upright, honest, brisk and efficient, a tower of
strength, a 'pukka' type, qualities which were greatly needed during
the last days of the British Raj in India when there was enough
violent death to satisfy even Aries at the time of the partition. Her
progressed Sun reached natal Mars then, indicating bloodshed,

~ Aries ~

alarums and excursions. She didn't like her face which was bony and tough-looking. She admired courage because she felt she lacked it. She admired soldiers who, in ancient times, fell upon their swords rather than admit defeat, and the scorpion which she thought she saw one day sting itself to death in a ring of fire. She relaxed by horse riding early in the mornings.

For some reason most of the best known Arien birthdays occur during the first week of the sign. Some days attract more than one. Today for example.

1829, Cumberland, England
Birth of **LAURA FAIRLIE**
(from <u>The Woman in White</u> by Wilkie Collins)

Another 'Surely not!' No one could be less of an Arien than the sweet and gentle, trusting and passive Laura. Well, although the Sun was in Aries, Mercury and Venus were in sweet and gentle, trusting and passive Pisces, while Sun ruler Mars was in the Venusian sign of Taurus sextile Venus - a soothing effect. Again, it was through her (first) husband that the Arien danger manifested. As a wealthy orphan she was married off by her hypochondriac guardian uncle to the arch-villain Sir Percival Glyde who exhibited all the worst traits of Aries. Helped by his friend Count Fosco he robbed Laura, not only of her fortune, but of her very identity, having her committed under another name to a lunatic asylum. Of course the baddies got their come-uppances in the end and horribly Arien they were too. Sir Percival burnt to death while pursuing his criminal business in a church and Fosco was knifed by an assassin. Pluto conjoined her Sun which, for a woman, can signify the removal of the men in her life or their violence towards her. The Moon was quite possibly in Capricorn under the governance of Saturn while Saturn itself was at home in Capricorn making for a tragic chart. In her 20th year Laura's progressed Sun would have aspected Saturn bringing all the implicit ill-luck to a head. She was 20 when she had to give up her true love and marry Sir Percival. Such an important configuration is effective for 2/3 years, both while it is approaching and while moving on, and this was the most miserable period of her life.

WILKIE COLLINS' Moon, signifying women, was almost certainly in Aries and he was far more deft with the character of the mannish Marion Halcombe, Laura's friend. (Do very feminine Arien women attract domineering, possibly lesbian friends? Remember Margaret Godfrey?) The positive Marion could easily illustrate Aries but Wilkie never revealed her birthday.

~ Aries ~

MARCH 28

Sometime in the future, Pacific Ocean
Explosion!
(from The Floating Island by Jules Verne)

A Jules Verne fantasy. A man-made luxury Island designed for pleasure-bent billionaires sailing wherever fancy dictated. Unhappily, the two plutocrat owners were deadly rivals and began giving contradictory orders. One wanted to go NE, the other SW, resulting in the Island being driven round and round its centre by 6 million hp. It spun for a week, the VIPs and nabobs getting sicker and sicker. Quarrels raged between the factions. Eventually, on the 28th (and naturally Jules Verne chose an Arien date for the disaster), at a little before daybreak (Sun in Aries coming up in the east/ascendant)

> '.. a terrific explosion shook the air. Driven beyond the pressure they would bear, the boilers of the larboard section blew up with the buildings and machinery. And as the source of electrical energy suddenly gave out on this side, half the Floating Island was plunged into profound darkness.'

MARCH 29

1943, 9.00 a.m., Prague
Firing Squad
(from The Secret Miracle in Labyrinths by Jorge Luis Borges)

Jaromir Hladik is to be shot, but he asks God the favour of another year of life so he may finish writing his drama, The Enemies or Vindication of Eternity. The favour is granted between the sergeant's arm beginning and completing the gesture to fire. Jaromir died at 9.02 a.m. after having lived through another year and finished his play. Quite apart from the Arien Sun, Gemini would have been ascending containing Saturn and Uranus. Together they signify violence and stress. Saturn limits the freedom of Uranus and the result is a shoot-out between them. Destiny v. free will. If there is a winner it's the one which is the stronger at a given moment. Mercury, the writing/mental planet, had just entered Aries and was opposed by Neptune. The forthrightness of Mercury in Aries was thus softened by

~ Aries ~

Neptunian fantasy, deceit and an imagination running riot. Jaromir's point of death experience was therefore, as far as astrology is concerned, 'all in the mind'.

MARCH 30

1820, Norfolk, England
Birth of **ANNA SEWELL**, author of the revolutionary <u>Black Beauty</u>

She was born into a Quaker family - a hard fate for an Arien. The 'waiting in silence upon the Lord' for a couple of hours on a hard bench takes a more phlegmatic nature to endure. "She never liked silent meetings; she chafed against them as purposeless," said her mother. In looks Anna had dark curly hair, a high complexion and a broad determined jaw. "She had a great deal of courage and independence of character, never burdened with any kind of fear," testified her mum. Her courage extended to the protection of ill-treated animals. Cruelty to them roused her to a frenzy. "Thee cruel man, thee shan't have it at all," she screamed at a man who came to the door to get a blackbird which he had shot and which had fallen into her garden. She seems to have had some sort of psychological illness which made her an invalid. In fact she was one of those indomitable Victorian spinsters who simply didn't have enough to do with all their energy. Her incandescent <u>Black Beauty</u> had a tremendous impact and did improve the lot of horses.

MARCH 31

1836, London
<u>Pickwick Papers</u> first appeared as a monthly serial

This was Charles Dickens' first big break. Originally intended to accompany a series of sporting illustrations, the adventures of Samuel Pickwick and his friends, Mr Snodgrass, Mr Tupman and Mr Winkle, took over and became a publishing phenomenon. Fresh, high-spirited and full of joie-de-vivre, it thoroughly deserved its Arien send-off. Pluto conjoined the Sun today which, in Aries, signifies record achievements paid for by physical breakdown through overwork, which certainly applied to Dickens from then on (see February 7).

~ Aries ~

1894, London
Return of Sherlock Holmes from the Dead!
(from <u>The Adventure of the Empty House</u> by Arthur Conan Doyle)

The affecting reunion between Holmes and Watson took place at about 7.00 p.m. For three years Watson had believed that the great detective had perished with Professor Moriarty at the Reichenbach Falls. However, Holmes had survived and turned up today to solve the murder of the Honourable Ronald Adair on March 30 in his rooms at Park Lane. Shot, of course. Close perusal of the <u>Adventure</u> might pinpoint Holme's return as being March 31 as the murder had obviously occurred the previous day but Watson recalls it as an April evening so April it must be. Heaven forbid that Conan Doyle forgot there were 31 days in March! The chart for the meeting shows Saturn rising in Libra. Saturn is the planet of separations and death but gives of its best in Libra, the sign of its exaltation. Additionally, it was nicely aspected to Venus, ruler of Libra. Libra is the sign of friends and partnerships and cheerful phrases like 'old friends' sum up this Saturn. Further, the Arien Sun was in conjunction with the Moon's North Node. This Node can relate to friends and associates and the configuration would denote the time as excellent to begin (or resume) associations between males. Upon his visitor throwing off his disguise, poor Watson fainted dead away for the only time in his life but was soon revived with brandy and rattling off in a hansom, his revolver in his pocket and the thrill of adventure in his heart.

Across the Channel, **EDMOND ROSTAND** was born in 1868. He wrote <u>Cyrano de Bergerac</u>, the enormous nose of the character evidently engaging this Arien's sympathies!

1920
Birth of **AMOS BREARLY** of TV's Emmerdale

Amos was considered eccentric and autocratic. He served in the Royal Artillery during the war. After a mild stroke he moved to Spain to enjoy the sunshine. More interestingly, he was landlord of the <u>Woolpack</u>. Anything to do with wool 'comes under' Aries the sign of the Ram. The Lord Chancellor sits upon the Woolpack in the House of Lords. It's a large square bag of wool. Wool was originally the symbol of England's wealth and her staple trade. England is traditionally an Arien country.

~ Aries ~

1967, England
Birth of **ADRIAN MOLE**, tormented teenager
(from <u>The Secret Diary of Adrian Mole aged 13 3/4</u> by Sue Townsend)

Adrian is really too full of frustration to be a true Arien but Saturn conjoined the Sun which, in one way or another, cramps and restrains the Arien drive. All the same, Adrian's troublesome skin eruptions are certainly Martian in origin and as for the matter of his poor nose getting glued to his model aeroplane and swelling to an enormous size - well, Ariens traditionally have impressive hooters and possibly trouble with them. **SUE TOWNSEND** has given Adrian her own birthday - she was born April 2, 1946 - greater love hath no author. Being born on the day of a New Moon she has both Sun and Moon in this sign of the young male adolescent, so knows what she's writing about.

1888, The Laurels, Brickfield Terrace, Holloway, London
Another Diary
(from <u>The Diary of a Nobody</u> by George & Weedon Grossmith)

Another diary. Aries is the sign of beginnings but not endings, which is the fate of most personal journals. Anyway, Charles Pooter had just moved into his new residence and decided to keep a diary. The astrological chart of any enterprise at its commencement should determine the fate of that enterprise. Detective work reveals that the year must have been 1888, although it isn't stated, and Uranus opposed the Sun, foreshadowing the catastrophic disasters which were destined to be confided to the diary's pages. Unruly cabmen, surly charwomen, blackguard butchers, the grave mistake of painting the bath red, Lupin Pooter's engagement to Daisy Mutlar, the neighbours, the humiliations, accidents, annoyances, ill-timed buffoonery... all minor domestic upsets and agitations on a world scale but as earth-shattering to Mr P. as Sun opposition Uranus working in its grand opera mode. Mr Pooter's birthday is not known but the September/October pages of his diary were used to light the fire ('<u>Monstrous!</u>') so it could well have been in Virgo's span which would have fitted the fussy Mr Pooter beautifully.

~ Aries ~

1818, Ireland
Birth of **MAYNE REID**, adventure story writer

He was the eldest son of a clergyman but was too restless and adventurous to follow in father's footsteps. In 1840 he sailed to New Orleans and worked as store clerk in the lawless town of Natchez, Missouri. He then moved around working as a trapper, trader, actor, tutor and reporter up the Platte, Missouri and Red Rivers, befriending the Red Indians. He joined the US Army, fought in the Mexican War and sent newspaper dispatches from the front. In 1847 he was severely injured and returned home. During convalescence he wrote The Rifle Rangers quickly followed by some 70 more - The Scalp Hunters, The Bush Boys, The War Trail, The Headless Horseman... In 1855 he married a 15-year old girl (Ariens like them young). His obituary in The Times read, 'Every schoolboy and everyone who has ever been a schoolboy, will learn with sorrow of the death of Captain Mayne Reid.' They could have added... Arien!

1837, London
Birth of **ALGERNON SWINBURNE**, poet

Another flouter of convention who scandalised and terrified the Victorians with his insistent drumbeat rhythms and galloping metres. 'When the hounds of spring are on winter's traces...' is one of his. So is, 'Change in a trice! The lilies and languors of virtue. For the raptures and roses of vice.' He was tiny but had a large head thatched with shaggy red hair to match his fire-brand Arien temperament. Vehement and passionate, he especially hated the monarchy, the House of Lords and restraint of any kind. Sadly, in the end, he took to drink and had, for his own good, to be restrained himself.

1930s
Splat!
(from Money in the Bank by P. G. Wodehouse)

Lord Uffenham had an accident today. He was a man who would not accept conventions and took a resolute stand against them. He was driving on the right of the road, taking a resolute stand against the English convention of driving on the left, when an orthodox thinker in a lorry came round the corner. When they let his lordship out of hospital the stitches were healing nicely but his memory was a blank and where he had put the family (Arien) diamonds the day before the occurrence was a mystery. A day on which to drive extra carefully.

APRIL 6

Regency period, Brighton
Cometomania!
(from <u>Bostock and Harris</u> by Leon Garfield)

This was the night when Piggott's Comet was due to appear at its brightest, and the best part of Brighton went up to Devil's Dyke to do it honour with music, dancing and food. 'Comet' comes from the Greek 'kome' meaning hair, an Arien connection. Hairy star. They aren't looked on with much favour by astrologers. Transit of one over a natal point presages trouble so try not to get one on your birthday.

Although, if you're one of the 'mere' people, you're probably safe. As Shakespeare said in <u>Julius Caesar</u>, 'When beggars die there are no comets seen; The heavens themselves blaze forth the death of princes.' A particularly bright comet was recorded at the time of the Battle of Hastings, it can be seen on the Bayeux Tapestry, and you can read all about it in <u>1066 and All That</u> by W.C.Sellar and R.J.Yeatman. Although a Bad Thing for King Harold, who got an arrow in his eye, it was a Good Thing for William the Conqueror who won, so comets aren't disasters (<u>astra</u> means a star; disaster = evil star) for everyone, however high up.

APRIL 7

1923, France
Gallic Interlude
(from <u>Clochemerle</u> by Gabriel Chevallier)

Another opening ceremony for today. The public urinal in the village of Clochemerle was inaugurated in an appropriate way. The Water signs were well represented in the chart. Pluto in Cancer was trine Jupiter in Scorpio which was trine Venus and Uranus in Pisces which were trine Pluto in Cancer... Neptune was trine the Sun. Very harmonious.

~ Aries ~

WILLIAM WORDSWORTH (born today in 1770, at 10.00 p.m. in Cockermouth) was, in his youth, very taken with France. He went there on walking tours and admired the Revolutionaries to the extent of writing in one of his best poems, The Prelude, 'Bliss was it in that dawn to be alive and to be young was very heaven.' He had a passionate affair with a mam'zelle and a daughter resulted. He was completely self-centred - 'devoured by his own ego' and admitted to a violent temper. Still, he could throw off smashing Arien poetry like -

> 'It was an April morning; fresh and clear
> The rivulet, delighting in its strength,
> Ran with a young man's speed.'

He was appointed Poet Laureate yesterday in 1843.

He had an enormous nose.

APRIL 8

1943, 8.45 a.m., London
Birth of **JAMES HERBERT**, chiller-thriller author

His first, The Rats (which are ruled by Aries of course), led the way into all the ensuing violent films and books. He's not a bit sinister himself; people like him, and his wife fell in love with him because he was so funny - the result of a close aspect between the Sun and jolly Jupiter no doubt. He doesn't plan his books, if he does they lose their freshness. Aries is all for spontaneity. Herbert was a street-wise kid born in Bethnal Green. He got ideas for some of his stories from his mother who was a night nurse at an East London Children's Hospital, where she had some weird experiences.

1896 or 1898, New York
Birth of E. Yipsel ('**YIP**') **HARBURG**, librettist

Another who recognised the seamy side of life. His electrical business crashed during the Depression and he turned to versifying. 'Buddy, Can You Spare a Dime' was his first big hit. He later won an Oscar for his lyrics in The Wizard of Oz. Another clear-cut Arien, politically and racially aware. 'Yipsel' means squirrel which, in the tangle of the astrological zoo, 'comes under' Cancer not Aries. Cancer is the hoarder. However, Aries caught up with him in the end. He was killed in a car crash - but not until he was 85!

~ Aries ~

1821, 3.00 p.m., Paris, France
Birth of **CHARLES BAUDELAIRE**, poet, genius
and a very different kettle of Arien

Les Fleurs du Mal got him tried and fined for blasphemy. He was that sort of writer. Pornographic. His is a famous horoscope with Mars, Venus, Jupiter, Saturn and the Sun all crammed into the first twenty degrees of Aries. His appearance was equally striking - jet black, close cropped hair coming to a point on his forehead, covering his head 'like a kind of Saracen helmet'. He always dressed in black. He died of drink and drugs when 46 after shocking the bourgeoisie, squandering a fortune and attempting suicide with a knife. A precocious child, a brilliant talker. His rebelliousness was blamed on childhood trauma; he hated his stepfather who was a General. He wasn't successful with women, his best known mistress was the mulatto actress Jeanne Duval. Syphilis resulted in two strokes which left him half paralysed.

> 'Long let me bite your heavy black tresses. When I gnaw your elastic and rebellious hair, it seems I am eating memories.' (Hair again.)

A far more worthy citizen was the English poet, **EDWARD THOMAS** who was killed today in 1917 at Arras by an exploding shell.

1901, U.K.
Birth of **COLONEL TUSKER SMALLEY** (Ret'd)
(from Staying On by Paul Scott)

The Smalleys, Tusker and Lucy, stayed on in India after Independence. When Ibrahim brought their tea today in 1972 he hung a wet and ripely scented garland of flowers around Tusker's neck and a smaller one around Lucy's. Not that Tusker appreciated it, he was bad-tempered, drank, used bad language and had a combative manner. In the course of a quarrel, Lucy went for him and, rather astonishingly, hammered home her point with astrology. "You were born under the sign of Aries - and you do not want to be left out because people, born under this sign, hate being left out of anything but are utterly selfish, always trying to control and order other people

~ Aries ~

about to suit themselves." Tusker amiably remarked that she was "pissed". He did have a sense of humour of the knockabout, pantomime kind. Nothing subtle. He died a few days later on April 24 of a massive coronary in a fit of rage after receiving a notice to quit their home.

1818, England
Births of **SIMON** and **SOPHIE**
(from <u>Dido & Pa</u> by Joan Aiken)

1931, England
Births of **RUPERT** and **CHARLES**
(from <u>First Among Equals</u> by Jeffrey Archer)

Obviously a birthday for twins, aristocratic twins at that. Simon and Sophie were positive, cheerful, brave characters. Simon was 5th Duke of Battersea. If Charles Seymour had been born nine minutes earlier he would have become an earl, inherited a Scottish castle, 22,000 acres in Somerset and a merchant bank in London. As it was, Rupert got them and Charles had to scrape by as a Conservative MP.

LORD ARCHER is an Arien himself - April 15, 1940, 11.45 a.m., Mark, Somerset - and has Sun in Aries conjunct Jupiter denoting healthy ambition, courage, optimism, the wealthy VIP syndrome in fact. It also shows he doesn't have to worry about those who can't stand him!

| APRIL |
| 11 |

1929, New York
Birth of **POPEYE**

Today is the birthday, or first appearance if you prefer, of the comic strip hero. An Arien plus spinach - look out! For astrologers 'into' mid-points, Mercury in the birth chart is at the mid-point of Sun and Uranus, all in Aries. This promises quick movements and swift action, which seems apt, especially when Popeye's girl friend, Olive Oyl, is in trouble.

Still in the States, **EDWARD SYLVESTER ELLIS** was born today in 1840. He was described as the perfect writer of dime novels. What <u>we</u> would call penny dreadfuls or shilling shockers. In 1860, he published <u>Seth Jones</u> or <u>The Captives of the Frontier</u>. It sold half-a-million copies in six months. He specialised in exciting yarns about Red Indians, bear hunters, trappers and cowboys. All good, gory Arien fun.

~ Aries ~

In thirty years, he turned out nearly one hundred, with titles like <u>Captured by Indians</u>, <u>Pony Express Rider</u>, <u>Blazing Arrows</u>, <u>Redskin and Scout</u>. He would have been a wonderful scriptwriter for Popeye!

APRIL 12

Year 3018 of the Third Age in Middle Earth
The Beginning!
(from the <u>Lord of the Rings</u> by J.R.R. Tolkien)

After an absence of nine years the wizard, Gandalf the Grey, returned to Bag End in the Shire to visit the hobbit, Frodo Baggins, and to tell him a strange tale about the ring which Frodo's Uncle Bilbo had reluctantly left him before vanishing from the Shire for ever. There were a number of these rings, made by the Elven smiths, all magical and very, very dangerous. Some still existed, some were lost. Then, to Frodo's horror, Gandalf threw the ring into the fire. The flames revealed Elvish letters which translated into the Common Tongue read: 'One ring to rule them all, One ring to find them, One ring to bring them all and in the darkness bind them.' As Gandalf has suspected, Frodo's ring is the Master-ring, which rules all the rest. It is being sought by Sauron the Great, the Dark Lord, who once owned it. Then, for a time his dominance was broken and the ring taken from him. It was lost for years but eventually reached Bilbo who, to a great extent, managed to withstand its destructive powers. Sauron has returned to his old stronghold in the Dark Tower of Mordor and his gaze is coming closer and closer to the peaceful Shire and the country bumpkin hobbits. Gandalf tells Frodo that the ring must be destroyed before Sauron gets it and the only way this can be done is to cast it into the Cracks of Doom in the depths of Ododruin, the fire-mountain, and Frodo, little Frodo Baggins, has been chosen as the Ring-bearer in this perilous venture. We're well into this classic Arien tale of dungeon, fire and sword which has become a cult.

1771, Weybosset Point, U.S.A.
Time for a Lynching
(from <u>The Case of Charles Dexter Ward</u> by H.P. Lovecraft)

At 10.00 p.m. a lynching party set out. A company of about 100 men fell silently into military order in the street shouldering their flintlocks, fowling pieces and whaling harpoons. They were on their way to demolish the farmhouse of Joseph Curwen, warlock, and Joseph Curwen himself.

~ Aries ~

APRIL 13

1922, England
Birth of **JOHN BRAINE**, author

His first and, almost, only book, <u>Room at the Top</u>, made him a fortune by the standards of 1957. The story of the rise of rough, working class Joe Lampton was fresh, vigorous, and based partly on himself. Braine's comments and politics were forthright and uncompromising (Moon in Scorpio); he moved from extreme left to extreme right which Aries does easily. In 1975 he joined a Civil Assistance organisation founded to aid Britain in any crisis in which law and order broke down (which looked feasible then). Advocated the return of hanging and was anti-immigration.

APRIL 14

1950, England
Birth of **DAN DARE**

This is the birthday or first appearance of our very own comic strip hero in <u>The Eagle</u>.

On the world stage, **ABRAHAM LINCOLN** was shot in 1865 while at Ford's Theatre, Washington. He died the next day. Walt Whitman, much affected, wrote the poem: 'O Captain! My Captain! Our fearful trip is done! The ship has weather'd every wrack, the prize we sought is won...'

APRIL 15

1982, Kingsmarkham (Chief Inspector Wexford country)
Mad Hysteria!
(from <u>An Unkindness of Ravens</u> by Ruth Rendell)

Today, Sara Williams and her half-sister murdered their father. It was a case of <u>folie à deux</u>, a kind of madness that overtakes two people only when they are together, each egging on the other. "I told her to get me a knife. I wasn't serious then, it was fantasy. I was angry and I was excited - high like when you've had a drink."

~ Aries ~

She had raised the knife and stuck it in her father's neck, right in hard using both hands. That woke him up so she stabbed him a few more times to stop the noises he was making and the blood from spraying over everything. Dear Ruth Rendell always gives dates or makes them easy to discover. On this day Pluto opposed the Arien Sun and Mercury, which is a time for arrogance, fanaticism, physical suffering, murder.

RENDELL herself - born on February 17, 1930 - has Aries ascending containing her Sun-ruler, Uranus.

1927, U.S.A.
Good Friday Shenanigans!
(from <u>The Case of Charles Dexter Ward</u> by H.P. Lovecraft)

In the late afternoon young Ward began some strange rite which set all the neighbourhood dogs howling and produced a hideous smell. There was a flash of lightning and a <u>voice</u> the like of which no one had ever heard before. It shook the house... 'Mr and Mrs Ward conferred at some length after dinner and the former resolved to have a firm and serious talk with Charles that very night.' He'd left it rather late. The Sun was trine Neptune, a splendid time for mystical, magical practices.

```
┌──────────┐
│  APRIL   │
│   16     │
└──────────┘
```

1758, Dorset
A Baying-for-Blood Day!
(from <u>Moonfleet</u> by J.Meade Falkner)

Another bloodthirsty day. Thomas Maskew JP of Moonfleet Manor was shot at Hoar Head, a lonely place in the Parish of Chaldron. He had been caught spying on the smugglers. He got no mercy for he had shot Elzevir Block's son and outbid Elzevir for possession of the <u>Why Not?</u> inn.

FALKNER, born May 8, 1858, worked for an arms manufacturer and became Chairman of the company. He usually wrote County Guides in his spare time, and was a great walker and cyclist. <u>Moonfleet</u> was a one-off. This children's adventure story was first published in 1898 and soon became a classic with a loyal band of devotees, including Chris de Burgh who has read it dozens of times and chose it as his Desert Island book. Falkner's chart shows Sun, Mercury, Jupiter and Uranus conjoined in rural, placid Taurus, but all were opposed by a

~ Aries ~

vicious Mars in Scorpio, which just had to let off steam occasionally.
And how!

1922, London
Birth of **SIR KINGSLEY AMIS**, author of <u>Lucky Jim</u>

One of the original Angry Young Men. A sharply satirical writer,
unsympathetic towards his characters and everyone else. Wrote a funny
but hurtful collection of anecdotes about his friends - he could draw blood
easily without a firearm. Mars is in Sagittarius - in good aspect to Sun
and Mercury in fiery Aries - in his horoscope which is a telling vignette.

APRIL
17

1660, a Desert Island (without the Discs) off Barbados
An Earthquake!
(from <u>Robinson Crusoe</u> by Daniel Defoe)

> 'The ground I stood on shook three times at about
> 8 minutes' distance, with three such shocks as
> would have over-turn'd the strongest building
> that could be suppos'd to have stood on the earth;
> a great piece of the top of a rock, which stood
> about half a mile from me next the sea, fell down
> with such a terrible noise as I never heard in all
> my life. I perceiv'd also, the very sea was put into
> violent motion by it; and I believe the shocks were
> stronger under the water than on the island...
> After the third shock was over, and I felt no more
> for some time, I began to take courage.'

But Crusoe was not out of the wars yet.

> 'While I sat thus I found the air was over-cast and
> grow cloudy as if it would rain; soon after that the
> wind rose little by little, so that, in less than half
> an hour, it blew a most dreadful hurricane. The
> sea was all of a sudden cover'd over with foam
> and froth, the shore was cover'd with the breach
> of the water, the trees were torn up by the roots,
> and a terrible storm it was...'

Oddly enough, and this is fact not fiction, in the early hours of April
18, 1906, the great San Francisco earthquake began.

~ Aries ~

1906, East Poland
Birth of **ABEL ROSNOVSKI**

1906, Boston, U.S.A.
Birth of **WILLIAM LOWELL KANE**
(both from <u>Kane and Abel</u> by Jeffrey Archer)

Astro-twins whose lives were entwined. Each, making allowance for his circumstances, was a true Arien. Abel was straight-forward enough. He had to fight every inch of the way and was soon blooded. The family who took him in when he was found, newly-born, in a field beside his dead mother, was slaughtered by the Germans and the Russians in World War 1. Still only nine he found himself in charge of a few peasant survivors and spent harrowing years in prison camps. He was bayoneted in the leg and limped for the rest of his life. Eventually he got to New York and worked as a waiter, scratching and biting his way up until he owned a chain of restaurants, but still wasn't safe from Arien-type disasters. Arsonists got him! Kane was the son of a wealthy banking family, spared the early physical bloodshed, but fuelled by a ruthless drive for power. They ran up against one another in the course of business but did not get on. Both served in World War 2 where, unwittingly, Abel saved Kane's life by carrying him off the battlefield. Aries, at its most primitive, had caught up with Kane who was badly wounded. Kane's son marrying Abel's daughter only added fuel to the Arien flames. Well, Ariens are too independent and competitive to get along with each other. Rivals - yes; friends - not really.

1986, London
Entertaining Mr Sloane opened at the Royal Court Theatre

This was a black comedy written by the much reviled Joe Orton. Mr Sloane was a violent, nasty piece of Arien work. When he took the stage for the first time, Pluto was ascending in its own sign of Scorpio, a sinister touch. The Arien Sun was aspected by Uranus denoting excitement, upset, rebelliousness, innovation. Orton wrote black comedies dwelling on violence and perversion and contributed to <u>Oh! Calcutta!</u>, which one critic said gave pornography a dirty name. He met a bloody end himself, battered to death with a hammer by his lover.

~ Aries ~

1900
Birth of **RICHARD HUGHES**

1901
Birth of **GLADYS MITCHELL**

Two well-known English authors born today. In 1929 Richard Hughes' A High Wind in Jamaica was published. A famous adventure story of children kidnapped by bloodthirsty pirates and taken out to sea. In 1924 he had written Danger, the first radio play to be commissioned by the BBC. As well as Sun in Aries he had a conjunction of Mercury and Mars there. A real Jolly Roger writing combination.

Gladys Mitchell was a schoolmistress who wrote a crime or adventure novel a year, took two masculine pen-names and won a Silver Dagger Award. Her detective was Dame Beatrice LeStrange Bradley with her sidekick the Amazonian Laura Gavin. Dame Beatrice was attached to the Home Office but wasn't above producing a pistol when required while Laura would kick a docker in the teeth as soon as look at him. Gladys had Mercury in Aries and her Arien Sun was in good aspect to Mars in Leo so her choice of characters is not surprising.

1841, U.S.A.
The Murders on the Rue Morgue first published

This is considered to be the first modern detective story, and was written by the master of the macabre Edgar Allan Poe. The detective was Dupin and the villain - an orang-utan. The victims were an old woman and her daughter and a proper bloodbath it was. The story could only be pigeonholed under Aries which cannot be said of C. Auguste Dupin himself. It can only be gleaned from the three tales in which he appears that his family was illustrious but impoverished, that he was a snob and an intellectual, that he lived in seclusion shutting out the sun and reading through the daylight hours by the light of tapers, that he rambled about Paris during the hours of darkness. None of which proclaims him as a rumbustious, extrovert Arien. Aries only claim to him would have to be on the grounds of his being a pioneer, the first of the analytical fictional investigators,

~ Aries ~ Taurus ~

appearing two years before the word 'detective' had even appeared in the English language.

APRIL 21

1930s
Birth of **RICHARD HAWK-MONITOR** of Hautcourture Hall
(pronounced Howchiker), Howling, Sussex
(from <u>Cold Comfort Farm</u> by Stella Gibbons)

Dick was typical of the Taureans who are 'easy on the eye but slow on the uptake'. Bossy Flora Poste decided he should marry her cousin Elfine Starkadder. On this, his 21st birthday, there was a grand party at the Assembly Rooms at Godmere attended by the flower of the County. Groomed and schooled by Flora, Elfine was a knock-out and Dick was enraptured. He was very much the young country squire with a wind-reddened, open, boyish countenance.

> "It's been awfully jolly seeing you all here to-night... And this is a particularly jolly evening for me, because I've got something else to tell you all. I want to tell you that Miss Starkadder and I are engaged."

Success for Flora but when they arrived back at Cold Comfort Farm in the small hours of the next day, they found an ancient ceremony in progress...

APRIL 22

1930s, Cold Comfort Farm, Howling, Sussex
The Starkadder's Annual Counting
(from <u>Cold Comfort Farm</u> by Stella Gibbons)

You can't get more bucolic or Taurean ruralean than an assembly of Starkadders in the kitchen of Cold Comfort - Amos, Judith, Meriam the hired girl, Adam Lambsbreath the aged retainer, Ezra and Harkaway, Caraway, Micah, Daft Rennet and, of course the matriarch of the clan, Aunt Ada Doom, who tonight had left her room unexpectedly to hold the Annual Counting. Ada had seen something nasty in the woodshed when she was no bigger than a titty-wren and refused to let any of the family leave. This was Flora's first meeting with her and what with the disclosure of the engagement of Elfine

~ Taurus ~

sending Urk (to whom she had been promised by the water voles) off his trolly, Rennet trying to drown herself in Ticklepenny's well, Amos defecting to go and spread the Lord's word in one of they Ford vans, the elopement of Urk and Meriam, Aunt Ada lashing out with the <u>Milk Producers' Weekly Bulletin and Cowkeepers' Guide</u> and having an Attack (breath), it was a night to remember. Stella Gibbons was, of course, 'taking the mickey' on the popular Mary Webb type of novel, all elemental with Nature at is rawest. Very Taurean. She even starred the best passages so you don't miss them (Mary didn't go that far). '* Dawn crept over the Downs like a sinister white animal, followed by the snarling cries of the wind eating its way...' Stella was born January 5, 1902 and was a townee Capricorn without a drop of Taurus in her.

APRIL 23

St. George's Day
A Red Letter Day for the English Bookworm-Astrologer

George means farmer and, traditionally, this is also the Bard's birthday and death-day by the Old Style Calendar. Updated it would be in early May but still Taurus. **SHAKESPEARE** was a solid citizen with aspirations to become a 'gentleman' and was certainly no tormented genius. He made jolly old Sir Toby Belch in <u>Twelfth Night</u> a Taurean.

> Sir Andrew: Shall we set about some revels?
> Sir Toby: What shall we do else? Were we not born under Taurus?

Later he gives an indignant wail: Shall there be no more cakes and ale? Shakespeare saturates the day. **NGAIO MARSH** was born today, 1899, in New Zealand. She was a Shakespearian actress and producer and in her crime novel, <u>Light Thickens</u>, 'the Scottish play' was put on tonight at the Dolphin Theatre. Angela Carter, another Taurean, in her <u>Wise Children</u> gives it as a birthday to that grand Shakespearian actor, **MELCHIOR HAZARD**, and his twin daughters, **NORA** and **DORA**, also share the day and the celebrations. They were born in the morning in 1915, a Monday washday, bright and windy. All over Brixton long black stockings stepped out with gent's long johns. More! **PHIL ARCHER** of the famous radio farming dynasty was born today in 1928 and **NORMAN PAINTING**, who has played him from the beginning, in 1924. Both are musical and play the church organ.

~ *Taurus* ~

1815
Birth of **ANTHONY TROLLOPE**

1900
Birth of **ELIZABETH GOUDGE**

Two unmistakably English novelists. Trollope was a typically Victorian Englishman. He was a Post Office surveyor, familiar with the English and Irish countryside. Wherever he found himself working he plunged into the local life and was addicted to hunting. Anti-blood-sportspeople need not fear. He was so short sighted he could never even see the fox. Few men, he said, had investigated more thoroughly the depth and breadth and water-holding capacity of the Essex ditch. He is best known for the Barsetshire chronicles and his characters have all the satisfying solidity of Taurus. Some find him dull as his characters lead outwardly placid comfortable lives but, after a slice of Trollope, other authors' characters seem flimsy and see-through. Both Elizabeth Goudge and Trollope were at home in Cathedral cities amongst Anglicans. She wrote, amongst others, A City of Bells (Wells) and Towers in the Mist (Oxford). Her children's award winning Little White Horse, like her others, was set in Victorian times and leads us into magical evocations of the English countryside. She was staunch C of E, a spinster, handicraft teacher and resident of Rose Cottage. Both authors led unmelodramatic, full and busy lives.

1873, Woolwich, South London
Birth of **WALTER DE LA MARE**

And so the Taurean list of authors goes on. He gave up accountancy for literature. He is one of the fantastical Taureans writing fairy tale poetry and prose. There is also a reflection of opposing Scorpio in much of his work. Seton's Aunt has been called the most terrifying murder story ever written. The Listeners reeks of the supernatural

"Is there anybody there?" cried the Traveller
Knocking at the moonlit door

~ Taurus ~

His novel, <u>Memoirs of a Midget</u> records the adventures of a mysterious Miss M, a dwarf, who on the night of April 24/25, year unknown, disappeared. Her housekeeper was uneasy as she heard voices yet had let nobody in. When she went up to the large pleasant room at the top of the house it was empty. Nothing was disarranged, nothing unusual except that a slip of paper had been pinned to the carpet a little beyond the threshold with the message: 'I have been called away. M.' By whom? On what errand? For what purpose? Like yesterday's Trollope and Goudge, this author had Sun in Taurus square Saturn in Aquarius. He too livid quietly and productively, loved by all. However, Mars and Uranus joined in to make a fixed Grand Cross which added a chill factor.

APRIL 26

1794, (Year II of the New Calendar), Paris in the Terror
A Meagre Feast
(from <u>The Triumph of the Scarlet Pimpernel</u> by Baroness Orczy)

Robespierre, the orchestrator of the Terror, visited a psychic on the Rue de la Planchette today but all the soothsayer can see in the crystal is <u>Scarlet</u>! Beware! "That which is scarlet is shaped like a flower...five petals, I see them distinctly." Not surprising perhaps. In her ante-room sprawled a huge, ungainly coal-heaver, Citizen Rateau. THE SCARLET PIMPERNEL! That evening open air meals were held all over Paris. Fraternal Suppers these family outings were called. They were an innovation of Robespierre's who realised that the riff-raff must be entertained lest they mope around and talk themselves into the belief 'that they are more wretched, more indigent, more abused, than they were in the days of monarchial oppression.' Huge braziers and torches were lit and tables set out with such food as was available. It wasn't much but, being French, they managed to make a banquet out of a few herrings sprinkled with shredded onions and vinegar, boiled prunes, pottages of lentils and beans and bread and cheese. In the Rue St Honoré a young hothead tried to stir up the crowd and things were getting ugly when an incensed Citizen Rateau knocked out the orator, pushed him under the table in the milieu and saved his four companions from being dragged <u>à la lanterne</u>, while apparently denouncing them louder than anyone else.

1935, Severn Hall, seat of Lord Severn, Gloucestershire
A Lady Vanishes
(from <u>Lord of the Sorcerers</u> by Carter Dickson)

Severn Hall was something like Strawberry Hill but much larger and more battlemented. It reeked of money. On this rainy afternoon Lady Helen Loring had returned from an archaelogical dig in Egypt with a lamp filched from a Pharaoh's tomb and his curse to go with it. She vanished - as prognosticated - and she wasn't the last. This is a Carter Dickson locked room mystery at which he excelled. This is said to have been his favourite. Sun and Mercury were in Taurus conjunct Uranus for sudden disappearances. Virgo was probably rising with Neptune, planet of illusions and deceptions, on the ascendant. It was opposed by Saturn smacking strongly of ancient curses.

1948, Bucks
Birth of **TERRY PRATCHETT**

Terry Pratchett has created an alternative universe, Discworld, which is flat and balanced on the backs of four elephants which are balanced on the back of a giant turtle. The cosmology is worked out in detail and the whole place crammed full of wizards (sorry - wizzards), trolls, dryads, druids, barbarians, elves, Luggage (which runs after its owner on hundreds of little legs) and other assorted loonies. One hero is the wizzard Rincewind who was born under the Small Boring Group of Faint Stars lying between The Flying Moose and The Knotted String. Discworld's Professor of Astrology found it fascinating that even a wizzard of Rincewind's poor calibre should have a horoscope which contained nothing magical at all. Terry Pratchett's own horoscope is in the same situation. There are no planets in the Water element which is a prerequisite for magic, no shadings, no nuances. A very prosaic chart. Why should he worry? His novels are hugely popular. The last word goes to Mr P. who remarks that as a typical Taurean he doesn't believe in all that astrology stuff. Work that out!

1863, around 6.00 a.m., San Francisco, USA
Birth of **WILLIAM RANDOLPH HEARST**, newspaper proprietor

He lowered public taste to raise his circulation figures and succeeded brilliantly. In the 1930s he owned the world's biggest publishing company. His life inspired fellow Taurean Orson Welles' film masterpiece Citizen Kane (premiered on May 1, 1941, when Jupiter and Uranus crossed over Hearst's ascendant). For Hearst everything had to be BIG, on the grand scale. He had to live in a castle, had to buy castles, even if he just put them by for possible future use. A steamroller of a Taurean and not very nice example of the Taurean desire for money, power and possessions.

Year unknown
Birth of **PRINCESS MARY**
(from The Artificial Princess by Ronald Firbank)

This is Walpurgis Night when witches run riot attended by the Devil himself and it seems that it was the Princess's birthday too and a lavish party was held. The princess certainly lived in a magical fairy tale setting in a real family castle, not a bought one like William Randolph's. From the little we learn of her she was cocooned in luxury and loved dancing. At one point she dances a Tarantella before a mirror in just a bracelet and a rope of pearls. She apparently entertained some hopes of dancing before her step-father, the king, and demanding the head of the local prophet à la Salome but it's a strange tale (although Firbank's simplest) and hard to grasp. **RONALD FIRBANK** was a rich, 'precious', neurotic homosexual. He died when only 39 unknown outside his own aristocratic eccentric circle. Apparently the Princess' birthday celebrations on Walpurgis Night were to tie in with the black arts which were being conducted in the shrubbery, and a forerunner of our own Mystic Meg was there too. 'In the chiaroscuro of a shrubbery, a Society crystal gazer, swathed in many shades of violet was predicting misfortunes by the light of the stars.' Her solitary secret was to look uncanny. People expect '...moonstones, Veils, and a ghoulish cut to one's skirt.' On a practical note she found it tiresome not to be able to wear out her professional clothes in the street.

~ Taurus ~

1848, London
Birth of **SARAH RAINBOROUGH**
(from The Houses in Between by Howard Spring)

Sarah tells the story which spans 99 years. She didn't quite make it to her century. Her parents were wealthy and she had a comfortable life. On her 3rd birthday (1851) she was taken to the opening of the Great Exhibition at the Crystal Palace. Queen Victoria was there in pink and silver, Prince Albert (whose idea it was) and the Royal children. It was a memory that would remain with her always. It was the day of a New Moon, both Sun and Moon in Taurus, plus Pluto and Uranus. The Great Exhibition as a showcase for material wealth and heavy, monumental artifacts was truly Taurean. And it made a profit! An important day in the country calendar too. 'In the morning,' reported Prudence Sarn, 'ploughing one of the far meadows with Gideon, I saw yellow nut catkins in the hedge.' She picked them and tied a bunch to each of the ox's horns so 'all that day of sad-coloured weather, the white cattle went up and down the red field, which was white-over in parts, so that they looked yellow, with ruddy gold plumes on their heads as if it was a fair. When we unspanned, Gideon said - "What'n you been after, bedizening the cattle?" "It's May Day," I says.' That's from Precious Bane by Mary Webb, which Stella Gibbons sent up so mercilessly in Cold Comfort Farm.

1859
Birth of **JEROME K. JEROME**, humorist

He wrote Idle Thoughts of an Idle Fellow and founded a magazine called The Idler. Not surprising that his Sun and Moon, conjunct in Taurus, were squared by Saturn from Leo which slows down an already easy-going Taurus. 'It's impossible to enjoy idling thoroughly unless one has plenty of work to do.' But his most famous book is Three Men in a Boat, a very English tale of three very English men and their very English mishaps as they rowed down the Thames. They were connoisseurs of the English pub but didn't fare so well when self-catering. 'We were very fond of pineapple all three of us. We looked at the picture on the tin; we thought of the juice. We smiled at one another, and Harris got a spoon ready. Then we looked for the

~ Taurus ~

knife to open the tin with.'

They had forgotten it. After hours of fruitless - and bloody - battering there was one great dent across the top that had the appearance of a mocking grin which drove them mad and Harris went into a field 'and got a big sharp stone, and I went back into the boat and brought out the mast, and George held the tin and Harris held the sharp end of the stone against the top of it, and I took the mast and poised it high up in the air, and gathered up all my strength and brought it down..It was George's straw hat that saved his life that day.'

MAY
3

1896, England
Birth of **DODIE SMITH**, actress, novelist and playwright

She wrote the much-loved I Capture the Castle and Dear Octopus - usually stories of comfortably-off middle-class Taurean families. Her book for children, The One Hundred and One Dalmations, was wildly successful when it was filmed by Walt Disney (released 25 January 1960). Cruella deVil was obviously the enemy, not only of dalmations, but of all right-thinking Taureans. A nasty conjunction of Saturn and Uranus in Scorpio opposite the Sun in her horoscope gave Miss Smith the ability to create such a beastly woman. An unaided Taurus could never have done it!

MAY
4

1891, Switzerland
Death of Sherlock Holmes
(from The Final Problem by Sir Arthur Conan Doyle)

In the afternoon Sherlock Holmes met his doom going over the Reichenbach Falls locked in the deadly embrace of his arch-enemy, Professor Moriarty. What was Dr Watson thinking of to let him out alone? No astrologer would have allowed it. The Sun in Taurus was powerless. Pluto was at the mid-point of Mars and Neptune, which denotes brutality to others or to suffer from it oneself. Additionally, Pluto was in conjunction with the Dragon's Head, a karmic link, and not a pleasant one.

Not at all a Taurean day but Sir Arthur must have fancied this as a Day of Doom because he had Sir Charles Baskerville of Baskerville

~ Taurus ~

Hall, Devon, die today. 'His features (were) convulsed with some strong and dreadful emotion and nearby the footprint of a gigantic hound.'

MAY 5

1818, 2.00 a.m., Trier, Germany
Birth of **KARL MARX**

He was the author of <u>Das Kapital.</u> Capital in other words. Again that side of Taurus which is fascinated by money and economics pops up. Marx was not one of the famous Brothers but an earnest philosopher who settled and wrote his socialist bible in London. He came from a solid, respectable family and fell in love once and for all, marrying after a courtship of 7 years. Taureans don't rush things. When she died he described himself as a moral cripple. Marx was born on the day of a New Moon, so the Moon joined the Sun in Taurus. Both were excellently aspected by Jupiter which increases the Taurean influence even more, and brings out its best side. As if that weren't enough, Venus ruler of Taurus was also in the sign, so Karl had a predominance of the Bull in his horoscope and, Communist or not, must have been a very nice man.

MAY 6

1893, Early hours, Transylvania
Meet Count Dracula!
(from <u>Dracula</u> by Bram Stoker)

This was when Jonathon Harker first met Count Dracula, his new employer. Sun, Venus and Jupiter were conjoined in Taurus but were opposed by Uranus. Pisces was probably rising so ruling Neptune at the nadir conjoined Pluto which doesn't bode well. At first all seemed fine to the young man who received a warm welcome from the Count. He was conducted to a well-lit room in which a table was spread for supper and a great fire of logs flamed and flared. "I pray you, be seated and sup how you please. You will, I trust, excuse me that I do not join you, but I have dined already," said the Count. (Ooooh!) Jonathon, half-famished after his journey, fell at once on an excellent roast chicken, cheese, salad, and a bottle of old Tokay and a cigar. Refreshed, he began to notice little things however - the peculiarly strong white teeth which protruded over the remarkably ruddy lips of his attentive host, in particular.

~ Taurus ~

1812, London
Birth of **ROBERT BROWNING**, poet

He was the one who wrote: <u>Oh to be in England, now that April's there</u>. A very proper sentiment for a Taurean. He delighted in music, was charming, popular and sociable, had adoring parents and a besotted wife, Elizabeth Barrett Browning. Their romance, she was a Miss Barrett of Wimpole Street, is famous. They eloped to Italy where they lived happily ever after. The only cloud in their relationship was that she (mystic Pisces) was attracted by the occult while he (down-to-earth Taurus) was decidedly not. He wrote a very stinging poem called Mr Sludge the Medium which was obviously aimed at Daniel Dunglas Home, a very fashionable occultist of the time, who either was genuine or was never found out. Mrs Browning was one of his fans. Robert didn't publish the poem until after her death - very wise!

1927, Leningrad
Birth of **MARIA ANDREYEVNA OSTRAKOVA**
(from <u>Smiley's People</u> by John L. Carré)

She defected from Russia in 1956 and went to Paris where her husband lived. He had defected some time before and for assisting him she was sent to a forced labour camp where she broke her leg in three places after a coal slip. Once in safety she worked as a checker in a warehouse until 1978 when she was rescued and co-opted by George Smiley, an English intelligence agent. She was short and stout, very brave and capable of great affection. Her horoscope is a typical one of the period when, in many spring/summer charts of the late 1920s/early 1930s, Saturn in Sagittarius is a singleton planet, quite capable of slewing the entire nativity to its wishes. It certainly showed its doom and gloom side to poor Maria. Her brother hanged himself, her daughter disappeared, she spent many years in - at best - dull, routine work, at worst, slave labour. She was separated from her husband for many years and soon after their reunion he died from cancer. She limped because of her injury which is all of a piece with Saturn (bones) in Sagittarius (hips and thighs). One ray of hope, the nice trine to Saturn from Uranus, which helped her survive assassination attempts.

~ Taurus ~

1711, in the land of Houyhnhnms
A Taurean Banquet
(from <u>Gulliver's Travels</u> by Jonathon Swift)

Gulliver's ship was taken over by the seamen who had turned pirate and he was put down on a strand where he was set upon by Yahoos. 'I never beheld in all my Travels so disagreeable an Animal, or one against which I naturally conceived so strong an Antipathy.' However, they were frightened off by a horse who was very kind to him and took him home. It was a Houyhnhnm, gentle and very Taurean. 'About Noon, I saw coming towards the House a kind of Vehicle, drawn like a Sledge by 4 Yahoos. There was in it an old Steed, who seemed to be of the Quality; he alighted with his Hind-feet forward, having by Accident got a Hurt in his Left Fore-foot (perhaps he'd got Saturn in Sagittarius!). He came to dine with our Horse who received him with great Civility. They dined in the best Room and had Oats boiled in Milk for the second Course... Their Mangers were placed circular in the Middle of the Room and divided into several Partitions, round which they sat on their Haunches upon Bosses of Straw.'

1925, Cambridge, England
A Pact with the Devil
(from <u>The Devil in Velvet</u> by John Dickson Carr)

In the evening, about 8.00 p.m. BST, Professor Nicholas Fenton sold his soul to the Devil. As an historian he had become obsessed with something which had happened in his home in 1675. On June 10 of that year, someone had died from poison administered over a period of time there but the outcome was unknown. His pact with the Devil allowed him to return to the scene on May 10, 1675 to investigate the murder and prevent it. Oddly enough the owner of the house at that time was also Nicholas Fenton, a baronet, and they shared the same birthday, December 25, the professor in the year 1866 and the baronet in 1649. At the time of the pact the middle degree of Scorpio would probably have been rising - the most accursed degree of the most accursed sign, according to one ancient authority. An inharmonious aspect to the Sun from Neptune gives a glimpse of the mystery and deception. Saturn would have been rising which was prophetic as the victim was still going to die. Jupiter trine the Sun stands for the high society circles into which the professor was plunged with the devil-may-care Sir Nick, whose persona the sober professor assumed. As a Capricornian he hated the 20th century and yearned for the past.

```
MAY
11
```

1897, London
Reunion
(from <u>Raffles, The Amateur Cracksman</u> by E.W.Hornung)

Today Raffles and his great friend Bunny were reunited. Bunny had just come out of jail after an 18 month sentence, Raffles had got away. They celebrated by going out to supper and gourmet Taurus comes into its own!

> 'It was no mere meal, it was no coarse orgy, but a little feast for the fastidious gods, not unworthy of Lucullus. And I who had bolted my skilly at Wormwood Scrubs, and tightened my belt in a Holloway attic, it was I who sat down to this ineffable repast! Where the courses were few, but each a triumph of its kind, it would be invidious to single out any one dish; but the <u>jambon de West-phalia au champagne</u> tempts me sorely. And then the champagne we drank, not the quantity, but the quality! Well, it was Pol Roger '84 and quite good enough for me, but even so it was not more dry, nor did it sparkle more, than the merry rascal who had dragged me thus far to the devil, but should lead me dancing the rest of the way.'

By the end of the evening Raffles pulled off another coup and they were back in a life of crime. Well, Saturn conjunct Uranus rising in Scorpio signals rebellion against Society, Taurus or no Taurus.

```
MAY
12
```

1901, London
Birth of **JON FORSYTE**
(from <u>The Forsyte Saga</u> by John Galsworthy)

He was the son of 'Young' Jolyon and Irene, former wife of Soames Forsyte. With Sun conjunct Venus in Taurus it wasn't surprising that

~ Taurus ~

'there never was anyone born more loving or more loveable.' Inevitably Fleur Forsyte (a Scorpio), daughter of Soames and his second wife, fell for him. His open, affectionate nature was averse for an intrigue which could only bring grief to others. Fleur, his direct zodiac opposite, was all for it but for once in her life she failed. Irene, her older and more experienced Scorpio rival, won the day. Jon decided to take up farming and went to Canada. He married someone else and was saved.

Today is also the birthday of **HOMER SIMPSON** from the popular cartoon series. Obviously a day for devoted husbands and dads to be born! Homer is the loving husband of Marge and an affectionate, if sometimes misguided, father of three. He has something of the portly Taurean figure, too!

MAY 13

1907, London
Birth of **DAPHNE DU MAURIER**

Another very English novelist - if Cornwall will allow it as her love was all for that county and her most famous books have Cornish settings. She was born into the famous du Maurier theatrical family and was very Venusian being blonde, blue-eyed, very pretty, attractive, charming and highly-sexed. Her best known book must be Rebecca which is narrated by an unnamed heroine, put across as gentle, loving and unassuming - the best type of Taurean. Rebecca herself is her opposite, obviously a Scorpion. Daphne du Maurier herself, and her horoscope, were very complex. One un-Taurean corner of her chart shows clearly her interest in a psychic dimension to life, particularly reincarnation. She saw herself as having been a shepherd boy in some ancient kingdom and that, at any rate, is Taurean.

MAY 14

Late 1890s, Germany
Gardening Interlude
(from Elizabeth and her German Garden by Elizabeth von Arnim)

An eventful afternoon. Elizabeth was in her garden with her three little daughters, the April baby, the May baby and the June baby, when the April baby, who had been sitting pensively on a tree-stump, got up suddenly and began racing about, shrieking and wringing her hands. A herd of young cows had got through the hedge and was grazing dangerously close to the roses. Before they could be chased away, they had trampled down a border of pinks and lilies, made great holes in a bed of China roses and nibbled a Jackmanii clematis. 'The June baby, who is two feet square and valiant beyond her size and years, seized a stick much bigger than herself and went after the cows.' The cows were astonished and stood staring at her. The June baby's description and action smack of Taurus and would have been more appropriate to the May baby, but perhaps she was eating!

MAY
15

1827, Rochester, Kent
First Appearance of The Fat Boy!
(from <u>Pickwick Papers</u> by Charles Dickens)

The Pickwickians, who had begun their travels on May 13, rose early to witness a Grand Review which was to take place upon the Lines. The manoeuvres of half-a-dozen regiments were to be inspected by their commander-in-chief. A huge concourse had gathered but somehow the Pickwickians found themselves under the levelled muskets of half the British Army and in a state of panic. They were rescued by a stout old gentleman in a blue coat with bright buttons. This was Mr. Wardle, who was to become a good friend. He had several relations in his party, also a hamper of spacious dimensions - 'one of those hampers which always awaken in a contemplative mind associations connected with cold fowls, tongue, and bottles of wine' - and 'a fat and red-faced boy, in a state of somnolency, whom no speculative observer could have regarded for an instant without setting down as the official dispenser of the contents of the before mentioned hamper, when the proper time for their consumption should arrive.' The whole scene is Taurus personified at its highest level by the bluff, hearty, hospitable Mr. Wardle and at its lowest by the Fat Boy whose sole aim in life was to eat. The 'spacious hamper' itself ascends to a spiritually gastronomic plane - the apotheosis of Taurus!

c. 1877/8, China
Excessive Caution
(from <u>The Tribulations of a Chinese Gentleman</u> by Jules Verne)

The gentleman, one Kin-Fo, having heard he was financially ruined, resolved to kill himself on May 1 with the aid of opium and poison, but he was an unimaginative soul and was upset because he couldn't feel any emotion about dying. He therefore arranged with his old tutor to kill him with no intimation beforehand so he might spend his last days in an agony of anticipation. The tutor duly disappeared to prepare but today news came that Kin-Fo was not ruined after all and, naturally, he no longer wished to snuff it. Unluckily the tutor could not be found and Kin-Fo had to be guarded by two representatives of the life assurance office who stood to lose heavily if Kin-Fo died before his birthday on June 25. They started by putting him on a diet of boiled eggs because of the risk of the tutor attempting to poison him.

1909, Lower East Side, New York
Birth of **HARVEY METCALF** formerly HENRYK METELSKI
(from <u>Not a Penny More, Not a Penny Less</u> by Jeffrey Archer)

Henryk Metelski was born dirt poor, but with the Sun and probably the Moon in Taurus, the pursuit of money came naturally to him He rose swiftly from stockbroker's messenger boy to tycoon by unethical methods which were a disgrace to all respectable Taureans. However, Henryk had Mars square his Sun which can scratch and claw with the best. Having made his first million, Henryk changed his name and proceeded to live a life of luxury becoming grossly overweight in the process. He was not unaffectionate; he doted on his daughter Rosalie. He discovered that Art was not only a good investment but the source of great pleasure. His hobby was the cultivation of rare orchids. For a villain, Harvey doesn't come across badly. He's generous and charitable and quite likeable. But, even when rich beyond the dreams of avarice, he couldn't resist his shady financial dealings and, in the course of one of them, he ruined four men. Jeffrey Archer's first and best-known novel details how the four banded together and pursued Harvey to recover their money - not a penny more, not a penny less.

~ Taurus ~

1872, 5.45 p.m., Trelleck, Wales
Birth of **BERTRAND RUSSELL**, 3rd Earl Russell, philosopher,
mathematician

In 1950 he won the Nobel Prize for Literature. His most popular and
accessible book was his successful History of Western Philosophy
(1945). His Principia Mathematica, upon which his scientific
reputation rests, is a book which perhaps twenty people have read
right through although, as Bernard Miles would have said, "not to
understand it". The peace-loving side of Taurus manifests in his
passionate quest for nuclear disarmament. He was imprisoned
during World War 1 for his outspoken pacifism. On the other hand,
his rising Scorpio, with co-rulers Mars and Pluto, in explosive
conjunction with the Sun, sums him up as a militant pacifist.

c.1874, Prince Edward Island, Canada
Birth of **EMILY STARR**
(from Emily of New Moon by L.M.Montgomery)

Emily has been overshadowed by L.M.Montgomery's more famous
creation, Anne of Green Gables, but Emily too was orphaned. She was
sent to live with her mother's people, the Murrays of New Moon Farm.
Her mother had thought Emily was the prettiest name in the world.
It was quaint and arch and delightful - as was Emily herself.
L.M.Montgomery was an astro-twin of Sir Winston Churchill. She
died in 1942, just as he had found his true niche in life. Both she and
her Emily loved the natural beauty of their homeland and were nice.

1904, London
Birth of **MARGERY ALLINGHAM**, crime writer

1900, a Stately Home somewhere in England
Birth of **ALBERT CAMPION**, fictional detective

Another author who gave her hero her own birthday. Margery Allingham loved the country and enjoyed horses, dogs and gardens. She lived for many years in a lovely house in Essex. Albert Campion, her detective creation, came from the ranks of the landed gentry and presumably had a country background. He had the Taurean charm and kindness and was described by his wife as a useful, dependable sort. His good temper was proverbial. His rooms at 17 Bottle Street, Piccadilly W1 (entrance on left by Police Station) were luxuriously furnished. His 'man', Lugg, was a lumbering, working-class Taurean. Just occasionally, Campion experienced that 'deep anger which altered him and changed him from affable Universal Uncle to a man with an intolerable personal affront.' Then the bull's head went down with frightening effect. His creator's writing was rich and satisfying and wonderfully humorous.

Early 1930s, London
Balletomane
(from Ballet Shoes by Noel Streatfield)

The three Fossil girls - Pauline, Petrova and Posy - had quite a day on May 20 and the excitement continued today. Posy had been taken to see Manoff dance Petrushka (middle of the front row of the dress circle) where she was bewitched and determined that she would be taught by him even if it meant going to Czechoslovakia. Today she tricked her way into the theatre and danced for him. He said: '"You will come with me to Szolyva and I will make you into a beautiful artiste."' Dancing is a favoured Taurean profession or past-time. There was the little matter of money but Pauline signed a contract to go to Hollywood and Petrova was to have her flying lessons paid for so all was well. Petrova wondered if other girls had to be one of them, which one would they choose to be. Any one, Petrova, any one!

~ Taurus ~ Gemini ~

1906, England
Birth of **LADY ELIZABETH CARACOLES**, pronounced CRACKLE
(from Pirates at Play by Violet Trefusis)

An angelically beautiful English girl was sent as a paying guest to Italy to learn the language with a socially ambitious family who also had an angelically beautiful daughter, Vicca (no birthday given). Elizabeth was Geminian. She was eloquent about things she liked and wrote long, long letters. She liked the hair-breadth escapes of French taxi drivers. She was extrovert, unorthodox, undisciplined, thoughtless and loved parties. She was all for trying new things, like getting engaged for an afternoon to make someone happy. She was thoroughly at home in the frenetic 1920s when this novel is set. Violet Trefusis (June 6, 1894) is not a well-known author today, although Virago Classics have taken her up. She was the daughter of Mrs Alice Keppel, mistress of Edward VII (shades of Camilla Parker-Bowles who is also descended from that lady). Violet had a cosmopolitan childhood, was fluent in three languages, witty, a society hostess and a vivid writer. Her lesbian relationship and elopement with Vita Sackville-West caused a Society scandal (Venus opposes shocking Uranus). Both heroines in this novel were modelled on herself, and her horoscope is uncannily similar to Elizabeth's.

1827, London
Twin Geminians
(from Pickwick Papers by Charles Dickens)

Today marks our first acquaintance with Sam Weller. The Pickwickians were in hot pursuit of the rascally, philandering Mr Jingle who had persuaded Rachel Wardle, the maiden aunt, to run away with him. They had got as far as the White Hart where Sam was the bootboy. Both Jingle and Sam are out-and-out Geminians although their birthdays are unknown. Both run on like ha'penny books, are droll, streetwise and staccato. Jaunty impudence sums up both of them. Today they met for the first time. Jingle asked Sam the way to Doctors' Commons where he wanted to get a licence to marry Rachel. Sam gave a long, lively account of his old father's encounter with the licence touters there and then it's Jingle's turn. "The licence," he exulted to Rachel. "In hurry, post-haste for a licence,/In hurry, ding dong, I come back." "How you run on!" said Rachel. "Run on - nothing to the hours, days, weeks, months, years, when we're united - run on - they'll fly on - bolt-mizzle-steam-engine-thousand-horse-power - nothing to it". Rachel enjoined him not to be long. "Long away from you? Cruel charmer," cried Mr Jingle, kissing her and dancing out. "Dear man!" said the spinster. "Run old girl," said Mr Jingle, walking down the passage, which makes his intentions clear enough. The spinster aunt had money!

MAY 24

1819, 4.15 a.m., London
Birth of **QUEEN VICTORIA**

At first sight this monumental figure does not qualify for membership of the Twins, but she had Sun, Moon and Ascendant all within four degrees in that sign. If born at dawn, as she was, with the Sun rising, you have a lot of royal Leo in you whatever the sign. So, plain and dumpy she might have become but nobody forgot she was Queen for a moment. And, in her youth, prior to Prince Albert, she was undoubtedly Geminian. She had a flashing smile, loved gossip, danced all night and, all her life, wrote volumes. Correspondence, diaries and journals weigh down yards of library shelves, but she had Gemini's lively, graphic pen and used constant CAPITALS, underlinings and exclamation marks!!! Leaves from Our Highland Journal was her high watermark. Of all her prime ministers she liked (Sagittarian) Disraeli best. He flirted with her and, being a novelist himself, could once say: "We authors, ma'am..." She was thrilled. Born into a different time and sphere, she would have made an excellent Court & Social Correspondent for a Society paper.

~ Gemini ~

1948, Oxford
Birth of **MRS JULIA STEVENS**

1977, Oxford
Birth of **KEVIN COSTYN**
(both from <u>Daughters of Cain</u> by Colin Dexter
- Oxford is Chief Inspector Morse country)

The story begins on May 25 too, in 1994. Julia and Kevin shared a birthday and their lives were entwined in a thoroughly Geminian way. In return for sexual favours, he disposed of the murdered body of her cleaner's husband. He was a pupil of Julia's in Form 5C but not a pupil to be proud of. He was, in fact, a young criminal, below the average in intelligence although he did have a talent for verbal repartee. His poor Geminian showing may have been because he was partially deaf and his horoscope shows Mercury in Taurus in poor aspect to Saturn and Uranus which may tie up with deafness or a speech defect. On the other hand, Julia had a Mercury/Uranus conjunction in Gemini opposite Jupiter and was an excellent teacher. Before their 1995 birthday, Julia was to die from a brain tumour and Kevin be facially scarred in a car crash after a ram raid. Inspector Morse sorted out the murder although how Colin Dexter could make him a Libran (which he evidently is) is beyond belief!

1795, England
Birth of **JUDGE THOMAS NOON TALFOURD**

He was a member of Parliament and a Judge but his real love was literature. He was a critic, biographer and dramatist and in his judicial capacity did much to get the law of copyright amended in favour of authors. A dazzling conversationalist. "Listening to Mr Talfourd is like looking at the sun, it makes one's mind ache with excessive brilliancy. To say that he harangues is nothing. All his talk is one harangue. It is impossible to slide in a word," said Miss Mitford. He looked the part, too, being thin, long-nosed and delicate.

~ Gemini ~

1863, Hamburg
Setting Out
(from <u>Journey to the Centre of the Earth</u> by Jules Verne)

On May 24, Professor Lidenbrock had found an old manuscript giving instructions on how to reach the centre of the earth, the first step being to descend the crater of an extinct volcano in Iceland. Today, the excited Professor and his nephew Axel left their home in Hamburg on the first stage of their amazing journey. They had packed scientific instruments, firearms and electrical apparatus. Their poor old housekeeper didn't know what was happening. "Is the Master out of his mind?" she demanded. Axel nodded. "And he's taking you with him?" Axel nodded. "Where?" Axel pointed towards the centre of the earth. "Into the cellar?" she exclaimed. "Further down than that," said Axel. Sun, Mercury and Uranus were all in Gemini for a lively start but an inharmonious aspect to them from Saturn should have given somebody pause. It wasn't going to be easy.

1908, London
Birth of **IAN FLEMING**, creator of James Bond

We know Ian Fleming's birthday but not that of his famous character, the spy James Bond. We do know that he was born in the Year of the Rat which must have been 1924 so why not May 28, 1924? Other authors have given their heroes their own natal days and Fleming and Bond were alike in many ways. Fleming was a fine athlete and Bond's physical exploits leave the rest of us goggling. They both loved gadgets, fast cars and high living. Fleming was good Geminian company, a great raconteur and said to know something about everything. Bond's proposed horoscope would conjoin Venus and Pluto in Cancer, bringing the girls along in bus loads, while Ian Fleming had Mercury and Pluto conjoined in Gemini which has a similar effect on editors. Bond <u>must</u> have had a Scorpio ascendant. The actors who have played him have been Virgo (Connery and Lazenby), Libra (Moore), Aries (Dalton), and Taurus (Brosnan).

~ Gemini ~

A Diversion

' 'twas the twenty-ninth day of May, 'twas a holiday,
Four-and-twenty tailors set out to hunt a snail;
The snail put forth his horns, and roared like a bull,
Away ran the tailors, and catch the snail who wull.'

The holiday would have been Oak Apple Day, the birthday of Charles II and the day when he entered London in triumph at the Restoration in 1664. Parliament commanded that it be observed as a Day of Thanksgiving and up until recently it was obligatory to wear a buttonhole of oak leaves. (Charles was saved from Cromwell's men by hiding in an oak tree after his defeat at Worcester in 1651.) He was very Geminian - a flirt, frivolous and irresponsible but with a quick wit and an interest in science. As for the slur on the tailoring business, the verse was first recorded in Gammer Gurton's Garland in 1784 and has many variations. Before they became grand fashion gurus, tailors were despised. They defended themselves against the proverb, Nine tailors make but one man, by declaring that 'tailor' was really 'teller' a stroke of the bell at funerals, nine being the number they rang for a man. No one believed them. Scissors, needles and pins come under Gemini and so does the dextrous cutter and stitcher. Adam and Eve were the first tailors. They sewed fig leaves together and made themselves aprons. As they are also the perfect pair, we must assume that our first ancestors were Geminians!

1835, Yorkshire
Birth of **ALFRED AUSTIN**, Poet Laureate

There are a very few Geminians who think they are dab hands with pen and word processor but ain't! One such was Alfred Austin, a pompous leader writer on a newspaper and failed politician. When offered the laureateship after the death of Lord Tennyson, he did not subscribe to the general derisive view that it was a botched-up political appointment. To his 'armour plating of self-satisfaction' it was simply recognition of his position at the head of English literature. There is some doubt as to whether he actually did write the immortal lines, on the illness of the Prince of Wales -

~ Gemini ~

'Along the wires the electric message came,
He is no better, he is much the same.'

It may have been a spoof but Alfred had no need of spoofs to put
forward his application to be the worst poet in the English language.

'O thou nation, (France, he didn't like the French), base
besotted, whose ambition cannon shotted,
And huge mounds of corpses clotted with cold gore alone
can sate!
May the God of Battles shiver every arrow in thy quiver,
And the nobly-flowing river thou dost covet drown thy hate.'

Some of his verse became a music hall turn to the general hilarity. He
put it down to jealousy. He had no great opinion of Tennyson or
Browning and even doubted that the latter <u>was</u> a poet. Browning
called him a filthy little snob and 'Banjo Byron' - he was on the small
size. Austin nearly did for the laureateship. Worse, he could nearly
do for Gemini so we'll pass on - quick!

MAY 31

Late 1920s, London
Inland Revenue v. Haddock
(from <u>Misleading Cases</u> by A.P. Herbert)

Today, Mr Albert Haddock took a large cow of malevolent aspect to the
office of the Collector of Taxes. On its back and sides was written an
order to his Bank to pay the Collector the sum of £57. A twopenny
stamp had been affixed to the cow's dexter horn (which was then
necessary as another form of tax). Mr Haddock led the cow in and
demanded a receipt. The Collector refused to accept the 'open' cow as
valid payment. Mr Haddock led the cow away and was arrested in
Trafalgar Square for causing an obstruction. He was summoned by
the Inland Revenue for non-payment of income tax. The case was
heard by Sir Basil String, who found for the Defendant. A.P. Herbert
was not a Geminian (he was Virgo) but, with his impish sense of
humour, he should have been. He contributed to <u>Punch</u> and the stage
for many years. He also campaigned for author's rights. Mr Haddock,
though, <u>must</u> have been a Geminian!

~ Gemini ~

1785, Somerset
Birth of **MISS ELIZABETH ELLIOT**,
eldest daughter of Sir Walter Elliot of Kellynch Hall
(from <u>Persuasion</u> by Jane Austen)

However much we may admire Jane Austen, she was no good at birthdays. Miss Elliot is no flighty, delightful Geminian but an acidulated spinster, as puffed up with her own consequence as her pompous father. She was handsome, self-possessed and decisive but not a likeable person.

Today in 1938, USA, was the first flight of **SUPERMAN** in DC Comics (also see February 12). He was created by two college students. Today in 1936, **GERALD SCARFE** was born. Not exactly an author, but a book illustrator and caricaturist - an excellent example of the Geminian ability to 'capture' the essence of others.

Flying, students, lightning impressionism - much more Geminian than starchy Miss Elliot.

1953, London
Coronation of Elizabeth II

A number of authors have woven the event into their books, all bringing in the dismal weather on that day. In <u>Ulverton</u> by Adam Thorpe they watched on TV. Buckets of rain and a freezing wind hampered the festivities although Ulverton did its best with processions, tea in the village hall and a bonfire fuelled by all the old wagons from years ago and Mr Bateman's precious memoir, <u>The Life as Lived</u> thrown on by Violet Nightingale because she wasn't in it. Then there's Catherine Cookson's <u>A Grand Man</u>. Nowhere in Jarrow was the Coronation looked forward to and prepared for more than in Burton Street. But it took more than rain to damp the enthusiasm of the tenants of Mulhattans Hall. Both young and old were wild with excitement and, for once, Mary Ann's 'da' didn't get drunk and spoil everything.

At the time of the Coronation, the Sun and Jupiter were together in

~ Gemini ~

Gemini at the mid-heaven - a royal and successful augury. On the other hand, Mercury and Mars were also there, which may account for the hostile (Mars) press (Mercury) which the Royal Family has constantly experienced ever since.

JUNE 3

c.1880, South Africa
An Eclipse of the Moon
(from <u>King Solomon's Mines</u> by H. Rider Haggard)

Allan Quartermain and his companions, in search of the fabulous wealth of the legendary diamond mines, were in deadly peril having been captured by a hostile tribe. '"Now look here, you fellows, isn't tomorrow the 4th of June?" asked Captain Good. We had kept a careful note of the days' (which is a laugh as the Bookworm Astrologer is completely baffled by their reckonings, a common failure in authors) 'so we were able to answer that it was. "Very good: then here we have it - 4th June, total eclipse of the Moon commences at 8.15 Greenwich time, visible in Teneriffe, <u>South Africa</u>, etc."' (It may have been in Captain Good's almanac but it isn't in ours.) '"There' a sign for you. Tell them we will darken the Moon tomorrow night." I made out that the eclipse should begin here about ten o'clock tomorrow night and last until half-past twelve. For an hour-and-a-half there should be almost total darkness. "Well," said Sir Henry, "I suppose we had better risk it." I acquiesced, though doubtfully, for eclipses are queer cattle to deal with - it might be a cloudy night, for instance, or our dates might be wrong.' (They could say that again!)

Nevertheless, enough of these quibbles, it's a ripping yarn as they used to say, the eclipse did happen and put the fear of God up the King of the Kukuanas and saved the fairest girl of the tribe from being sacrificed to the tribal goods.

JUNE 4

1942, New York
A Neurotic Bridegroom
(from <u>Raise High the Roof Beam, Carpenters</u> by J.D.Salinger)

This was Seymour Glass' wedding day, his only relation present being his brother, Buddy. The ceremony was fixed for three o'clock but an hour and a quarter passed with the organist desperately plunging

~ Gemini ~

from Bach to Rodgers and Hart. Eventually the bride, flanked by a parent on either side, was escorted out to the waiting limousine. It transpired that Seymour, who was a bit peculiar, was <u>indisposed by happiness</u>. However, he was at the apartment when the bride and her parents returned and they eloped, Seymour having promised the bride's mother that he would go to an analyst and get himself straightened out. Well, it was a terribly Geminian day guaranteed to bring on 'nerves' in anyone. The planets in order of appearance in Gemini were Uranus, Saturn, Sun, Mercury and Jupiter. June is the month for weddings both real and fictional - twin hearts beating as one and all that guff.

JUNE 5

1884, Middlesex
Birth of **IVY COMPTON-BURNETT**

1939, Yorkshire
Birth of **MARGARET DRABBLE**

Miss Compton-Burnett is 'a writer's writer because she is fascinated by words and phrases as such, juggling with them like a logician. She challenges us with creatures that might inhabit another, colder and more intellectual planet' (Raymond Mortimer). Her books, <u>Brothers and Sisters</u>, <u>Men and Wives</u>, <u>Manservant and Maidservant</u> (Geminian double titles) are minus narrative and scenery. They are conversation pieces of highly artificial, stylized dialogue. Her father married twice and had twelve children all told. There were many tensions between them as there are in her books but she got on well with her own brothers. She always had to have one special person to devote herself to. She hated being alone but never married; described herself as 'a neuter' but was very interested in homosexuality. Witty and brilliant. Had small, delicate hands and feet and a tendency to bronchitis. Margaret Drabble lectures, broadcasts and appears on TV. She has no wish to be a literary recluse and is afraid of being socially cut off and isolated. Strange, un-Geminian link between both ladies - a dislike of the telephone!

~ Gemini ~

Early 1840s, Thornfield
Reader, I married him!
(from <u>Jane Eyre</u> by Charlotte Bronte)

The wedding day of Mr Rochester and Jane Eyre. Not at all Geminian but one of the great dates of English romantic fiction. 'A quiet wedding we had: he and I, the parson and clerk, were alone present. When we got back from church, I went into the kitchen of the manor-house, where Mary was cooking the dinner, and John cleaning the knives, and I said - "Mary, I have been married to Mr Rochester this morning." The housekeeper and her husband were both that decent, phlegmatic order of people, to whom one may at any time safely communicate a remarkable piece of news without incurring the danger of having one's ears pierced by some shrill ejaculation, and subsequently stunned by a torrent of wordy wonderment. Mary did look up, and she did stare at me but she said only - "Have you, miss? Well, for sure!"' (No Geminian she!)

1895, Saltey, Essex
The Devil Visits Essex
(from <u>Cargo of Eagles</u> by Margery Allingham)

Yesterday was the birthday of that little devil **DAMIEN**, from <u>The Omen</u> (6-6-6). Today the village of Saltey was visited by a Demon who 'rushed down the road, smashed gates and windows, broke moorings, took tiles off roofs, destroyed crops and generally had such a ball that the place took years to recover.' The legend was handed down from generation to generation and, inevitably, got a bit embroidered on the way. It's doubtful that a baby <u>was</u> found in the middle of a haystack, or that a two-headed calf and a plague of bats <u>did</u> appear, although there were undoubtedly cloven hoofmarks in the churchyard and mysterious cakes were found cooking in the bakehouse oven. The cold, prosaic facts were that all of Saltey had gone off to see the Royal Review of the troops and militia in the grounds of Sparrows Manor at Nine Ash. All, that is, except the baker who had to stay with his ovens and the publican. <u>They</u> had a little celebration of their own, got tipsy, ran riot and then had to invent a tale to explain it. An excellent Geminian tarradiddle too.

~ Gemini ~

JUNE 8

c.1790, Highbury
Birth of **ROBERT MARTIN**
(from <u>Emma</u> by Jane Austen)

He was the young farmer who was enamoured by the foundling, Harriet Smith, and who eventually married her despite Emma's poor opinion of his breeding. He was very good humoured and obliging. He went three miles round one day to bring Harriet some walnuts because she had said how fond she was of them... and in everything else he was so very obliging. Mr Knightley also had a high regard for him. Nevertheless, he exhibited no signs of being Geminian, such reading as he did undertake was on practical matters, not romantic and high-flown. Once again we have to doubt Jane Austen's grasp of zodiacal principles.

JUNE 9

1780, London
Rescued!
(from <u>Barnaby Rudge</u> by Charles Dickens)

The anti-Popery Gordon Riots terrorised Londoners in 1780. They were real enough but, of course, Dickens' people were fiction. Today saw Emma Haredale and Dolly Varden, the locksmith's daughter, held captive by the rioters and fast losing hope. At least, Dolly was. No birthday is given for Dolly but Dickens was able - unknowingly - to paint the shadowside of Gemini in her. 'Unmindful of all her provoking caprices, forgetful of all her conquests and inconstancy, with all her winning little vanities quite gone...' Dolly pined slowly away like a poor bird in its cage. 'Light hearts, light hearts, that float so gaily on a smooth stream, that are so sparkling and buoyant in the sunshine - down upon fruit, bloom upon flowers, blush in summer air, life of the winged insect, whose whole existence is a day - how soon ye sink in troubled water! Poor Dolly's heart - a little, gentle, idle, fickle thing; giddy, restless, fluttering; constant in nothing but bright looks, and smiles, and laughter - Dolly's heart was breaking.' However, they were rescued in the nick of time and coquettish Dolly Varden hats became immensely popular.

~ Gemini ~

JUNE 10

1890s, London
Another Wedding (and a Very Grand one too)
(from <u>The Young Visiters</u> by Daisy Ashford)

The Wedding of the Year took place between Mr Bernard Clark and Miss Ethel Monticue at Westminster Abby and afterwards for refreshments at the Gaierty Hotel.   Daisy Ashford wrote this charming tale when she was nine and got herself into Eng.Lit. without ever having to pen another line. It's a far cry from our previous June weddings. Ethel's wedding dress cost a good bit.   It was 'rich satin with a humped pattern of gold and a long train edged with Airum lilies.' Bernard was in 'an <u>elligant</u> black suit with coat tails lined with crimson satin, pale lavender tie, opera hat, violets in his buttonhole, his best white spats, diamond studs and a few extras of costly air.' He gave Ethel a very huge <u>tara</u> made of rubies and diamonds.   The wedding refreshments were indeed a treat. Not only the sparkling wines and lovely wedding cake of great height, but 'countless cakes also ices jelly merangs jam tarts with plenty of jam on each some cold tongue some ham with salid and a pig's head done up in a wondrous manner.'   Ethel could hardly contain herself as she gazed at the 'sumpshious' repast.

JUNE 11

1940, the Jura, France
Journeys Start
(from <u>Pied Piper</u> by Nevil Shute)

It was today that John Sidney Howard, retired solicitor, decided that, with German troops pouring into France, it was no use attempting to continue the fishing holiday which he had set out upon in April, and started for home. Rather odd that, with Great Britain declaring war on Germany in September 1939, anyone in their senses should have left England for a holiday on the continent the following spring. but it <u>was</u> 'the phoney war' and he did. Thomas Cook arranged it for him. Having no car, he started his journey home on foot, which was bad enough, but on the way he found himself becoming a Pied Piper to a motley crew of children who were also trying to get to England. He began by agreeing to take the two children of an acquaintance back with him and off they went in a taxi to the station. It was a nerve-wracking experience trying to get one step ahead of the Germans and the chart for the start of the journey - early morning today - is crowded and packed with incident which is how the journey turned out. The tally of youngsters increased to seven. They arrived back in a London now definitely at war, cold, tired, hungry, penniless and lousy, but they arrived.

The original **PIED PIPER** (see July 22), setting off, playing a catchy tune, in his dual coloured outfit and surrounded by children, is a very Geminian figure.

JUNE
12

1929
Astro-Twins
Births of **ANNE FRANK** in Germany
and **BRIDGID BROPHY** in England

They both had Sun and Mercury in Gemini, Mercury's own sign, so this common conjunction is quite potent and brings out the Geminian-ness of the sign. Both began writing very young. Brigid Brophy was the daughter of a novelist. She became a ferocious intellectual writing witty, satiric novels, often exploring the psychology of sex. Her first was Hackenfeller's Ape. She has also written biographies of Ronald Firbank and Aubrey Beardsley. Jewish Anne Frank wrote her famous Diary while in hiding from the Nazis. After two years of concealment the Gestapo were tipped off by an informer and Anne and her family were sent to various concentration camps. Anne died in Belsen of typhus. After the war her writings, precocious and emotionally perceptive, were found and published as The Diary of a Young Girl. In both charts Saturn throws an opposition to the Sun, which Anne certainly got the full force of.

JUNE
13

1923, London
A Nice Walk
(from Mrs Dalloway by Virginia Woolf)

At about 11 a.m. Mrs Dalloway set off to buy flowers for her party that night. The author merely says it is mid-June and a Wednesday (ruled by Mercury) but from little clues this seems the most likely date. The novel consists of one day in the life of Mrs Dalloway. Not only the Sun

~ Gemini ~

but the Moon and Mercury were in Gemini personalising a lively, intelligent woman. Another character thought how enchanting London was looking, how fresh and slim the women. Mrs Dalloway's birthday is not given but she must have been a Gemini. She was charming - 'a touch of the bird about her, of the day, blue-green, light, vivacious.' She loved life and she loved walking in London (which is 'under' Gemini). She enjoyed the carriages, motor cars, vans and buses and especially the aeroplane sky-writing overhead. As she walked round the Westminster shops (her husband was an M.P.) she liked the thought of the messages zinging from the Fleet to the Admiralty. Although over fifty she felt young. She was tall and upright, adored dancing and riding and had a passion for gloves. Her christian name was Clarissa meaning bright and clear. Gemini! She was pointed, dart-like, definite. She helped young people and irradiated dull lives. An ill-wisher considered she had trifled her life away. Rubbish! The party (Mrs Dalloway loved parties) was a great success.

JUNE 14

1914, London
The Mystery Solved
(from The Thirty Nine Steps by John Buchan)

After three weeks of being on the run, Richard Hannay solved the mystery of the 39 steps and thereby foiled the German plan to cause disruption and dismay in the civilised world on the following day. All Europe trembled on the edge of an earthquake but so far as he was concerned this was a waiting day although he knew that 'Hell was afoot!' He could only drive and walk though London, getting more and more restless and irritated because of the lack of action. Sure enough, Saturn was exactly conjunct the Sun all day, damping down all the natural bobbishness of the sign. Things livened up in the evening when Uranus in its own sign of Aquarius rose, promising shocks and surprises, while Jupiter in good aspect to the Sun/Saturn conjunction brought a successful conclusion.

~ Gemini ~

1814, Chiswick Mall
A Scholastic Farewell
(from <u>Vanity Fair</u> by W.M.Thackeray)

Miss Pinkerton's Academy for Young Ladies lost two of its pupils today
- Miss Amelia Sedley, beloved by all, and Miss Becky Sharp,
thoroughly disliked.   Becky's farewell consisted of flinging the
customary parting gift of the great Dr Johnson's <u>Dictionary</u> out of the
coach window and into Miss Pinkerton's garden. A year later, Amelia
and Becky, now married ladies, attended the famous Ball at Brussels
on the eve of the Battle of Waterloo. This time it was Becky who was
fêted and Amelia who was neglected. What a difference a year makes.
Just to keep up on the wedding front, today in the 1920s, Eleanor
Hodgman Porter's **POLLYANNA** married her childhood sweetheart
and was glad, Glad! GLAD!

1940, Dublin
Bloomsday
(from <u>Ulysses</u> by James Joyce)

This famous novel, banned in the U.K. for 14 years on account of its
'glaring obscenity and filth', records a day in the life of Leopold Bloom.
It's a working class re-hash of Homer's story of Ulysses. The Homeric
Ulysses moved through Greek mythology in an epic way.   Joyce's
Ulysses is on a kitchen sink level but the parallels are there, although
the non-classical reader will need a crib to relish them. For example,
the real Ulysses' encounter with the Sirens is transposed to the bar of
the Ormond Hotel presided over by the delicious barmaids, Miss
Douce and Miss Kennedy. It is said that Joyce chose the date because
it was the day he first went out with his partner, Nora Barnacle. Well,
the chart for the day is impressive whatever the reason for the choice.
Together with the Sun in Gemini are Venus, Mars and Pluto in a tight
conjunction, which can be passionate love or, alas, 'glaring obscenity
and filthy' depending on how you look at it. Uranus opposes them for
excitement and sheer wackiness. At 8 a.m. when the book starts,
Jupiter is right on the mid-heaven smiling down on all and sundry
auguring well for international success. With six planets in Air signs
and two or three in Fire, it's a positive, forward-looking, intellectual

~ Gemini ~

affair. They do a guided tour in Dublin to follow Leopold Bloom's footsteps on that day. London should do the same for Mrs Dalloway!

JUNE 17

1930s, England
Two Deaths
(from <u>A Blunt Instrument</u> and <u>Death in the Stocks</u>,
both by Georgette Heyer)

Georgette Heyer's largest following is for her Regency romances which she is alleged to have despised. She much preferred her crime novels. For some reason she favoured today for the demise of her victims. In <u>A Blunt Instrument</u> at about 10 p.m., Ernest Fletcher was found dead in his study, his head battered in. The local bobby, the bible-thumping P.C.Glass identified him. "'I believe him to have been wholly given up to vain show, double of heart, a fornicator, a...'" "Here, that'll do," said the Sergeant, startled. "We're none of us saints.'" In <u>Death in the Stocks</u>, the disliked Arnold Vereker was lured into Ashleigh Green's village stocks by his girl friend, Violet, so she could stab him without too much trouble.

JUNE 18

1799, Hayslope, Derbyshire
A Single Drop of Ink
(from <u>Adam Bede</u> by George Eliot)

'With a single drop of ink for a mirror, the Egyptian sorcerer undertakes to reveal to any chance comer far-reaching visions of the past. This is what I undertake to do for you, reader. With this drop of ink at the end of my pen, I will show you the roomy workshop of Mr Jonathan Burge, carpenter and builder, in the village of Hayslope, as it appeared on the 18th of June in the year of our Lord 1799.'

That single drop of ink would have told the sorcerer that Jonathan was going to lose his first love, Hetty Sorrel, but would end up with a lady Methodist preacher, Dinah Morris, instead. The two girls are contrasted throughout the novel - to Hetty's detriment. She is vain and self-centred; Dinah is calm and serious. One can't help thinking though that Hetty would have been more fun!

~ Gemini ~

1947, 342 Lawn Street, Ramsdale, New England
Nubile Young Girls!
(from <u>Lolita</u> by Vladimir Nabokov)

At the end of May, middle-aged Humbert Humbert took up lodgings with Mrs Haze in order to be near her 12-year old daughter Dolores, the Lolita of the title. This is the book which caused tremendous controversy and introduced the world 'nymphet' into the language. Once installed, Humbert kept a journal which he says covered most of June and by using slide rule, fingers and toes, it can be deduced that it was today that he found a mimeographed list of names of Lolita's classmates - a veritable poem of nubile young girls running from Angel, Grace to Windmuller, Louise. In the middle, bracketed by a bodyguard of roses - Hamilton, Mary Rose and Honeck, Rosaline - was his fairy princess, Haze, Dolores, his 'dolorous hazy darling'. The Sun, Venus and Uranus all in Gemini represent a delicious titillation of the senses. In his Notes, Nabokov recalls this class list of Ramsdale School with pleasure as one of the nerves of the novel, one of the secret points, the subliminal co-ordinates by means of which the book was plotted.

1921, Wales
Birth of **TOBY JUGG**
(from <u>The Haunting of Toby Jugg</u> by Dennis Wheatley)

Today, in 1942, was the 21st birthday of Toby Jugg, D.F.C., the day in which he was to come into his fortune. For years he had visualised it as a time of rejoicing, a carnival of flowers and music, not just for himself but for the thousands of people employed by or connected with Jugg Enterprises. He meant to surpass all that he received in gifts by what he returned in the way of bonuses, grants and pensions. Unluckily Toby, paralysed from an air crash, is being held captive by villains whose wicked plans will culminate on Midsummer's Eve with Satanic rites, initiations, murder... This is one of the cases where the author chose the birthday to fit the plot so we can't expect Toby to be particularly Geminian and the fact of his immobility would certainly go against it. Dennis Wheatley wrote many novels with occult themes and your astrologer takes modest pleasure in having gently nudged him into writing the factual <u>The Devil and All His Works</u>.

~ Gemini ~

JUNE 21

1830, England
Birth of **RACHEL VERINDER**
(from <u>The Moonstone</u> by Wilkie Collins)

On Rachel's 18th birthday she received a legacy from her late uncle - a Moonstone which disappeared the same night. Moonstones are, naturally, Cancerian gems, but we are right on the cusp of Gemini and Cancer so it's all right, and Wilkie Collins knew what he was doing because Rachel is undoubtedly still a Geminian. She was slim, pretty and poetry in motion.

> 'To see her sit down, to see her get up, and especially to see her walk, was enough to satisfy any man. She carried her head as upright as a dart, in a dashing, spirited, thoroughbred way.'

Additionally, she had a clear voice, a lovely smile, a host of graces and attractions but - ideas of her own! The Moonstone was originally stolen from a temple in India and had a curse on it so it wasn't the happiest of gifts.

JUNE 22

1911, London
Coronation of George V
(from <u>A Horseman Riding By</u> by R.F.Delderfield)

Paul Craddock and his wife went. Paul was gripped by a sense of climax about the spectacle, as though it symbolised the extreme high tide of the Victorian and Edwardian eras and had been deliberately staged to advertise the enormous thrust and weight of British Imperialism. 'He said aloud, "My God! It's like a Roman triumph!"'

Sebastian went (from <u>The Edwardians</u> by Vita Sackville-West). 'His robes spread their red velvet and miniver over the back of a chair; his coronet and gloves stood ready on a neighbouring chair. His valet, attaining the apotheosis of a valet's life, hovered round him with tunic and boots...'

And chorus girl Elsie Marina went (from <u>The Sleeping Prince</u> by

~ Gemini ~ Cancer ~

Terence Rattigan and <u>The Prince and the Showgirl</u> starring Olivier and Monroe). She deputised as lady-in-waiting to the Grand Duchess of Carpathia in place of the Countess von und zu Meissenbronn (Maud) who had a cold.

Royalty, romance, history, patriotism - the apotheosis of Cancer, let alone the valet.

JUNE 23

c. 1800
Birth of **HARRIET SMITH**
(from <u>Emma</u> by Jane Austen)

And, for once, Jane got it right! Harriet can easily be accepted as one type of Cancerian. 'Harriet certainly was not clever but she had a sweet, docile, grateful disposition, was totally free from conceit; only desiring to be guided by anyone she looked up to.' Her first idol was the strong-willed Emma, which was a disaster. The next, Robert Martin, a pleasant young farmer, whose birthday we also know. '"He was four-and-twenty the 8th of last June and my birthday is the 23rd - just a fortnight and a day's difference! which is very odd!"' Odd too that adjoining signs (he was a Geminian) are much more dissimilar than those in opposition which have much in common. Anyway, they married. Emma, always patronising, saw that - 'She would be placed in the midst of those who loved her, and who had better sense than herself; retired enough for safety, and occupied enough for cheerfulness. She would be respectable and happy.' And the luckiest creature in the world to have created so steady an affection in such a man.

JUNE 24

1928, U.S.A.
Summertime
(from <u>Dandelion Wine</u> by Ray Bradbury)

Douglas Spaulding decided to start a notebook keeping track of things. Every summer they did the same things over and over which they had done every summer before. Like making dandelion wine. He divided it into RITES & CEREMONIES and DISCOVERIES & REVELATIONS. Under today's date he recorded in the former his first argument and licking of the season by his dad.

~ Cancer ~

Year unknown, Moominland
Birth of **LITTLE MY**
(from <u>The Exploits of Moominpapa</u> by Tove Jansson)

She's a strange little person, very sharp and scratchy when contrasted with the gentle, billowy Moomins.

In some books, today is Midsummer Eve; in others, Midsummer Day. Others, again, call June 21 Midsummer Day, but that's usually the day of the Summer Solstice when the Sun moves into Cancer and brings the longest day to the northern hemisphere. It all becomes very confusing when trying to date literary events. The official line is that today is St. John the Baptist's Day and Midsummer Day.

| JUNE |
| **25** |

1847, China
Birth of **KIM-FO**
(from <u>The Tribulations of a Chinese Gentleman</u> by Jules Verne)

A somewhat moody gentleman and with reason. On his 31st birthday today (1878) he had intended to take his own life. Then things improved and he was going to marry. Then court mourning was imposed and he couldn't. Saturn was in poor aspect to the Sun which is delay and frustration. He should have checked!

1903, India
Birth of **GEORGE ORWELL**

He wrote the darkly depressing <u>Animal Farm</u> and <u>Nineteen Eighty-Four</u>. A difficult character with an over-plus of Cancer. The Sun, Moon and Neptune are there, within a few degrees of each other, which suggests acute sensitivity, moodiness, and deep inner discontent. All can lead to self-inflicted suffering. His biographers speak of his tragic pessimism. He was 'the Jeremiah of the Thirties'. He sympathised passionately with the underdog and fought against Franco in Spain where he was wounded.

1966, New York
Birth of a Little Devil
(from <u>Rosemary's Baby</u> by Ira Levin)

Just after midnight, "'exactly half the year round from you-know'" exulted the Satanic cult Rosemary had been drawn into. The little one's horoscope seems innocuous, one expects something more

~ Cancer ~

startling for a baby with talons. One corner, though, looks promising. The practically exact conjunction of Uranus and Pluto was common to all charts in the 1960s. It means transforming and extraordinary powers of creation if it is well placed and aspected. But Rosemary's baby had Mars in inharmonious aspect to them which is violence and devastation - the transforming is then painful and the powers of creation more likely to be powers of destruction. The conjunction is also opposite the ascendant, suggesting the power he would perhaps one day wield over others.

JUNE 26

1970, U.S.A.
Birth of **EUGENE DINGMAN**, America's Answer to Adrian Mole
(from The Amazing and Death Defying Diary of Eugene Dingman by Paul Zindell)

There's little to say about Eugene himself, he's completely colourless. On his 15th birthday (1985), though, he decided to begin writing his first, extremely personal diary. Not an auspicious start. He had to record that he threw a spoon at his mother's left leg (and a Crab attacking its mum is awful) when she persisted in talking about the lodger whom she evidently had in mind to take her ex-husband's place. After this Oedipal outburst, his mother called his aunt who was something big in the New York State Employment Agency and she got him a summer job as a waiter at The Lake Henry Hotel in the primitive Adirondack Mountains.

Something to go in the diaries of Jane Austen's Emma and her friends today was the death of **MRS CHURCHILL**. She was the handsome Frank Churchill's aunt and completely smothered him. He had to dance to her tune because she paid the piper and held the purse strings. Apparently, a whining hypochondriac who used her ill-health to get what she wanted, but today the great Mrs Churchill was no more! One has a nasty feeling that Mrs Churchill was a Cancerian of the worst type. However,

> 'In one point she was fully justified. She had never been admitted before to be seriously ill. The event acquitted her of all the fancifulness, and all the selfishness of imaginary complaints.'

Vindication of a Crab!

~ Cancer ~

1914, Essex, England
The Day before the Bomb Exploded
(from <u>Mr.Britling Sees It Through</u> by H.G.Wells)

Mr. Direck, an American, was travelling to Matching's Easy on the little old Great Eastern Railway to stay with Mr. Britling. Suddenly he was in the heart of Washington Irving's England - a Cancerian dream. The countryside was so tidy and bright with cornfields surrounded by dog-rose hedges. There were thatched cottages, coaching inns, a vicar driving a governess cart. 'It wasn't like any reality he had ever known. It was like travelling in literature.' Mr. Britling was waiting to drive him home in his automobile. Mr. Direck suspected he hadn't driven before and indeed they were soon sitting in a sloping car which had ascended the bank and buried its nose in the hedge. But worse things were happening at Sarajevo in Bosnia where men whispered together and one held nervously to a black parcel and nodded as they repeated his instructions. So what sort of day was it astrologically, this last day of an era? Mercury conjunct Neptune in Cancer is peaceful but reeks of self-deception and heads-buried-in-the-sand. The other notable aspect, also taking place in the Crab, was Pluto's slow progress into that sign where it would stay for over twenty years. A few days earlier the Sun had conjoined it which, during that week, released all manner of nasties from their Cancerian cave and set the war drums beating.

1854, late afternoon, Manchester
Nymphs and Fairies
(from <u>The Rag Nymph</u> by Catherine Cookson)

Abandoned by her mother who was in flight from the police for soliciting, 7-year old Millie Forester was taken home by Raggie Aggie, a trader in old clothes. Millie never saw her mother again because she hanged herself in her cell and Aggie had perforce to take in the child. Today wasn't Millie's birthday but it began her new life and the Grand Trine of Venus, Mars and Jupiter was an excellent omen for a loving relationship. Millie was well brought up and strikingly pretty, completely out of place in Aggie's slum, but Aggie had a heart of gold beneath the dirt. It was one of the men who had evil intentions

~ Cancer ~

towards Millie who called her 'Rag Nymph'. Aggie knew what rags were, but nymphs? "A nymph is a kind of fairy, I think. I've read about them in one of my stories. They live in woods and dance around toadstools," said Millie.

Which fits in with **CICELY MARY BARKER** who was born today in Croydon in 1895. She is the well-known illustrator of the Flower Fairy books. She was fascinated by fairies, living in woods and dancing round toadstools or anywhere else. She used children as models, making their twig and gauze wings and dresses herself. The Flower Fairies have always had their devotees and, recently, have become immensely popular.

| JUNE |
| **29** |

1960, Paradine Hall, East Walsham, Norfolk
Things Going Bump in the Night
(from Too Many Ghosts by Paul Gallico)

The hauntings began. For the previous two days there had been a ferocious East Anglian gale screaming around the house, banging doors and shutters, moaning around corners, gables and chimney stacks. Tonight it stopped abruptly. Then, someone or something violently shook the carved fourposter bed in which slept the Hon. Isobel Paradine. Water signs and planets gang up to portend strange manifestations of the supernatural. Here, Sun and Venus in Cancer aspect Neptune in Scorpio, and over the next few days the ghostly occurrences continued to terrify everyone. However, 'natural' has to replace 'supernatural'. No malevolent body was throwing things about. The highest tide in 18 years coupled with the June gales was to blame. A subterranean stream ran close to the foundations of the Hall. The pressure of the tide on the coast flooded the watercourse which affected the walls and this had caused all the trouble. BUT it didn't explain away the harp playing without the aid of human hand, cries the true Cancerian triumphantly.

~ Cancer ~

JUNE 30

1936, U.S.A.
Publication of <u>Gone With The Wind</u> by Margaret Mitchell

The romance of Scarlett and Rhett has kept generations of Cancerians palpitating. Both book and film were enormously popular from the start. The book became the largest selling novel in the history of U.S. publishing up to that date, and the film - well, the film broke all records. Sadly Margaret Mitchell, whose only novel it was and who took ten years to write it, died at the age of 49 after being run down by a car. The title comes from the steamiest of romantic poems by Ernest Dowson, one of the most gifted of the Decadents as they were called in the 1890s - <u>I have been faithful to thee, Cynara! in my fashion</u>.

> Last night, ah, yesternight, betwixt her lips and mine
> There fell thy shadow, Cynara!.......
> I have forgot much, Cynara! gone with the wind,
> Flung roses, roses, riotously with the throng,
> Dancing, to put they pale, lost lilies out of mind;

(They don't write 'em like that any more!)

JULY 1

c.1840, Schloss Rosenbad
Conception
(from <u>Ehrengard</u> by Isak Dinensen)

It was a ritual for Herr Cazotte to spend tonight out of doors because he believed he had been conceived then. If astrology was logical our conception date would be more important than our birthdate but, in that event, few of us would have a chart. It has often been tried using complex calculations, taking 280 days for gestation and noting when the degrees of the ascendant and the Moon were interchangeable with the degrees of the ascendant and the Moon at birth. Or their opposites. Others maintain that the true moment of conception is the so-called 'quickening'. So, most of us are stuck with our birthdays, except Herr Cazotte who, when the household had retired, walked out 'below pale stars in a pale sky' and philosophised on the unfathomable power of the imagination which had formed the smallest detail before

~ Cancer ~

him. 'I venture to believe that... I might have invented the dusk, but could I have invented the stars? I know that I could not have invented the nightingale.' Pity he wasn't a Cancerian. He was, of course, an Arien.

JULY 2	

1950s, Hillsdale, U.S.A.
Come Home, Eleanor!
(from <u>The Haunting of Hill House</u> by Shirley Jackson,
filmed as <u>The Haunting</u>)

On June 21 Dr. Montague, ghost hunter, arrived at Hill House with his assistants to investigate the reported paranormal occurrences there. It was a good time, astrologically, the Sun was just moving into Cancer. Cancer being the Cardinal, or leading, Water sign, gives the sensitivity necessary to pick up psychic emanations which is why those born under the Crab are able to 'sense' atmospheres. The researchers had some terrifying moments - thunderous knockings, cold, voices, messages written in blood on the walls, but the experiment ended today in tragedy. Hill House itself was insane. Rooms were built inside rooms and every angle was slightly wrong. Stairs and doorways were all at a slight slant. Was it evil from the start or did it become so because of the sad and warped lives of its previous owners? Eleanor was drawn to it. She had been invited because she had been at the centre of poltergeist activity when a child and as the disturbances crystallised they focussed on her to the extent that the whole party, fearing for her safety, told her she must leave at once. They packed her bags, put her into her car and watched her drive off. But I won't go, she thought.

> 'Hill House is not as easy as <u>they</u> are, just by
> telling me to go away they can't make me leave,
> not if Hill House means me to stay.'

And Hill House did. At the curve of the driveway her car crashed into the great tree there, scene of former fatal accidents, and Eleanor drifted back into <u>her</u> house.

~ Cancer ~

1883, Prague
Birth of **FRANZ KAFKA**, novelist

1937, Czech Republic
Birth of **TOM STOPPARD**, playwright

Two Czechs. Probably Tom Stoppard's best-known play is Rosencrantz and Guildenstern Are Dead, the nub of which is that humans are only minor players in an overall, incomprehensible scheme. On a more mundane level he has described himself as a very domestic person. Kafka was a Cancerian from the Tormented Genius drawer. His father made him feel inadequate which contributed to his timidity, sensitivity and introspection. He was haunted by fear of failure. As a German-speaking Jew, an atheist, a socialist and an intellectual, he was isolated from practically everyone and escaped through writing dream-like surrealist fantasies of despair and absurdity like The Trial and The Castle. Most of The Castle takes place in the dark, wintry landscape of a village where 'K' is unable to get a hearing with the Castle authorities while The Trial metaphorically takes place in the dark as 'Joseph K' is arrested for no given reason and goes to his execution still in the dark yet accepting his fate, like Rosencrantz and Guildenstern. Kafka was charming and humorous but neurotically disturbed when it came to deeper relationships. Kafka means jackdaw and he described himself as a jackdaw who longed to disappear among the stones. He should have made it a Crab!

The Current Year, Castledean, England
Birthday of **APPLEBY MENNYM**
(from The Mennyms by Sylvia Waugh)

It's always Appleby's 15th birthday today. She never ages, she's always a rebellious adolescent in jeans, long sweater, shades, floppy hat and loads of make-up. She's a bit moody and truculent but very nice, helpful and inventive in a crisis. "She's the one you'd be glad of if you were shipwrecked on a desert island," declared her grandfather. She's adventurous, going out to the market and Post Office regularly. She collects things - stamps, fashion photos, anything - and is part of

~ Cancer ~

a close family group who are none the less for being - lifesized rag dolls. They were made by Kate Penshaw, a gifted needlewoman from scraps of cloth and kapok. There's Sir Magnus and Lady Tulip Mennym, their children and grandchildren. When Kate died, her spirit somehow went into them and they took over the running of the house by a number of ingenious devices, mostly thought up by Appleby. She's Sir Magnus's favourite and spoilt by him. Despite being stuffed with kapok she's a genuine Cancerian and a great pretender. Although not exactly lying, Cancerians can live in pretend worlds, which is all very well until something goes wrong as Appleby discovered.

JULY 5

1898 Apalachia, U.S.A.
Birth of **JOHN SLADE**, poet
(from Pale Fire by Vladimir Nabokov)

Pale Fire is a classic although some say it is unreadable, 'a self-indulgent book of tricks.' The title is a Shakespearian quote and very appropriate for Cancer. 'The Moon's an arrant thief and her pale fire she snatches from the Sun.' Some Cancerians do tend to live on or through others. It has been described as a melodrama about 'a lunatic who intends to kill an imaginary king, another lunatic who imagines he is that king, and a distinguished old poet who stumbled into the line of fire and perishes in the clash between the two figments.' Several lunars there! Anyway, the poet Slade is given a Crab-like, if very unflattering, description. He had a slight limp and a curious contortion in his way of walking. He shambled. He was not handsome. His face 'reminded one of a fleshy Hogarthian tippler of indeterminate sex.' He had a misshapen body and bags under his lustreless eyes. He liked his glass, as they say. He had a dominant wife and held old-fashioned family values. He began his poem, called Pale Fire, at the dead centre of the year, a few minutes after midnight on July 1, 1959. Not the best of times with Saturn in direct opposition to the Sun.

~ Cancer ~

1880, Copenhagen
Birth of **ASTA WETHERBY**
(from <u>Asta's Book</u> by Barbara Vine)

She married an engineer and settled in London. She was always homesick, always yearning for the green roofs of Copenhagen. On her 25th birthday she began keeping a journal, her 'Book', a record not only of what she did but of what she thought. Stories too. "I've always liked stories, telling them to myself, true and made up." At night they helped her sleep, in the day they helped her to escape from reality. She made up magical stories for her children as she considered Hans Christian Andersen too cruel. Not that she was a dreamer - far from. She did feel weepy at times but hid it under a self-assured Cancerian shell. She changed with the Moon's phases being 'sensitive and insensitive, gentle and hard, tough and vulnerable, aggressive and shy... the writer of fiction and non-fiction.' She was proud of her two daughters who both married well, one romantically too, which gladdened her heart! She loved clothes but until she died at 93 she kept to the fashions of the '20s. Chanel, Lelong, Schiaparelli. Sheer nostalgia. High-heeled shoes, a showy Persian lamb trimmed with a white fox, a white fox muff, a cream pongee coat with green linen revers, all lovingly detailed in the 'Book'. She had the Sun and Venus in Cancer square Jupiter which denotes lush living and extravagance.

1971, Amity, Long Island, U.S.A.
Dangers of the Deep
(from <u>Jaws</u> by Peter Benchley)

Cancerian days aren't all spent splashing about on the beach. Today, Hooper went down in a shark cage to take a close look at the killer shark which was terrorising the residents and threatening their tourist trade. As the fish drew near Hooper was paralysed by the beauty of its colour in its natural element. It passed to and fro only a few feet in front of the cage as if showing off its huge mass and power. The nose; the jaw, slack and smiling, row upon row of saw-like teeth; the black deep eye fixed on him. He stuck a hand through the bars and felt it - cold, hard and smooth. It seemed to have no end. Then it swam back - and got him!

~ Cancer ~

JULY 8

1962, London
Birth of **GRANT MITCHELL** of TV's EastEnders

The macho-type Cancerian male, dominated by his old mum! He's very possessive about his girl friends and dotty about his little daughter. First wife Sharon tired of his moods, while Tiffany actually died running away from him. Public houses and catering establishments are second homes to Crabs, although it's hard to imagine Grant bringing in much trade. His horoscope shows a very nice Grand Trine in the Water element between Sun, Jupiter and Neptune, which isn't a bit Grant-like. It's extra-sensitive and saps the vitality although it promises success without much effort.

Another soap Crab was born today in 1955. **DEIRDRE** of Coronation Street united the nation on two occasions - in 1983, during her love triangle with Libran husband Ken and Aquarian Mike Baldwin; and again in 1997, when she was falsely imprisoned. Deirdre's alter-ego, Geminian actress Anne Kirkbride (June 21, 1954) casts the horoscopes of all the actors on the set of the show.

JULY 9

1938, Canada
Birth of **ELIZABETH SCHOENHOF**
(from <u>Life Before Man</u> by Margaret Atwood)

A Cancerian born 'in the Scorpio decanate, as some pretentious little fraud told her.' This further breakdown of a sign into three decanates of ten degrees each with a further planetary ruler is an astrological refinement which had much importance attached to it in previous times. There are a number of ways of doing this, each with its own adherents. The 'pretentious little fraud' had used a modern system. This gives dominion of the first decan of a sign to the natural ruler of the whole sign - e.g. the Moon rules the whole of Cancer but particularly the first decan. The rulers of the two following signs of the same triplicity have rulership over the next two decans. The next Water sign after Cancer is Scorpio so Pluto rules the second decan, followed by Pisces ruled by Neptune which thus rules the third decan. A decan is roughly ten days. Elizabeth was in the second decan with Pluto as a sub-ruler which gives (roughly) July 1-10 folk very powerful

~ Cancer ~

emotions and possibly violent sexual problems. This was certainly so for her. In the October before her 1977 birthday, her lover had blown his head off because she wouldn't leave her husband and family for him. She was shattered and, Cancer-like, felt like a 'peeled snail'. She wanted her shell back - a shell 'like a sequinned dress, made of silver nickels and dimes and dollars, overlapping like the scales of an armadillo.'

JULY 10

1792, London
Birth of **CAPT. FREDERICK MARRYAT**, naval officer and author

1871, 11.30 p.m., Paris
Birth of **MARCEL PROUST**, psychological novelist

Both true Cancerians but what a difference!

Marryat hated school and ran away to sea when only 14. He rose rapidly in the service, attaining the rank of captain. He was heroic and saved several people's lives and was awarded the RHS gold medal for courage. On retirement he wrote adventure stories in a simple, humorous style. They were ripping good yarns and very popular. He firmly believed that Britain should Rule the Waves and considered home and religious teaching the centre of life. He drew on his naval training for Mr. Midshipman Easy. The Children of the New Forest, a tale of the English Civil War (historical), became a classic. Proust's monumental classic, The Remembrance of Things Past, is a good old nostalgic wallow. He was a sickly child, dependent on his mum. After her death he became completely neurotic, a melancholic invalid, a hypochondriac and a homosexual. He was hypersensitive and eventually lived in a cork-lined room as a virtual recluse. He could be labelled selfish but he was a genius and so perceptive, with such delicate antennae, that he charmed everyone.

JULY 11

1900, Ambridge
Birth of **DORIS ARCHER**, matriarch of the radio Clan

Wife of Dan, mother of Phil, grandmother of Shula. The pivot of the entire family. Nice, homey, protective, Cancerian. Unimaginable without a pinny and a couple of sick or abandoned lambs drying out

~ Cancer ~

under the kitchen stove. Lovely. And it goes on...

Today was one of the happiest days of Charles Pooter's life. His employer, Mr. Perkupp, gave him the deeds of his house! Looks as if Mr. P. was a Crab, which he wasn't! (from Diary of a Nobody by George and Weedon Grossmith). Then Elizabeth, in her German Garden, told her three babies - the April baby, the May baby and the June baby - the story of Adam and Eve. She got as far as the angel with the flaming sword when the April baby exploded with her own version. And greatly improved too! '"Once upon a time there was Adam and Eva, and they had plenty of clothes, and there was no snake, and lieber Gott wasn't angry with them, and they could all eat as many apples as they liked and was happy for ever and ever - there now!"' (from Elizabeth and her German Garden by Elizabeth von Arnim).

JULY 12

1960s, Belfast
Dissent
(from The Twelfth of July by Joan Lingard)

The Protestants were astir early, polishing their shoes, laying out their clothes, their sashes and their bowler hats, but Sadie and Tommy Jackson wouldn't eat any breakfast and shattered their parents by refusing point blank to go on the Orange Day Parade. Tommy was to have played his flute in the band and Sadie to have been a drum-majorette in purple velvet. They were left at home in disgrace. They heard the music beginning: 'the drums tapping soft, then loud, the tootle of the flutes, the deeper tones of the pipes. Tommy's foot tapped. '"It's a pity," he said. "For Brede too," said Sadie.' Brede was their friend, a Catholic; she was in hospital after being hit on the head by a brick the night before. Cancerians in general are not violent, like the crab they're more inclined to scuttle away from trouble, but there's an awful lot of mayhem and misery goes on under the Moon's rays.

~ Cancer ~

1827, Ireland
Birth of **GRACE MARKS**
(from <u>Alias Grace</u> by Margaret Atwood)

Pretty Grace Marks was a real person. She was born in impoverished Ireland and emigrated to Canada with her family, losing her mother on the voyage. She hated her father. In Canada she worked as a servant and at 16 was condemned to death for the murder of her employers. Her fellow servant and accomplice (if indeed he was) was hanged. She was given a life sentence but later pardoned and disappeared from the records. Margaret Atwood has woven a story around the few known facts of this controversial figure, making out quite a good case for Cancer although she probably didn't intend to. Today, in 1843, Grace was given her birthday afternoon off (she was a good domestic worker). She went for a walk, dozed off and dreamed deeply and vividly as she usually did. She was psychic and very sensitive to impending doom. Later, in prison, she was subjected to hypnotism and terrified those present who could only assume she was capable of being possessed, of being taken over and used by another entity. Cancer runs Pisces a close second for this 'open-ness'. Her dreams were so vivid that she couldn't distinguish them from reality so whether she did the murders herself, or incited them, or was victimised into doing or helping with them is never clear. At the end of the novel she is married to a small farmer and very proud of her neat, white farmhouse, embellished with cross-stitch pictures, patchwork quilts and white summer curtains. She liked white. She made them on her treasured sewing machine. She could have had a hired help but no way! Grace ran the house herself and didn't tempt Fate!

1789, Paris
Fall of the Bastille
(from <u>A Tale of Two Cities</u> by Charles Dickens)

The Parisian mob stormed the hated Bastille and released the prisoners. 'Every living creature there held life as of no account, and was demented with a passionate readiness to sacrifice it. As a whirlpool of boiling water has a centre point, so, all this raging circled

~ Cancer ~

round Defarge's wine-shop, and every human drop in the cauldron had a tendency to be sucked towards the vortex where Defarge himself, already begrimed with gunpowder and sweat, issued orders, issued arms...laboured and strove in the thickest of the uproar.' He was ably supported by his wife, the lady who knitted at the foot of the guillotine but had now exchanged the needles for an axe, a pistol and a knife. Once in the Bastille, Defarge made the turnkey take him to the cell which had been occupied for years by a Dr. Manette and there he found concealed a document which had been written and hidden by the prisoner - a document which, years later, was to condemn the doctor's son-in-law to the guillotine and ultimately lead to Sydney Carton doing a far, far better thing than he had ever done. A bloodbath of a day for Cancer, but it's a sign which stands for the masses and the hoi polloi, and the mob can easily become vicious or soppily sentimental, just like Cancerians.

JULY 15

1990s, St. Julian's, Smithfield, London EC1
The Fourth Wedding
(from Four Weddings and a Funeral by Richard Curtis)

Wedding day of Charles and Henrietta ('Duckface'). At least, it was to have been but romance triumphed and he jilted her for the American Carrie who had told him, at the last moment, that she and her husband had split up. Duckface gave Charles a black eye but it was worth it. There was a violent storm. Tom said that it was a wedding no one would forget. Charles proposed to Carrie but not quite in the traditional manner.

> "Do you think, after we've dried off, after we've spent a lot of time together, you might agree...not to marry me? And do you think not being married to me might maybe be something you could consider doing for the rest of your life?"

Carrie did. A thunderbolt lit the sky and the sentimental old Crab reaches for the tissues.

JULY
16

1959, New York
No Place Like Home
(from <u>Mrs. Harris Goes to New York</u> by Paul Gallico)

Mrs. Harris, the loveable Cockney charlady, sailed from glamorous New York back to ugly old Willis Gardens in London's East End. Even if Mrs. Harris herself wasn't Cancerian, the day is. Going home, be it ever so humble, is a Cancerian dream when in foreign parts and to sail there on the magnificent Queen Elizabeth puts the icing on the cake. The Sun in Cancer was in excellent aspect to the lucky planet, Jupiter, and the Moon was in Jupiter's own sign of Sagittarius, a voyaging sign. Mrs. Harris had, as usual, made loads of friends and a super party took place in Cabin A59, the largest and best apartment in Tourist Class amid a welter of roses and orchids. 'Even though it takes place almost weekly in New York, there is always something exciting and dramatic about the sailing of a great liner.'

JULY
17

1930s, South England
Holiday Weather
(from <u>Diary of a Provincial Lady</u> by E.M.Delafield)

Her husband saw her off by an early train for London 'after a scrambled and agitating departure exclusively concerned with frantic endeavours to induce suit-case to shut.' The cook, maid and gardener assembled at the front door to wave her off, Cook giving it as her opinion that it was blowing up for a gale and, speaking personally, she had always had a 'Norror' of death by drowning. In London the Provincial Lady observed - with Norror - that the trees in Grosvenor Gardens were swaying with extreme violence and the train journey to Folkestone was entirely occupied by seeing from the window quite large trees bowed to earth by the force of the wind. Later she reflected on the dissimilarity of journeys undertaken in life and those undertaken in fiction where everyone either has a romantic encounter or discovers a body in mysterious circumstances. Neither enlivened her own journey which, however, improved remarkably as her French train headed south. Cancerians are travellers but find home hard to shake off.

~ Cancer ~

13,000,085 A.D., quarter to 13 in the afternoon, Greenwich, now Grenija
The Last Day of the World
(from <u>The Last Days of Earth</u> by George C. Wallis,
collected in <u>Beyond the Gaslight</u> by Hilary and Dik Evans)

Alwyn and Celia are the last inhabitants of a dying earth. Alwyn reflects on the long association of the place with recording Time and that all the labour has been in vain. They have a last look round at the world on the Pictorial Telegraph before shooting off into space. Icebergs drift slowly; everywhere ice, snow and shallow, slowly-freezing seas, countries black and plantless or covered with glaciers.

> 'No sign of life save the vestiges of man's long fight with the relentless cold - the ruins of his Cities of Heat; moats excavated to retard the glaciers, canals to connect the warmer seas; the skeletons of floating palaces; and in every daylight scene, the pale ghost of a dim red sun.'

It was like that at Clacton one year.

So, according to this, the world, as we know it, will end on July 18 - you will have to work out the chart yourself but it's surprising to see they will still be using our humble old dates and times. Cancer, because of its connection with the 4th house of the horoscope, rules births and deaths, beginnings and endings, the cradle and the grave, so it's not too surprising to find it pinpointed like this.

c.1820, 3.10 a.m., Devonshire
Birth of **KATE NICKLEBY**
(from <u>Nicholas Nickleby</u> by Charles Dickens)

Dickens had two types of heroine, one lively and kittenish and one sweet and sad. Kate, being a Cancerian, falls into the latter category. Like all true Cancerians she was closely bound to her mother and never an unkind word although that garrulous old soul must have been a trial. On the other hand she is worth her weight in gold to the astrologer for being able to give her daughter an exact time of birth, pity about the year. After many vicissitudes Kate married the nephew

~ Cancer ~

of the wealthy Cheeryble brothers. Whatever her birth year the Sun
would have been near the cusp of the second house of her horoscope -
money! - so it all worked out fine.

JULY 20

2019, 4.15 a.m., Comprehensive Fertility Institute,
Beverley Hills, California
Birth of **JASON LAWRENCE MILLER**
(from Arthur C. Clarke's July 20, 2019)

Data taken from the Certificate of Life and no more 'if's' and maybe's'
for the astrologer to contend with in future. Every detail is given:
time of conception, November 15 2018, 12.15 p.m.; details of the three
parents; full history of the conception and pre-natal care and surgery;
genetic profile, showing Jason would be completely grey by age 22 and
would live to be 82. High risk professions to be avoided, sports to be
cultivated, weak spots to be circumvented. Personally, we astrologers
prefer the old astrological hit-or-miss method. There's something
chilling about inevitability. Anyway, with Pluto in Capricorn conjunct
Saturn opposing the Sun, Mercury, Venus and Dragon's Head in
Cancer, we have no opinion of young Master Miller. All the nice
Cancerian qualities will be twisted into travesties. He will be
arrogant, quarrelsome, callous and unbelievably unlucky. At age 6,
his sperm donor will order him from home. His mothers will be
candidates for grief therapy. He will smash up the Comprehensive
Fertility Institute.

Back to sanity, Arthur C. Clarke chose this date for his Day in the Life
of the 21st Century because it was exactly fifty years on from the day
man first landed on the Moon - it's already coming horribly true!

JULY 21

1899, 8.00 a.m., Oak Park, Illinois, U.S.A.
Birth of **ERNEST HEMINGWAY**, author

An apparently macho-type Cancerian male, big, strong, handsome.
His themes were courage, violence, war and death, but the persona
was carefully built up. Out of sight of the public he suffered from
acute depression and a persecution complex. His virility was
criticised as 'fake hair on the chest'. He was turned down for the army
in World War I because of poor eyesight (inherited from mother) but

~ Cancer ~

he drove an ambulance and was wounded in 1918, later receiving an award for gallantry. He then became a journalist and writer studying violence at close quarters in the Spanish Civil War, World War II, in the bullring, big game hunting, fishing in Cuba where he became a cult figure and in...four marriages. His books, like <u>A Farewell to Arms</u> and <u>For Whom the Bell Tolls</u> have had a great influence on all literature from the best to the worst. He suffered from insomnia <u>and</u> nightmares. Karsh found him the shyest man he had ever photographed and guessed that the veneer was self-protective. He could be charming yet horrible to those he saw as rivals. Cancer was a fateful sign for him. He was born on the 21st, was badly wounded on July 8, and on July 2, ill with diabetes, anxiety-ridden and depressed, he went out and shot himself exactly as his father had done.

JULY 22

1860, London
Birth of **FREDERICK ROLFE** (pseudonym BARON CORVO),
author and eccentric

Leo has a foot - perhaps both feet - in the door now and Baron Corvo is a good mix of the two signs. He was raised a Protestant but joined the much more colourful and dramatic (Leonine) Roman Catholic church. He wanted to be a priest but his life style was not to the religion's liking and they weren't having any. He was homosexual, paranoid and a scrounger, not a likeable man. He wandered about trying a variety of careers and wrote a successful book of legends of Catholic saints, <u>Stories Toto Told Me</u>. His best known work was his ornate autobiographical fantasy <u>Hadrian the Seventh</u>, from which comes this <u>cri de cœur</u>:

> 'Under his shell, in fact, your crab is as soft as butter, and just one labyrinthine mass of the most sensitive of nerves. From which pleasing experiment (i.e. dissecting a crab) you should learn to be as merciful as God to all poor sinners born between the twenty-first of June and the twenty-fourth of July: for they are born under the constellation Cancer; and their nature is the nature of a crab. They are the cleverest, tenderest, unhappiest, most dreadful of all men. Clever men and dreadful men are not invariably unhappy; but crab-men are all three...'

The antidote, according to him, was union with the opposite sign of Capricorn, 'soft outside, hard within'.

~ Cancer ~ Leo ~

1376, Hamelin, Brunswick
Piping Times
(from <u>The Pied Piper of Hamelin</u> by Robert Browning)

Everyone knows the story of the rats which plagued the town of Hamelin and of the contract between the Council and a stranger in a long coat of red and yellow (Leo colours) who offered to rid the town of the rodents for a thousand guilders. Of how he went into the street and played a few notes on his pipe, of how the rats rushed out in droves and followed him to the River Weser where they all plunged in and drowned, and of the shameful aftermath when the Council refused to pay up. Of how the piper went out again and led away the children to a doorway in the Koppelberg Hill never to be seen more. There are other versions and other dates - Midsummer Day and 1284, for example, but this is the date given in Browning's famous poem. Legend has it that the exodus is linked to the Children's Crusade when so many innocent, unequipped youngsters went off, as they thought, to fight the infidel but their fate was so sad that it's nicer to stick to Browning's version.

> ... In Transylvania there's a tribe
> Of alien people that ascribe
> The outlandish ways and dress
> On which their neighbours lay such stress,
> To their fathers and mothers having risen
> Out of some subterranean prison...

So off goes the Crab with all the children - dancing.

JULY
23

1888, Chicago
Birth of **RAYMOND CHANDLER**, author

Although born in America he came from Anglo/Irish stock and was an unrepentant Anglophile. He even listed tea-drinking as a hobby! The family circumstances were comfortable and he received an English classical education. He seemed more at home in monarchist Britain than republican America. In 1917 he joined the Canadian army and tried to in 1939, but was too old. He didn't begin writing seriously until his 40s when he jumped up into the classics himself as a crime writer with <u>The Big Sleep</u>. It introduced his detective, Philip Marlowe, and you can't have a more pukka English name than that. Marlowe was based largely on Chandler himself. He was an attractive charmer, a gentleman, a man of honour, but a heavy

~ Cancer ~ Leo ~

drinker. (Chandler's father was an alcoholic and Chandler, although he married, was glad he never had children because he feared they would inherit the taint.) Both Chandler and Marlowe were classics-quoting chess players and those mimic battles of Court grandees should appeal to all right minded Leos. Despite the wise-cracking and violence, no one could deny that Chandler wrote brilliantly. All his books were filmed successfully, Humphrey Bogart (although Chandler wanted Cary Grant) making Marlowe his very own. 'Down these mean streets a man must go who is not himself mean, who is neither tarnished nor afraid...'

JULY 24

c. 1710, England
Birth of **CLARISSA HARLOWE**
(from Clarissa by Samuel Richardson)

One of the great English classics which nobody has ever read. An enormous book consisting mostly of letters to and from the various parties. Clarissa was a young lady of great beauty, daughter of a wealthy family who were set on her marrying an elderly rich man of their choice. Clarissa, a virtuous, high-minded maiden, refused and fell into the clutches of the disreputable Colonel Lovelace who, with seduction in mind, bore her off to London. If Clarissa had been a soppy Cancerian she would have reformed Lovelace, they would have married and lived happily ever after, but she was a Leo and the story proceeds along a troubled course. Unable to overcome the saintly Clarissa's defences, Lovelace eventually lost patience and raped her. Clarissa did the 'only decent thing' and prepared to die. She ordered her coffin and had it taken to her room for her inspection, then said farewell in extremely long letters to everyone and expired in an exemplary Christian manner. Lovelace was challenged to a duel by her cousin and killed, filled with remorse. Serve him right! (By our calendar this birthday would be eleven days later, but Clarissa would still be a Leo.)

JULY 25

c. 1890, England
St. James the Great
(from China Court by Rumer Godden)

Cook's niece Lily, an unattractive little Cockney, was graciously allowed to spend her summer holidays at China Court. Ripsie avoided

~ Leo ~

her until she saw her today on the driveway laying out a curious pattern of oyster shells on a bed of ferns edged with pebbles. It was 'a grotter'. '"A - a grotter?" asked Ripsie. "Yus." "What do you do with it?" "Git coppers." "Coppers?" "Pennies, stoopid... Every year, twenty-fifth of July, we mikes grotters of oyster shells on the pivement, see? Mike 'em pretty, see, and we gits coppers...sime as Guy Fawkes, see?" "The twenty-fifth of July? Why?"' But Lily had never heard of Saint James the Great, nor seen a representation of him carrying his palmer's shell and she did not know that her 'grotter' was an echo of the ancient shell grottoes erected with an image of the Saint, for the benefit of those who could not afford to make the pilgrimage to his shrine at Compostella in Spain. However - 'They work all morning and Ripsie discovers she is better at this than Lily. She does not throw the ferns down carelessly, or mass them, but plants each one, letting every frond show and sets them off with scarlet pimpernels, lady's slippers and clover.' The grotto was destroyed under a horse's hoofs but Ripsie built another secretly by the waterfall and then another, bigger and better, which grew into a wonderful garden, so this Leo day was a fine start for it.

JULY
26

1875, Switzerland
Birth of **CARL JUNG**, psychiatrist

1895, daybreak, Wimbledon
Birth of **ROBERT GRAVES**, poet and novelist (Might be 24th.)

These two prodigious writers come to us out of the realms of myth and legend. Both large, handsome men. Jung's great works like <u>Analytical Psychology</u> and <u>Psychological Types</u> introduced the concept of archetypes, extroversion and introversion, complexes and neuroses, and have influenced literature ever since. He believed we all share the Collective Subconscious which proves the existence of a spiritual world beyond our own. He analysed thousands of dreams and travelled the world studying mythology and religions. He felt that, 6000 years before, he had lived with the Masai tribesmen. Archaeological research now indicates that it was at that precise spot in Africa where man originated. He said that magic was the science of the jungle. Graves exiled himself to Minorca. Buses stopped outside his house for the drivers to point him out to tourists. He looked like 'a battered Zeus' with his shock of white hair topping a large head. He wrote love poems, humorous poems, children's poems, historical novels and is best known to today's TV audience for <u>I, Claudius</u>. Like Jung he had a strong attachment to the heroic past.

~ Leo ~

For him it was Roman times. All of which leaves no space for **GEORGE BERNARD SHAW**. Not physically large but mentally - yes. He said we shouldn't have minds like villagers which is Leonian enough for us.

JULY
27

1887, Salisbury, Wilts
Birth of **LEO** (Lionel) **COLSTON**
(from <u>The Go-Between</u> by L.P. Hartley)

At Christmas 1899 the aptly named Leo received a diary from his mother to record the events of the new century. The signs of the zodiac embellished the cover. The Fishes sported deliciously, the Crab had a twinkle in its eye and even the Scorpion carried its pincers with a gay, heraldic air. 'The Ram, the Bull and the Lion epitomised imperious manhood, they were what we all thought we had it in us to be; careless, noble, self-sufficient, they ruled their months with sovereign sway.' That summer the fatherless Leo was invited to spend the holiday with a school friend at Norfolk where he mixed with the gentry and found that he enjoyed himself immensely. He became a go-between carrying messages for two-star-crossed lovers, his god Ted Burgess a tenant farmer, and his goddess Maria Maudsley, the daughter of the house who was engaged to Viscount Trimingham. On his 13th birthday in 1900, the lovers were discovered and Leo because of his part in the affair had a nervous breakdown which affected the rest of his life. He never married and led a secluded existence, although there is a ray of hope for him at the end if he takes one last message as a go-between.

JULY
28

1905, London
Birth of **SWANHILD ASTA KJAER**
(from <u>Asta's Book</u> by Barbara Vine)

A sweet, gentle, beautiful child with Nordic-goddess looks befitting her Nordic-goddess name. She was always called 'Swanny' and swans are royal birds. Her 'father' ignored her because he knew she wasn't his, but Swanny bore no grudge against him or her favoured younger sister. She was genuinely good and generous. She was elegant and beautifully dressed, tranquil, sleek and well-groomed. Her husband fell in love at first sight and would have married nobody else if she had

~ Leo ~

refused him. He was pompous but rich. She lived on a Leo pedestal in his eyes. In a roomful of people they only had eyes for one another. They had no children and neither wanted them. She gave parties for his great friends in rooms like jewel boxes, warm, fresh-smelling, glittering and burnished, so many chandeliers and glass ornaments that they were filled with tiny moving lights. She revelled in the publicity generated by the publication of her mother's best-selling diaries (Asta's Book). But Swanny was one of those unfortunates who find out late in life that they are adopted. An anonymous letter brutally informed her that her airs and graces were a joke. She was trash, a nobody's child. Alas for Swanny's Leonian pride, she never recovered.

JULY 29

1981, London
Wedding of Prince Charles and Lady Diana Spencer
(from Kate's House by Harriet Waugh)

At 123 St. Luke's Road, Westbourne Green, all was excitement on the royal day. Princess Lily had been invited and was swept off in a Rolls. The others were watching telly or in The Mall except Eleanora who was going to Ken Livingstone's alternative festival. 'She was wearing a canvas striped dress of red, white and blue - it was very short with a deliberately jagged edge. With it, despite the warm gleaming weather she wore blue woollen tights. Her hair was sprayed in stripes of red, white and blue and was arranged in the shape of a crown on her head. "It's not supposed to be pretty exactly. More fancy dress."' Well, it was patriotic and this was a very Leonine day.

DENNIS the MENACE of Beano fame would have been celebrating his 43rd birthday - also in stripes - in his usual anarchist fashion.

JULY 30

1778, Hayslope, Loamshire
Birth of ARTHUR DONNITHORNE
(from Adam Bede by George Eliot)

Captain Donnithorne, gorgeous in his regimentals, was heir to the local squire. The farmhands approved his choice of birthday, which fell at a time of leisure on the farm when they could give their undivided attention to the great cask of ale which had been brewed

~ Leo ~

(the autumn after he was born) for tapping on his 21st birthday today in 1799. Tradition played a big part in Arthur's life. An unsolicited testimonial to him - and to all Leos - was paid by a village worthy at the celebration dinner.

> "We've pretty nigh all on us known you when you were a little un, an' we've niver known anything on you but what was good an' honourable. You speak fair an' y' act fair, an' we're joyful when we look forrard to you being our landlord, for we b'lieve you mean to do right by everybody, an' 'ull make no man's bread bitter to him if you can help it."

It was very agreeable to Arthur who 'liked to feel his own importance. Anyway, he cared a great deal for the good-will of his people: he liked to think they felt a special regard for him.' He saw himself as good natured and a model English gentleman.

JULY 31

Year Unknown, Verona
Birthday of **JULIET CAPULET**
(from <u>Romeo and Juliet</u> by William Shakespeare)

"Come Lammas-eve at night shall she be fourteen," rambled the garrulous old Nurse. Lammas Day was one of the old Quarter Days and fell on August 1, so Juliet must have been born today getting on for midnight. She was a member of the wealthy Capulet family, beautiful, radiant, bewitching and - unlucky in love! At first sight Romeo completely forgot the old love he had been moping for.

> "O, she doth teach the torches to burn bright!
> Her beauty hangs upon the cheek of night
> Like a rich jewel in an Ethiope's ear;
> Beauty too rich for use, for earth too dear!"

And he must have known a bit of astrology!

> "But soft! What light through yonder window breaks?
> It is the east, and Juliet is the sun!
> Arise, fair sun..."

But Juliet was a Capulet and Romeo a Montague and the stage was set for the most famous romantic tragedy in the world.

~ *Leo* ~

1980s, England
Birth of **HARRY POTTER**
(from <u>Harry Potter and the Philosopher's Stone</u> by J.K. Rowling)

Another bright star! Latest icon for juvenile readers is Harry Potter the young wizard who is studying at Howgarts School of Witchcraft and Wizardry. He becomes a Seeker in the complex game of Quidditch, the youngest player for his House in a century on his Nimbus Two Thousand broomstick. A wonder boy, obviously destined to be a hero.

AUGUST
1

1683, Bodmin, Cornwall
Battle of the Giants
(from <u>Lorna Doone</u> by R.D. Blackmore)

A wrestling match took place between a Cornish giant (height 7 feet and three-quarters, chest 70 inches, weight unknown as there were no scales big enough to weigh him) and John Ridd (a mere 6 feet and three-quarters tall and 60 inches round the chest). The Cornish giant's backers and boasters had issued a haughty challenge that John Ridd should meet him in the ring or else return his championship belt. Mrs. Ridd and Lorna were sure that John could beat any man alive so off he went. 'Now this story is too well-known for me to go through it again and again. Every child in Devonshire knows, and his grandson will know, the song which some clever man made of it...Enough that I had found the giant quite as big as they had described him and enough to terrify anyone. But trusting in my practice and study of the art, I resolved to try a back with him; and when my arms were round him once, the giant was but a farthingale put into the vice of blacksmith.' A Leonian day (even when translated to the New Style calendar) for an epic struggle, however modestly John Ridd recounted it.

AUGUST
2

1868, London
Birth of (William) **LUPIN POOTER**
(from <u>The Diary of a Nobody</u> by George and Weedon Grossmith)

On August 5 1888, Lupin arrived at Brickfield Terrace, Holloway, his parents' home, to appal his respectable father with the news that the

~ Leo ~

Oldham bank had given him 'the chuck'. Lupin, who had ideas above his junior clerk status, was not downcast and with his happy knack of inspiring confidence in men of standing, got a job in the City where he speculated, winning and losing large sums. His disapproving father could only watch helplessly as Lupin rose late, wore loud check suits, played billiards ("a walk round the cloth will give me an appetite for dinner"), indulged in low music hall entertainments, smoked huge cigars and started a pony-trap. "'Are you justified in this extravagance?" thundered Mr. Pooter. "Look here, Guv.," said Lupin, "excuse me saying so, but you're a bit out of date. It does not pay nowadays, fiddling about over small things...'" His conduct when driving the pony-trap was questionable - passing everything and shouting to respectable people walking quietly in the road to get out of the way. His engagement to Daisy Mutlar of the low-cut dresses foundered, but her successor was the richer Miss Posh. Lupin is last heard of taking furnished apartments in Bayswater as Brickfield Terrace was a bit 'off'. One never lost by a good address and he wasn't going to rot away <u>his</u> life in the suburbs. Lupin was a Leo all right!

AUGUST 3

1887, around 7.00 p.m., Rugby
Birth of **RUPERT BROOKE**, poet

'The handsomest young man in England', the darling of the literary world. When war came in 1914 he joined the Navy and wrote memorably patriotic poetry:

> If I should die, think only this of me:
> That there's some corner of a foreign field
> That is for ever England.

But it is his poetic tribute to The Old Vicarage at Granchester in Cambridgeshire that stays in most minds:

> Unkempt about those hedges blows
> An English unofficial rose;
> And there the unregulated sun
> Slopes down to rest when day is done,
> And wakes a vague unpunctual star,
> A slippered Hesper...

Hesper (Hesperus) is Venus when she sets after the Sun and puts in a stint as the lovely evening star. Appearing before sunrise she is the morning star, then sometimes known, poetically, as Lucifer. Everyone knows the last lines of the <u>Granchester</u> - Stands the Church clock at ten to three?/And is there honey still for tea? - and Peter Sellars' immortal and irreverent rejoinder - "Sorry dear, honey's orf!" Poor Rupert Brooke died in 1915 on active service of blood poisoning from an infected mosquito bite, not helped by - cruel irony for a Leo - sunstroke!

AUGUST 4

1906/7 (?), England
Birth of Detective Inspector **ALAN GRANT**
(from <u>A Shilling for Candles</u> by Josephine Tey)

He was a policeman of the old school. A real gent. He inherited money from an aunt so had no financial problems, went to public school and looked like the old Army officer type. He was egalitarian, at home with anyone, anywhere, well liked by his subordinates. His smile and manner could make them work their fingers to the bone for him but he could be intimidating when occasion demanded. In <u>The Daughter of Time</u>, immobile and bored stiff in hospital, he set out to clear King Richard III of the murder of the two little Princes in the Tower. He succeeded and it has been said that the research made a most interesting contribution to scholarship. Obviously a monarchist! "'Now you, Mr. Grant, are a Leo person. Am I right?" asked Lydia Keats the gossip columnist. "You have all the stigmata." "I hope they're not deadly?" asked Grant. "Deadly! My dear Mr. Grant! Don't you know anything of astrology? To be born in Leo is to be a king. They are the favourites of the stars. Born to success, predestined to glory...I should say that you were born in the first weeks of August." Grant hoped he didn't look as surprised as he felt.' Lydia fancied herself as an astrologer but in fact resorted to murder to make her predictions come true! (N.B. We take great exception to this.)

AUGUST 5

1939, Gibraltar
Barbary Ape
(from <u>Scruffy</u> by Paul Gallico)

It was a humid, hazy morning when Scruffy the ape went on a gigantic spree into the town of Gibraltar and caused mayhem. He was the largest, meanest, ugliest ape on the Rock and he wasn't getting his

~ Leo ~

ration of peanuts as laid down in an Order dated March 28, 1932. The O/c of Apes, Captain Tim Bailey, had a disastrous day - not least because the Nazi sympathiser, Dr. Ramirez, had his hair piece snatched by Scruffy - but he did meet his future wife which was romantic. The apes on Gibraltar, no matter how mean and scruffy, are nevertheless royal. It is well known that if they leave the Rock, the English will go too (although that looks more and more likely despite having been held by Great Britain since 1704). So the creatures have been pampered and quietly replaced over the centuries, just in case. They are Barbary apes, a different breed from the usual run as they are tail-less and the only European monkeys. A colony of them was found on Gibraltar and they are called Barbary as they were probably originally taken there from the land of the Berbers.

| AUGUST |
| 6 |

1849, 1 a.m., Finchley Road, London
An Apparition
(from <u>The Woman in White</u> by Wilkie Collins)

Walter Hartright was walking home on this oppressively hot night and had arrived at a crossroads. He mechanically turned towards the city and was strolling along the lonely high road when - 'in one moment, every drop of blood in my body was brought to a stop by the touch of a hand laid lightly and suddenly on my shoulder from behind me'. This is one of the great classic meetings in fiction. Walter Hartright had encountered Anne Catherick, the Woman in White herself. The chart drawn up for that moment is illuminating. The Moon, our original Woman in White if you look at it poetically, was full as was only to be expected, but it was also in the sign of Pisces the Fishes in almost exact conjunction with Neptune, Pisces' ruler. This doesn't help with Leo and the Sun - they are tucked harmlessly away 'under the earth', but it does give a fascinating Piscean aura of the mystical and supernatural to that particular time and place Anne's birthday is unknown but this configuration, marking her first appearance, describes a weak, defenceless, disillusioned woman, which she certainly was. She had just escaped from a lunatic asylum where the evil Sir Percival had her unlawfully confined.

~ Leo ~

1852, England
Birth of **JOHN WATSON** M.D.

Fans of Sherlock Holmes and Dr. Watson have their own societies devoted to the minutest minutiae relating to the famous pair and overlooked by Sir Arthur Conan Doyle. It is from the researches of the acknowledged authority, Mr. William Baring-Gould, that the birthday of Dr. Watson has been gleaned. Do we agree? Was Dr. Watson a Leo? We see him as thickset, dignified and bowler-hatted, with an open, ingenuous countenance and gentlemanly manners, the soul of honour and probity. His Sun comes under attack from all directions but this undoubtedly refers to his violent exploits with Holmes and in the army where he collected a Jezail bullet of such virulence that it rarely stays in the same limb for longer than one adventure. The poor aspect from Jupiter merely relates to his over-appreciation of 'dusty, cobwebby bottles' and his reliance on brandy as a panacea for all ills and injuries. Jupiter in this mode tends to overdo the fleshpots. His love life did not run smoothly. There appears to be a sorry procession of Mrs. Watsons, first to the altar and then to the grave. Children are never mentioned, but he certainly had a tender, affectionate heart and his courage and loyalty to Holmes can never be in doubt. On balance, Mr. Baring-Gould was probably right.

c. 1938, Nigger (not politically correct) Island, off coast of Devon
Come and be Killed!
(from <u>Ten Little Niggers</u> - not politically correct either so usually amended to <u>Ten Little Indians</u> or <u>And Then There Were None</u> by Agatha Christie)

The ten victims - murderers every one - arrived on their mysterious weekend invitation, cut off from the mainland had they but known it. All were destined to be executed one by one. The first, the dangerous driver, got his today with cyanide in his whisky. <u>One killed his little self, then there were nine.</u> Reluctantly the survivors exchanged goodnights, went into their rooms and locked their doors. The most frightening thing of all was that it wasn't an old, creaking Gothic mansion lit by candles in darkest winter. It was Leonian high summer, everything was new, bright, shining, modern and luxurious.

~ Leo ~

1953, Pennsylvania
Birth of **Dr. SAM BECKETT**
(from TV series <u>Quantum Leap</u>, created by Donald P. Bellisario)

Sam was a quantum physicist whose time travel experiment went "a little ca-ca". He found himself trapped in the past and impelled to try and change history for the better - to put right what once went wrong. "Oh boy!" the ebullient Sam would remark after each dematerialising out of one body into another. He explained to the viewer that life was like a piece of string. "One end is birth, the other is death. Tie the ends together to make a loop. Ball the loop and all the days touch. Thus you can leap from one to another." Sam, surprisingly for a physicist, displayed the religious side of Leo by becoming convinced that his 'leaps' were controlled by God (God being a bartender with whom he discussed destiny in an enigmatic final episode). The series ran from 1990 to 1994. Note the importance of <u>eight</u> in the date. 8+8+(5+3). Eight is a very occult number relating to the astrological 8th house - life, death and rebirth. Placed on its side, it's the symbol of infinity.

AUGUST
9

1787, Kellynch Hall, Somerset
Birth of **ANNE ELLIOTT**
(from <u>Persuasion</u> by Jane Austen)

Again, Jane disappoints! Anne doesn't immediately register as a Leo lass. She does have the background for it being the daughter - however despised - of the pompous Sir Walter Elliot and sister of the equally stuck-up Elizabeth. But Anne completely lacked confidence in herself and was <u>persuaded</u> (title!) to reject the advances of the young naval officer, Frederick Wentworth, with whom she was deeply in love, because he wasn't rich or grand enough for her little circle. Seven years passed before Captain Wentworth returned home heaped with honours and wealth, still unattached and now a quite acceptable suitor. But Anne was no longer beautiful, her bloom had vanished and her 'elegance of mind and sweetness of character' did not immediately recommend her. However, after the usual romantic twists and tangles, true love triumphed and Anne glowed again, secure in the knowledge of loving and being loved, which is a very Leonian characteristic - so Jane was right after all!

~ Leo ~

1863, 88 miles down, 75 miles from Iceland
An Awe-inspiring Sub-scape
(from <u>Journey to the Centre of the Earth</u> by Jules Verne)

Today the travellers found themselves in a huge cavern containing a vast sheet of water which stretched away out of sight. There was a beach of golden sand strewn with shells and the waves broke on the shore. About 200 yards from the waves a line of huge cliffs curved upwards. It was light, the light being of an electric origin, like an aurora borealis, a continuous cosmic phenomenon, filling a cavern big enough to contain an ocean. The vault overhead was full of clouds, above which could be glimpsed the roof of granite. It was supremely melancholy and sad. There was a fountain of gigantic mushrooms, 30 or 40 feet high, the light could not penetrate between them. There were many other trees with colourless foliage. 'They were easy to recognize as the lowly shrubs of the earth, grown to phenomenal dimensions, Lycopodiums a hundred feet high, giant sigillarias, tree ferns as tall as fir trees in northern latitudes and lepidodendrons with cylindrical forked stems, ending in long leaves and bristling with coarse hair like monstrous cacti.' They could see no living creatures, only the bones of mastodons and megatheriums. The grandeur and immensity of the scene were Leonine.

1999, 10.a.m., Westmorland
Eclipse of the Sun
(from <u>The Hollow Land</u> by Jane Gardam)

Jane Gardam took a chance and wrote this story for children before the date of the Great Eclipse. According to her it was to be a queer summer, no two days alike. Grandpa Hewitson, however, said it had been like it in 1927, when there was a total eclipse visible from North Stainmore. The best place to see the 1999 phenomenon in the UK was Cornwall but the North was not going to be left out. Accordingly, the villagers of North Stainmore prepared to climb up the fells to the Nine Standards this morning. It was said that the Nine Standards were Roman Soldiers turned to stone. Part of the Lost Legion of the Ninth. They were never quite where you expected them to be, very mysterious they were. You could wish for things on the Standards but

~ *Leo* ~

you had to be very, very sure you knew what you were wishing for. So off they went with their picnics to spread out around the Standards and to wait. It became very quiet, the bogs turned purplish, then the stone walls. Then everyone turned bronze. The birds stopped singing, it became darker. Anne Teesdale leaned against one of the great rough Standards and wished (and it came true!). The ancients held eclipses to be unlucky, the effect lasting as long in years as the eclipse lasted in hours.

AUGUST 12

c. 1920, Hampshire
Leo's Last Stand
(from Berry & Co by Dornford Yates)

At 2.30 p.m. the Great House called Merry Down was to be sold at the Fountain Inn. It was the nearest estate to the Pleydell's White Ladies and meant almost as much to them as their own. 'For more than two centuries a Bagot had reigned uninterruptedly over the rose-red mansion and the spreading park - a kingdom of which we had been free since childhood.' Not an ancient tree blew down but they knew of it and now the greatest of them all was falling, the house of Bagot itself. Sir Anthony Bagot, a gentleman of the old school, had stood firm until the last but WWI had cost him his only son and grandson in the trenches. His substance, never great, had shrunk and he could hold on no longer. The Pleydells drove there and on the way met the alien who was determined to buy it. Neither Dornford Yates (a Leo - August 7, 1885) nor the Pleydell family had any time for foreigners and they were not happy with the situation.

AUGUST 13

1920/1930, England
Friday the 13th
(from The Skin Chairs by Barbara Comyns)

The narrator, Frances, and her sister stole into the General's house to see the chairs. They were actually covered by human skin and he had brought them back from the Boer War. Frances was scared because of the date, and on the way someone told them to go home as it was going to pour with rain. 'We looked up at the sky and saw heavy rain clouds had gathered. It seemed as if they were filled with black rain and I was afraid again.' To their further horror they stumbled across the

General who was dying but they thought he was drunk and ran away, telling no one. Frances felt guilty for ever more. Chairs 'come under' the rulership of the Sun and Leo because of their importance as a seat of office, leading to Chairman or, rather, Chairperson!

AUGUST 14

1792, London
Noblesse Oblige
(from A Tale of Two Cities by Charles Dickens)

The two cities were peaceful, shabby old London and hectic, murderous Paris where the Terror reigned and the guillotine did its deadly work. Today, Mr. Lorry of Tellson's Bank, left London for Paris on the Bank's business. Drawn to the Loadstone Rock as the chapter heading has it, while, even more ominously, Charles Darnay, a member of the detested, aristocratic family of d'Evremont, received a desperate plea for help from an old servant of the family who was waiting to be called before the Tribunal and executed. Although married and living happily and safely in London, Darnay knew he had to go. He spent the evening writing letters, one to his wife and one to her father 'explaining the strong obligation he was under to go to Paris and showing, at length, the reasons that he had for feeling confident that he could be involved in no personal danger there.' Who was he kidding?

AUGUST 15

1947, 12.00 a.m. beginning the day, Bombay
Birth of SALEEM SINAI
(from Midnight's Children by Salman Rushdie)

He was born at the precise instant of India's arrival at independence surrounded by fireworks and cheering crowds. He had been 'handcuffed to history, my destinies indissolubly chained to those of my country.' Unhappily Saturn conjoined the Sun which invariably postpones the highest of hopes. Already, on August 13, Indian astrologers noted discontent in the heavens. Jupiter, Saturn and Venus were in quarrelsome vein; moreover, the three crossed stars are moving into the most ill-favoured house of all. Benarsi astrologers name it fearfully, "Karamstan! They enter "Karamstan!" All countries have their own astrological names and methods but the general principle holds good. For those born at midnight anywhere

~ Leo ~

the Sun is always near the nadir, on the cusp of the 4th house, which highlights the country of birth, the home, the family. The rich tapestry of Saleem's domestic life certainly justified his arrival at such a time! According to him, 1001 Indian children were born, like him, in the first hour after midnight. And 'what made the event noteworthy was the nature of those children every one of whom was, through some freak of biology, or perhaps owing to some preternatural power of the moment.... endowed with features, talents or faculties which can only be described as miraculous.' Magic children with powers of transmutation, flight, prophecy and wizardry. Salman Rushdie was also born in 1947 but too soon - June 19 - to be handcuffed to history. However, a New Moon in Gemini shackled to shock-horror Uranus is startling enough for anyone, as has so proved for Mr. Rushdie.

AUGUST 16

1965, Madison County, S. Iowa
Love Story
(from <u>The Bridges of Madison County</u> by Robert James Waller)

Francesca Johnson wrote out the story of her great romance for her children to read after her death. 'Robert Kincaid came to me on the sixteenth of August, a Monday, in 1965. He was trying to find Roseman Bridge. It was late afternoon, hot, and he was driving a pickup truck he called Harry.' He had stopped to ask for directions to the Bridge which was two miles away and she rode with him to direct him. Her husband and children were away at the State Fair. Kincaid was 52, a photographer for the National Geographic on an assignment. She was 45, a farmer's wife. They fell in love and spent four perfect days together but she would not leave her family for him and he drove away. He was something of a mystic. A former girl friend had the feeling that he'd been here for more than one lifetime, while his mother always felt he came from another planet to which he was trying to return. Immediately he and Francesca met he knew they had always been moving towards one another. Although they never saw or spoke to one another again they felt themselves bound for eternity and both directed that their ashes should be scattered by Roseman Bridge. A sad but beautiful Leonian romance. A gulp-a-minute book.

~ Leo ~

AUGUST 17

1953, England
Birth of **RUFUS FLETCHER**
(from <u>The Fatal Inversion</u> by Barbara Vine. Filmed by the BBC)

In 1976 it was his 23rd birthday and he and his friends celebrated, first in the Chinese Restaurant in Sudbury and then in the local pubs where he drank brandy, the tipple for heroes. Rufus could metabolise quantities of spirits. He could drink two bottles of wine in as many hours with little apparent effect. He saw no need for self denial, was macho, sexy and had a hearty rugger-player side to him. He would have made a good bad Roman Emperor, reflected one of his mates. They were camping out at the ancestral hall inherited by one of their number, scavenging and stealing the family heirlooms. Then something dreadful happened and they grew up and split up overnight, agreeing never to meet again. The agreement held for ten years by which time Rufus had become an expensive private gynaecologist. He still drank and smoked heavily but his looks, charm and personality endeared him to his patients. He had always determined to be a success and would let nothing stand in his way, least of all his disreputable old friends. He could be cruel. His wife knew that 'there was a lot of underlying violence in Rufus, and not all that underlying either, a <u>lion-like</u> aggression in times of stress that took the form of a whooping, destructive merriment.'

AUGUST 18

Late 1960s, U.S.A.
Birth of **CASSANDRA STEPHENS**
(from <u>The Pistachio Prescription</u> by Paula Danziger
'America's Greatest Comic Writer for Children')

A creative, artistic Leo. For her 13th birthday she wanted a silk screen and other art equipment but her mother took her out shopping for school clothes instead. Life was not good. Her parents were to divorce, she hated her sister, she had asthma and was a hypochondriac. Her only comfort was pistachio nuts, the red ones, which cured all problems. However, the new school term brought big improvements. She got a new boyfriend and won the election to be class president because she was bright and articulate, got along with the teachers, did well academically and cared about people. She

~ Leo ~

attributed her success to being a Leo - 'we're supposed to be leaders'. She was always smiling. Life was fun. She got the better of a hated teacher, to everyone's admiration. Her best enemy fell back, snarling. She had an active social life. She got healthier by the minute. She made it up with her sister. Her adored father seemed ready to call off the divorce. In short, she had found her Leonine paws and was able to give up the pistachios!

AUGUST 19

1902, New York
Birth of **OGDEN NASH**, writer

Author of witty, sophisticated light verse, full of charm and humour, who juggled dazzlingly with puns, tortured rhymes and line lengths, and is always good for a laugh from babies - A little talcum/Is always walcum - to the more mature - How easy for those who do not bulge/To not over-indulge. He had a happy, successful professional and private life as befits the nicest Leos.

AUGUST 20

45 B.C., Alexandria
Putting on the Style
(from The Ides of March by Thornton Wilder)

An imaginary reconstruction of the events leading up to the assassination of Julius Caesar. Today, Cleopatra wrote to her Ambassador in Rome: 'Cleopatra, the Everlasting Isis, Child of the Sun, Chosen of Ptah, Queen of Egypt, Cyrenaica and Arabia, Empress of the Upper and Lower Nile, Queen of Ethiopia, etc., etc., to her Faithful Minister. Benediction and Favour.' After that dream of a Leonine greeting, she informed the poor man that she was leaving Alexandria the next day for Carthage, a stop on her way to Rome. She demanded a number of Lists to be sent to her: the Lay Directresses of the Mysteries of the Good Goddess and the votaries of Hestia with notes as to family relationships, earlier marriages etc., Caesar's personal associates both sexes, particularly those he sees for other than official reasons, his confidential servants with length of service, previous employment and details of private lives (an on-going List this one!), the children, living or dead, who at any time have been attributed to Caesar with names of their supposed mothers and any relevant information. Also 'an account of the previous visits of all

~ Leo ~

Queens to Rome, together with precedents of etiquette, ceremonial, official receptions, gifts, etc.' Finally, 'The Queen trusts that you have not been negligent in ensuring that her apartment will be sufficiently warmed.'

AUGUST
21

Year of the Catastrophe, The Thames Valley
Destruction of London
(from <u>The Thames Valley Catastrophe</u> by Grant Allen (1897)
collected in <u>Beyond the Gaslight</u> by Hilary and Dik Evans)

'On the morning of the 21st of August I happened to be at Cookham, a pleasant village which then occupied the western bank of the Thames just below the spot where the Look-Out Tower of the Earthquake & Eruption Dept. now dominates the whole wide plain of the Glassy Rock Desert.' The narrator was on a cycling holiday. He rose early, inflated his tyres and set off along the river towards Oxford. He paused on Cookham Bridge and surveyed the charming scene, the last living man to see it. He heard a faint rumble then a red wall of fire advanced towards him. It was a volcanic fissure eruption! Fiery Leo incandescent! Everything, everyone in its path was shrivelled by the heat. It advanced faster than man could run. He rode for very life 'my pedals working as I had never worked them.' A sea of fire filled the valley. 'So glorious it looked in the morning sunshine that one could hardly realise the appalling reality of that sea of molten gold.' Despite a puncture and a policeman trying to stop him for frantic riding, he escaped, but London didn't. Or perhaps <u>doesn't</u> as, presumably, the Catastrophe is still in the future.

AUGUST
22

1920, 4.50 p.m., Waukegan, Illinois
Birth of **RAY BRADBURY**, poetic science fiction writer

1893, 9.50 p.m., West End, New Jersey
Birth of **DOROTHY PARKER**, humorist, critic, satirist

This is a changeover day when Leo and Virgo fight it out between them, or have to agree a compromise. Ray Bradbury comes out for Leo. He has Sun in exact conjunction with Jupiter there and his Neptune conjoins Mercury in the same sign. It's odd that a writer who dotes on Hallowe'en in his stories should be a sunny Leo but the latter

~ Leo ~ Virgo ~

conjunction would account for a spooky, fantasy, richly imaginative writing style. His <u>Fahrenheit 451</u> and <u>The Illustrated Man</u> have been made into films. Sun conjunct Jupiter in Leo is just plain success and good fortune all the way.

Dorothy Parker, on the other hand, is Virgo. Her Sun is just in that sign and, with Mars already there, is dragged in still further. It, plus a Mercury-Uranus aspect, gives a good astrological picture of the sharp, shocking, bitchy Mrs. Parker, noted for her cruel witticisms such as:

> Men seldom make passes
> At girls who wear glasses

and

> She ran the whole gamut of her emotions from A to B.

The latter remark was aimed at Katharine Hepburn. She could turn it against herself though. In 1922, separated from her husband and shrugging off an abortion, she quipped, "It serves me right for putting all my eggs in one bastard." At her 70th birthday party she said, "If I had any decency I'd be dead by now." She was a leading light in the 1920s of the Algonquin Round Table group, the literary <u>enfants terrible</u> of New York.

AUGUST 23

St. Wesel's Day, Oberweselberg on the River Rhine
Municipal Virgo
(from <u>Guilt & Gingerbread</u> by Leon Garfield)

Today the fountain in the middle of the market square flows with free beer in honour of the saint. Not that he is to be found in the Calendar of Saints or Oberweselberg in the atlas but Giorgio, a poor student in search of fortune found the place, and very Virgo-like it was. A pretty little town with quaint streets and houses with brightly-painted shutters, straight out of a fairy tale <u>but</u> it had modern sanitation and an excellent municipal transport system. The obligatory castle was surrounded by formally laid out gardens which 'looked like an impossible problem in green geometry.' Neat, tidy, law-abiding Virgo tourists welcomed. Early closing Thursday.

~ Leo ~ Virgo ~

In the future, Melbourne, Australia
Finis of Homo Sapiens
(from <u>On the Beach</u> by Nevil Shute)

Virgo dreads contamination and wages war on all germs, so it's ironic that Nevil Shute should have chosen the sign to see the end of civilisation in his novel. The world has been devastated by a nuclear world war which began in Albania. A few uncontaminated pockets of life remain. The various characters have been living as normally as possible but the radioactivity has now reached them and they are succumbing to the sickness and diarrhoea for which there is no cure. Today the last of our friends washes down her death pills with brandy while sitting at the wheel of her big car overlooking Port Phillip Bay. Everyone else will be dead too within hours - except the rabbits! The bitter irony (another!) for the Australians is that rabbits are the most resistant species known and they will survive us for a year or so. Other animals survive for a shorter period. This chiller was published in 1957 and so far its dire predictions have not materialised so let's hope this has all happened in an alternate universe and that we have wisely chosen another path. (Detective work and much counting on fingers has revealed the day but not, of course, the year.)

Late 1890s, London
A Birthday Feast
(from <u>Memoirs of a Midget</u> by Walter de la Mare)

The 'midget' is known only as 'Miss M' and her birthday was actually on August 30, but today she was given a birthday dinner which revolted tiny fastidious, vegetarian, Virgoan Miss M. She was an 'indescribably beautiful little figure in her bright coloured clothes.' The long table was heaped with silver dishes, corks popped and the fumes of meat and wine clouded the air. She was tongue-tied with nervousness, haggard and woebegone. "Angelic Tomtitiska," sighed her chief tormentor, "I wager when she returns to Paradise, she will sit in a corner and forget to tune her harp." A small silver dish of some sort of flavourless jelly was placed before her which she automatically picked at. Something in the guests' demeanour made her look for it on the menu and there it was - <u>Suprême de Langues de Rossignols</u>.

~ *Virgo* ~

This then was the jest. Nightingales' tongues. 'In an instant I was a child again at Lyndsey, lulling to sleep on my pillow amid the echoing songs of the nightingales that used to nest in its pleasant lanes. I sat flaming, my tongue clotted with disgust.'

AUGUST 26

1815, Milton Pangersbourne, Hampshire
Howzat!
(from <u>The Pangersbourne Murders</u> by Jeremy Sturrock)

By its elegance, formality and white flannels, cricket was, in those days, a Virgoan game. A noteworthy match took place today under a brassy thundery sky. The contest was on a knife edge (you either die of boredom at a cricket match or are carried off with heart failure). Pangersbourne needed fifteen runs to win with the last man in. The parson at the other end, tired but dogged, the crowd holding its breath as one man, and Jagger came out to bat. They won! Jagger's winning hit drove the ball over the boundary and smack into the face of the villain who was just about to dispose of an inconvenient witness. The bloodstained ball 'Jagger's Ball' is still preserved in a glass case in the taproom of the inn and is the centre of attraction for miles around.

AUGUST 27

1842, Forenoon at the Manse of Paradykes, Scotland
Jam-making
(from <u>Marigold</u> by F.R. Pryor & L.A. Harker)

And here's a scene of order and usefulness, plus a Maiden, to gladden any Virgoan heart. The last of the jelly for the year was being made. In the parlour of the Manse the round table in the middle of the room had been cleared for action and a smaller table stood beside it, bare except for pen and ink. Beenie, the serving maid, bustled about laying sheets of white paper, thick and thin, with two pairs of scissors on the smaller table, and a tray bearing jam-pots of many sizes on the round one. Mistress Pringle, the Minister's wife, was in the kitchen weighing out the sugar and the berries, two neighbours had come to help with the covers and labels and, in a little while, Marigold herself appeared carrying a basket of redcurrants. Her cheeks flushed by exposure to the sun were the delicate shade of a newly-opened China rose. Her thick curly hair was hidden under a sun-bonnet. Her sprigged muslin frock and pink apron were very becoming. She said in a soft young voice, "There's a gey wheen wasps about the rasps".

~ Virgo ~

1749, Germany
Birth of **JOHANN WOLFGANG VAN GOETHE**,
author of <u>Faust</u> and of <u>The Sorrows of the Young Werther</u>

He had immediate success as an author and the publication of his novel, <u>The Sorrows of the Young Werther</u>, led to a Europe full of young men wearing blue coats and yellow breeches and suffering from melancholy. The Virgo ideal of pure, unselfish, unrequited love led to an epidemic of suicides. Like many authors, Goethe gave Werther his own birthday and apparently a large helping of his own character and his knowledge of hopeless love affairs. Today in 1771 Werther wrote, 'This is my birthday and early in the morning I received a packet from Albert. Upon opening it, I found one of the pink ribands which Charlotte wore in her dress the first time I saw her and which I had several times asked her to give me.' Werther was completely neurotic but, at one point, he was honest enough to write, 'I will no longer, as has ever been my habit, continue to ruminate on every petty vexation which fortune may dispense.' A sentiment for every Virgo's calendar. Thackeray's robust kick-in-the-pants finished the Werther fashion:

> 'Werther had a love for Charlotte
> Such as words could never utter
> Would you know how first he met her?
> She was cutting bread and butter.'

It ended:

> 'Charlotte, having seen his body
> Borne before her on a shutter
> Like a well-conducted person
> Went on cutting bread and butter.'

Year Unknown, U.S.A.
Mechanical Gran
(from <u>I Sing the Body Electric</u> by Ray Bradbury)

This was the day the Body Electric arrived - a robot grandma to take care of the three motherless Simmons children. She had been built with loving precision to their own particular specification by the master puppeteer Guido Fantoccini. They unpacked the shell of the beautiful golden sarcophagus in which she arrived to reveal a mummy. They unwrapped the linen bandages and wound her up with the key provided and the Electrical Grandmother was born. Today. In the afternoon. And she was Virgoan perfect. Trust Ray Bradbury to get it right. She was beautiful. She was fun. She gave her complete attention to all of them. She could run, she could cook, she could sit up all night with a sick child, she could read stories, she could talk and philosophise. She never made mistakes, she was better than anyone they had ever known. She denied being perfect but admitted that, being mechanical... "I cannot sin, cannot be bribed, cannot be greedy or jealous or mean or small." She did not relish power for power's sake, was unattracted by speed or sex, was never tired nor irritable. "My eye stays clear, my voice strong, my hand firm, my attention constant." Even after saving one of the children's lives and being broken into bits by a car, she was able to reassemble herself! If this is your birthday, you have a lot to live up to!

AUGUST
30

1895, U.S.A.
Birth of **ADELE FESTE**
(from <u>Berry & Co</u> by Dornford Yates)

She was tall, slim, elegantly dressed and beautiful with soft dark hair, delicate well-marked eyebrows, bright brown eyes and a merry smile. She had a sweet voice, sang (mezzo-soprano), and played the piano. She had lovely hands and drove those great powerful cars of the 1920s fast and well. Even the Pleydell family, who usually closed ranks against strangers, took to her and welcomed her engagement to Boy Pleydell. "You beautiful darling," breathed Daphne, "Sargent shall paint you and you shall hang at the foot of the stairs." (Not literally of course.) Antonia Fraser, herself a Virgo (August 27) gave it as a birthday to her cool efficient **JEMIMA SHORE** billed on Megalith TV as Jemima Shore, Investigator. She has a non-conformist background, a Puritan streak and is convent educated. Nobody could be more Virgoan than a nun. Despite this heavy Virgo inclination, Jemima is glamorous, fiendishly intelligent, always top of the class. A non-smoker. Very attractive to men. Finally, it was the birthday of the elusive **MISS M** (see August 25).

1990s, England
Snap!
(from <u>Pictures in the Dark</u> by Gillian Cross)

'It was on the last day of August that Charlie Wilcox took the strangest photograph of his life.' It was midnight and he was waiting for his parents on the Old Bridge. Looking down at the smooth black surface of the river, he saw what a striking picture it would make with the pool of orange light from the street lamp reflected in it. He had his camera with him with just one shot left on the film. Mr. Feinstein, who ran the school camera club, was always nagging them to take more adventurous pictures and this was it. It was even more adventurous when, as he took the picture, an otter swam across the pool of light, fracturing the surface. And that's only the beginning of a scary story. Cameras and photographs come chiefly under Virgo, although other signs and planets may be involved. Photography is a good career/hobby for Virgoans. It combines technical skill with artistry. And of course, the best photographs are still black and white.

1878, East Grinstead, England
Birth of **ARTHUR KIPPS**
(from <u>Kipps</u> by HG. Wells)

Before becoming a genius, **H.G. WELLS** was a shop assistant and a Virgo (September 21, 1866). <u>Kipps</u> is part autobiography. Even the non-literate have heard of him, thanks to his musical translation in <u>'Arf a Sixpence</u>. His horoscope is extraordinary. Uranus, Sun, Mars and Mercury all in Virgo and so spaced as to denote sudden amazing changes in circumstances. Character-wise Kipps was very much a Virgo. Like his author, he was born in humble surroundings and apprenticed to a draper. He was a simple, decent, respectful, industrious and willing soul, exhibiting all the best old-fashioned Virgo working class virtues. He tried to improve himself by reading. <u>The Art of Conversing</u> loomed large in his life at one time. He could never see that he was worth more than all the surrounding snobbish characters of whom in was so much in awe. The first sudden change of circumstances came when he was left a fortune, the second when he lost it. In fact, Kipps was better able to cope with the second change

~ Virgo ~

than the first. True Virgos are never quite easy with unearned wealth. And it wasn't all bad. Enough was salvaged for him to buy a book-shop. He married his childhood sweetheart and they produced a commonplace but, to them, marvellous baby. "'I don't suppose there ever was a chap quite like me before." He reflected for just another minute. "Oo! I dunno," he said at last.'

SEPTEMBER 2

Early 1930s, Newton Abbey, England
Birth of **ATHENE PRICE**
(from <u>The Summer After the Funeral</u> by Jane Gardam)

Occasionally sharp-eyed people thought she was a bit too perfect. She was a vicar's daughter and it was he who chose her name. In classical mythology Athene was the mother-goddess of Athens, worshipped as Holy Virgin, Athene Parthenia in the Parthenon, her Virgin-temple - all of which marks out our Athene as a happy choice for a Virgo birthday. From being a sweet-tempered baby, through a sulk-free, tantrum-less adolescence, she was good at everything. She was learning Greek at the age of five and was set on becoming a scientist. She was effortlessly clever, played the piano like an angel, adored - and was adored by - her family. She was beautiful in every way. People remembered her and felt better for having met her, even if only fleetingly. She was an excellent cook and dressmaker. She didn't even get teenage spots. Her handwriting was Virgo too - small and black going across the page in impeccably straight lines. And somehow she managed to avoid being spoiled. Footnote: Following the strange events of the Summer after her father's Funeral, she cut off her hair so she looked like Joan of Arc, gave up the classics and the piano and became interested in socialism. She took to speaking her mind and called herself Anna. Still Virgo, but in a different mode.

SEPTEMBER 3

45 B.C., Baiae, Bay of Naples
Graffiti
(from <u>The Ides of March</u> by Thornton Wilder)

In this imaginative reconstruction of the last days of Julius Caesar, Clodia Pulcher wrote today to the Steward of her Household in Rome demanding a report on the matter of cleaning up the libellous scribblings about her in public places. Cicero recorded the 'verses of

~ Virgo ~

unbounded obscenity' which were scribbled about her over the walls and pavements of all the Roman baths and urinals and even in the Baths of Pompey. Three nightly cleaning men couldn't keep pace with the job, by next day the scurrilous verses had reappeared. Even the pie vendors had got them by heart! Virgo, of course, takes to the pen - or the air spray - rather than the sword or flick-knife - to air its grievances. Speaking of Caesar, his calendar was superseded in Great Britain today in 1752 in favour of the Gregorian which 'lost' us eleven days, brought us in line with the continent and caused astrologers much distress ever after in the determination of Old Style/New Style birth dates.

SEPTEMBER 4

1996, Kingsmarkham, England
Environmentally Friendly
(from Road Rage by Ruth Rendell)

Chief Inspector Wexford's latest grandchild was born on the 1st and Mrs. Wexford (Dora) set off to see mother and child yesterday. She phoned for a taxi to take her to the station and - disappeared. Four more people from the area disappeared at the same time. A message came through later to say they were being held hostage by Sacred Globe (which was Saving the World) until work was stopped on the new Kingsmarkham by-pass. The hostages were kept in a small room and spent today (Wednesday) making plans on how to escape. After ten hours without food they tried, but it didn't work and two of them were badly hurt. When the abductors found out who Dora was married to they released her on Friday. The others weren't so lucky. Virgo the Maiden is a sign closely associated with Demeter, Mistress of the Earth. In the country she was particularly concerned with the harvest and the final sheaf of corn was sacred to her - which is what Virgo traditionally carries. So Virgo is very much the environmentalists' sign.

SEPTEMBER 5

1903, England
A Rational Explanation
(from The Adventure of the Creeping Man by Arthur Conan Doyle)

Miss Edith Presbury, a bright, handsome, conventional girl, daughter of the famous Professor Presbury, was awakened tonight by the dog

~ Virgo ~

barking furiously. It was chained up outside having twice bitten her father although normally an amiable animal. Her room was on the second floor (third in the U.S.) and the blind was up allowing the moonlight to illumine the room. As she watched she was horrified to see her father looking in the window, his face pressed against the glass and one hand raised as if to open it. "If that window had opened, I think I should have gone mad. It was no delusion, Mr. Holmes." And there was no long ladder involved either. "The date being September 5th," said Holmes. "That certainly complicates matters." It turned out that the Professor's strange behaviour went in cycles and that his behaviour was indeed strange and improper for a hitherto respected old gentleman. Through-out the adventure, Dr. Watson had struggled to find some mundane explanation. On September 4, the Professor had been seen crawling along the passage on all fours. When challenged he swore horribly, sprang up and hurried off. Watson diagnosed lumbago - nothing could be more trying to the temper. "Good Watson. You always keep us flat-footed on the ground," said Holmes.

SEPTEMBER 6

Early 1800s, London
A Letter
(from Pride & Prejudice by Jane Austen)

Today Elizabeth Bennet's Aunt Gardiner wrote to her giving her the full details of Mr. Darcy's exemplary and noble conduct in getting the rascally Wickham and the shameless Lydia married. They had eloped thereby disgracing her family for ever. It's a lovely long copy-book Virgo letter which exonerated Darcy completely of Pride and dissolved Elizabeth's long-held Prejudice against him. We don't know either birthday which is just as well, as Jane wasn't very good at choosing birthdays, but Virgo can get very prejudiced against other people, being naturally inclined to see the world in black or white, good or bad.

SEPTEMBER 7

1858, New Jersey, U.S.A.
Birth of **IRENE ADLER**
(from A Scandal in Bohemia by Sir Arthur Conan Doyle)

Again we are indebted to Mr. Baring-Gould's researches. Irene was for Sherlock Holmes <u>the</u> woman. "She eclipses and predominates the whole of her sex," enthused Watson. "The daintiest thing under a bonnet on this planet," enthused Holmes. She was also as cool as a cucumber and a wily, skilful opponent. She was born on the day of a New Moon so had both Sun and Moon in Virgo, in-harmoniously aspected by Mars, which gives an adventurous, possibly criminal, twist to what should be a prim-and-proper chart. Rumour had it that she had an affair with Holmes from which a son resulted and the son was the detective Nero Wolfe, but it's not in character for either of them. She was an opera singer and is supposed to have been modelled on the Irish dancer and courtesan, Lola Montez (date unknown). Contemporaries said that Lola possessed 26 of the 27 points essential to female beauty - whatever they are. She was a charmer and her biggest conquest was King Ludwig of Bavaria. Irene similarly entranced the King of Bohemia, and Holmes crossed swords with her while getting back a compromising photograph for that gullible monarch after the relationship ended. Lola went out West and became an enthusiastic Evangelist. Did Irene emulate her? She could have done if her Sun sign is anything to go by.

SEPTEMBER
8

1964, Southampton
Birth of **OLIVE MARTIN**
(from The Sculptress by Minette Walters)

At first sight this 18¹/2 stone, plain, convicted murderess couldn't be less of a Virgoan but her horoscope shows Mercury, Uranus and Pluto all in somewhat dire conjunction with the Sun, causing no surprise that the psychiatrist wrote her off as severely disturbed. Her compulsion to eat was self-abuse. And on the Virgoan credit side? She had a wry sense of humour, it amused her that people were frightened of her. She was cynical, clever, and had no illusions. From her modelling of little figures from Plasticine and candlewax (from which she got her nickname) she had some aspirations to handicrafts, even though her object was to stick pins in them! She was not conventionally religious. If anything she was pagan and believed in natural forces like sun worship. It was on her 1987 birthday that things got ugly. Her mother and her lovely popular sister Amber did nothing for a birthday treat. The neglect festered away and next day she attacked them with savage ferocity and dismembered them in the kitchen. In her birthday chart Mars had reached the Virgo planets with devastating effect. It was devastating enough for us to be certain that Olive 'did' it. An investigative journalist believed not and secured a pardon, but from the last shot of Pauline Quirke as Olive in the TV adaptation, one feels very doubtful that the investigative journalist was right.

~ Virgo ~

SEPTEMBER 9

Mid-1980s, England
Nurse!
(from <u>Out of Season</u> by Barbara Gamble)

The narrator, Mrs. Hopkins, found herself in hospital after slipping on a wet pavement. The ward smelled of milk puddings and dedication, neither of which appealed to Mrs. H. She couldn't have been a Virgo or she would have felt at home, Virgo being a medical sign. But in Virgo fashion, she thoroughly objected to the gossiping nurses, the thermometer left so long in her mouth that she thought the mercury would melt, the ticking-off when she removed it, the refusal to give her her clothes and call a taxi ("This isn't the Grand Hotel, it's a hospital") and the final insult of cottage pie and chocolate pudding for lunch. She sneaked out and went home. Whatever the stars say, this definitely wasn't an NHS day.

SEPTEMBER 10

Late 1920s/early 1930s, England
Foreboding
(from <u>The Diary of a Provincial Lady</u> by E.M. Delafield)

'Unbroken succession of picnics, bathing expeditions, a drive to Plymouth Café in search of ices. Mademoiselle continually predicts catastrophe to digestions, lungs, or even brains - but none materialise.' 'Too much laughing turns to crying' is a well-worn Virgo theme, and Mademoiselle must have been one. It's usually, alas, only too true.

SEPTEMBER 11

2132.9 A.D., Space Lab. Common Room
Charge of Impurity
(from <u>Cards of Grief</u> by Jane Yolen)

Looking well ahead now and an inquiry into the actions of Aaron Spenser, an anthropologist First Class, is to be opened today. The charge is Cultural Contamination as defined by the USS Code #27.

~ Virgo ~

'The specification is that you, Aaron Spenser, did wilfully and unlawfully violate the Cultural Contact Contamination Act in regards to your relationship with an inhabitant or inhabitants of the newly opened planet Henderson IV in such a way that you have influenced - to the good or to the bad - all culture within their closed system forever.' In other words, Aaron Spenser is to fall in love with a girl of Henderson IV, a girl known as The Gray Wanderer, the Queen's Own Griever. On this planet, mourning is an art form and gifted grievers are revered. Well, 2132.9 or not, Virgo still seems destined to be going strong.

SEPTEMBER 12

1905, England
Birth of **LUCY SMALLEY**
(from <u>Staying On</u> by Paul Scott)

Her Virgo Sun was aspected by Mars which described her bad-tempered husband, Colonel Smalley. Her father was a clergyman and she was brought up very properly being known behind her back as the Virgin of the Vicarage. She learnt shorthand-typing and worked in a solicitors' office in Chancery Lane, where she met and married the Colonel and went off to India with him. There she lived through some tumultuous times but throughout it all she was lady-like, upright, modest, neatly dressed. Although brought up to know her place and by temperament somewhat shy and nervous, she nevertheless was able to command obedience without raising her voice. She was childless. The Indians regarded her as an English lady of the old school. Paul Scott obviously knew his astrology - see April 10 for the Colonel.

1930s, England
Birth of **SPIKE**, entertainer in the HI-DE-HI! TV comedy series

Although usually seen in a succession of ludicrous disguises to keep Maplin's campers happy, Spike was a very decent sort of young chap, very fair, straight and Virgoan. He could be believed when he said his birthday was today, unlike his rascally colleague Ted Bovis who had a birthday every fortnight in order to get as many presents as possible from the gullible campers.

~ Virgo ~

1957, England
Birth of **ALICE MORTHAMPTON**
(from <u>The Cloning of Joanna May</u> by Fay Weldon)

This novel is about genetic engineering. One day Joanna May, who
had always considered herself to be unique, a one-off, found that her
scoundrel of an ex-husband had cloned her and that she had four
'sisters' young enough to be her daughters. All four had been
implanted into women who wanted children and all four were born as
miniature Joannas. Their birthdays ranged from July to September
1957. Alice, born today, was the youngest. Gina, the oldest, a
Cancerian had, as astrologers well know, clone or no clone, a different
temperament from the other three who were Virgos. Alice was a
model, she would do anything for her career, including sleeping with
the photographer, but she didn't enjoy sex, hated children and found
the thought of marriage and continued companionship too onerous to
contemplate. She was unpopular but, then, she didn't like other
people either. Beautiful but 'sour' looks were her trade mark. She
didn't smoke or drink and was self-disciplined. Her mirror-lined
bathroom was packed with creams, unguents, oils and lotions. She
had a reputation of being 'a smart-arsed bitch' and could afford to turn
down film parts on moral grounds.

1955, England
Birth of **PAULINE MOLE**
(from <u>The Secret Diary of Adrian Mole aged 13 3/4</u> by Sue Townsend)

Unfortunately for Sue Townsend, Adrian Mole's mum is no Virgo so
she loses points for credibility! Mrs. Moles' efforts at housework are
sketchy, to put it mildly. She's far more likely to be having it off with
the man next door than hoovering. She smokes heavily and is not
concerned about Adrian's lack of vitamin C. 'She is not like the
mothers on TV,' complains Adrian. His Family Allowance goes on gin
and cigarettes. She dyes her hair red and reads sexy books. She is
given to wearing boiler suits covered in sequins and looking wanton
and so the sorry list goes on. The only astrological defence is that
Mars conjoins her Sun which is pretty rumbustious and rebellious
whatever the sign. She attended a women's workshop on assertive

training, which fits, and got a job as a security guard. The Spanish Inquisition was nothing to her.

SEPTEMBER 15

Early 1830s, Weydon-Priors, Upper Wessex
Hiring Fair
(from <u>The Mayor of Casterbridge</u> by Thomas Hardy)

Michael Henchard, an unemployed trusser with but twelve shillings in his pocket and tramping the countryside looking for work, today put his wife and their little daughter up for sale at the fair and got five guineas for them from a sailor. He was drunk but the bargain was struck and off they went. The next morning he bitterly regretted it and took a solemn oath not to touch a drop for 21 years. It's the usual tragic Hardy tale of poor, working class people and gritty realism, of high morality with bad deeds being paid out inevitably - in other words, Virgo.

SEPTEMBER 16

1954, England
Birth of **LADY ERICA ABDEN**
(from <u>The Green Flash</u> by Winston Graham)

As Erica Lease she was a pampered only child, 'a high-flying filly', who became an expert fencer. Fencing is a sport at which dextrous Virgo should excel. The finesse and formality, the virginal white contest apparel all appeal. And Erica had the Virgo temperament to match. She could keep to a rigid training regime and underneath all her practical jokes and impudence she had a laid-back, cool, down-to-earth streak. Her marriage was not a success. In fact, today, in 1980, on her 26th birthday, her husband killed her while fencing with her. She wasn't really cut out for wedlock. She wasn't much interested in sex and her best friends were gay. When her husband arrived at the Dorchester for her birthday dinner on the fatal day he found all 18 guests were homosexuals. Children she regarded as a form of pollution. She was great fun for those who liked a cynical, amusing, flippant companion with a razor sharp wit. She was devastated when she wasn't picked for England's Olympic team but she was too temperamental to please the selectors. She lived on her nerves and her nerves weren't always under control. She blamed her husband for being dropped and got very petty and sarcastic, as Virgo can. Erica is the posh name for heaths and heathers which 'come under' Virgo.

~ Virgo ~

c. 1925, England
Crime Sometimes Pays
(from <u>The Murder of Roger Ackroyd</u> by Agatha Christie)

Agatha Christie favoured Virgo for murder. Her corpses tumble over one another at this time. Today Roger Ackroyd copped it. In the early 1960s it was Fenella Rogers in <u>Endless Night</u>. Both are similar in the victims' names and the fact that the narrator is the murderer. **AGATHA CHRISTIE** was born on September 15 and was a Virgo. Her immortal creation, **HERCULE POIROT**, who solved both these murders and many more, was a typecast Virgo. He was cat-like and dapper from the top of his egg-shaped head to the pointed patent leather toes of his neat little shoes; shoes that were carefully encased in galoshes in inclement weather. He was prim, smug, neat and orderly, susceptible to draughts and fussy over his food. Virgo in the person of Poirot approves the cerebral approach, the analysis of character, the psychological deductions, the observations of tiny details, the stimulation of the little grey cells and the finger on the weakest spot. Poirot was conceited with the Virgo type conceit which knows its own worth. He preferred justice to compassion and never married. Like Sherlock Holmes, the woman he most admired was a beautiful adventuress.

1911, Cape Evans, Antarctic
Polar Cricket
(from <u>Tales from a Long Room</u> by Peter Tinniswood)

According to the Brigadier, admittedly not the surest source, Scott and Amundsen had an historic cricket match at the South Pole beginning today, which resulted in Norway's only Test victory over England. Months of meticulous preparation and training paid off for Amundsen and, on a perfect wicket, his team knocked up an impressive score. As soon as Scott's Eleven went out they were hit by blizzards, gales, hailstorms and sub-zero temperatures. Oates retired hurt and the English were in trouble at 78 for 8. Day after day the appalling weather took its toll. Scott wrote in his diary, 'Dear God, this place is terrible. Worse by far than the Thursday of an Old Trafford Test.' Worse followed. Virgo is generally good at individual ball games and cricket is both an individual and team game. The formality of it, the Gentlemen v. Players all in white flannels (well, it used to be), all appeal to the Virgo heart. Today saw the Sun aspected by both Saturn and Uranus and making up a Grand Trine. In Reinhold Ebertin's <u>Combination of Stellar Influences</u> this is designated as 'Physical exposure to severe tests of strength', and so it proved.

SEPTEMBER
19

Late 1940s, Swinly Dean
Christie's Favourite!
(from <u>The Crooked House</u> by Agatha Christie)

'On September 19 at the Three Gables, Swinly Dean, Aristide Leonides, beloved husband of Brenda Leonides, in his 58th year. Deeply regretted.'

There was also an interesting entry in Josephine Leonides' diary. 'Today I killed grandfather. Grandfather wouldn't let me do bally dancing so I made up my mind I would kill him. Then we should go to London to live and mother wouldn't mind me doing bally.' Agatha Christie was the Queen of Crime and must have produced enough corpses over 50 years to keep a jobbing undertaker in steady employment. Her clear-cut characterisations and minute attention to detail in her infuriating literary jigsaw puzzles are all Virgo. So are her sleuths - Hercule Poirot and Miss Marple, so lady-like yet so acute. Mrs. Christie was encouraged to write from an early age by her mother and a spell of nursing gave her her knowledge of poisons. She did not go in for overt violence. "It would be unpleasant to me and I should not like to read it. I don't like to see people hurting other people." Virgo has to have a more subtle approach to mayhem.

SEPTEMBER
20

1893, London
Death of LUCY WESTENRA
(from <u>Dracula</u> by Bram Stoker)

Dr. Seward recorded the melancholy event which followed a few days after the demise of Lucy's mother, both vampire victims. Lucy had to die. She had ceased to be pure, virginal Lucy and had turned into a vampire herself. It is well-known that vampires' victims become active in the bloodsucking business on their own account. 'Her open

~ Virgo ~

mouth showed the pale gums. Her, teeth in the dim, uncertain light, seemed longer and sharper than they had been in the morning...the canine teeth looked longer and sharper than the rest.'

SEPTEMBER 21

1850s, England
Birth of **GRANNY BEAN**
(from <u>Memento Mori</u> by Muriel Spark)

Great excitement today, sometime in the 1950s, in the Maud Long Ward. Granny Bean had attained her century! She sat up in bed in a new bedjacket and answered the reporters' questions in a distant, flute-like voice. Yes, she had lived a long time. Yes, it felt all right to be a hundred. Yes, she had seen Queen Victoria. She had started work at 11 as a seamstress, a Virgo occupation. Sister Lucy wore her service medal in honour of the occasion and Matron herself came down at 3 o'clock to read the telegram from the Queen. Everyone applauded although another granny said that 'on your hundredth birthday' didn't sound right. Queen Mary always said, 'on the occasion of your centenary.' Nag, nag... <u>she</u> should have been the Virgo-girl! They blew out the 100 candles on the cake between them and Miss Valvona read out Granny Bean's birthday forecast. "September 21st. You can expect an eventful year. People associated with music, transport and the fashion industry will find the coming year will bring marked progress." There! Granny Bean had been connected with the fashion industry! But Granny Bean had fallen asleep.

SEPTEMBER 22

2890 Third Age, The Shire, Middle-Earth
Birth of **BILBO BAGGINS**

2968 Third Age, The Shire, Middle-Earth
Birth of **FRODO BAGGINS**
(both from <u>The Lord of the Rings</u> by J.R.R. Tolkien)

To be born today at the autumn solstice means you can either be Virgo or Libra or a mixture, depending on your horoscope. Bilbo Baggins was unusually travelled and cosmopolitan for a hobbit and probably Libran. His nephew Frodo was Virgo. He never married, was quiet and thoughtful, a scholar and author, 'a very nice, well-spoken gentlehobbit.' Today, in 3001, the hobbit Bilbo held a great Party at

~ Virgo ~ Libra ~

Bag End for his relations to celebrate his 111th birthday and Frodo's 33rd. There were Bagginses, Boffins, Brandybucks, Tooks, the jumped-up Sackville-Bagginses, Proudfoots (or Proudfeet) and Gandalf the wizard to do the fireworks. As a climax Bilbo announced he was leaving NOW! and - vanished, leaving his real and personal estate whatsoever and wheresoever to his nephew Frodo. The personal estate included a plain gold ring which had strange properties, vanishing its owner being one of them. Seventeen years later to the day Gandalf returned to the Shire with disquieting news of Evil gathering in the outside world. Bilbo's ring was central to this and had to be destroyed in the fires of Mount Orodruin in Mordor, but none of the great ones of Middle-Earth dare touch it; possession would enslave and corrupt them utterly. Only one with no lust for power could be Ring Bearer on this perilous journey and that one was the frail, unassuming ordinary Virgo - Frodo Baggins!

SEPTEMBER 23

1799, London
Birth of **MISS ANN FORSYTE**
(from <u>The Forsyte Saga</u> by John Galsworthy)

She was the eldest daughter of old Jolyon 'Superior Dossett' Forsyte, a builder who founded the family fortune. She never married and was universally known as 'Aunt Ann'. She was very proud of the family and all its ramifications, and it was she who heard all the gossip and confidences and, in her quiet way, was its figurehead. Her life was cushioned, comfortable and entirely uneventful - a happy Libran! She had a sweet, calm disposition and, Libran to the day of her death, always wore a band of false curls on her forehead!

SEPTEMBER 24

1920s/1930s, Broadway, New York
Theatrical Interlude
(from <u>The Roman Hat Mystery</u> by Ellery Queen)

The sidewalk outside the Roman Theatre on 47th Street was jammed with a crowd of people in top hats and furs going to see the latest theatrical success, <u>Gunplay</u>. The lights dimmed, the curtain rose, a pistol coughed, a man screamed and the play was on. Later a real corpse was discovered lying between the rows. The murder, for such it was, was solved by author/narrator Ellery Queen and his father,

~ Virgo ~ Libra ~

Inspector Richard Queen of the New York Police, with their usual aplomb. Libra is the sign of partners and, in fact, the Ellery Queen mysteries were written by two American cousins each writing an alternate chapter so 'Ellery Queen' is a double-double partnership. As for the character of Ellery, who was by profession a writer but went along with his father for the ride, one researcher (Julian Symons) has declared that there were two of them as their/his character changed so drastically over the years - which makes a triple partnership! No birthdays are given for either Queen but Libra wouldn't be impossible for Ellery. He had an itch to see justice done, lived in a well-appointed brownstone New York apartment lined with books and retired to live in Italy with his glamorous Italian wife. He was very clever, well-educated and could be described as 'a Harvard snob'.

SEPTEMBER 25

1770s, Bristol
Courtly Passion
(from <u>Evelina</u> by Fanny Burney)

Evelina was very smitten with Lord Orville and he with her but as many mis-understandings could arise in 18th century literature as in today's soaps. They expressed themselves better, if more long-windedly, that's all. Today Evelina met Lord Orville unexpectedly and, in a far cry from EastEnders' "Can we talk?", began: '"There is no young creature, my lord, who so greatly wants, or so earnestly wishes for, the advice and assistance of her friends, as I do; I am new to the world, and unused to acting for myself, my intentions are never wilfully blameable yet I err perpetually!... and here there is not a human being whose counsel I can ask." "Would to Heaven," cried he, with a countenance from which all coldness and gravity were banished, and succeeded by the mildest benevolence, "that I was worthy, - and capable, - of supplying the place of such friend." "You do me but too much honour," said I; "yet I hope your Lordship's candour, - perhaps I ought to say indulgence, - will make some allowance, on account of my inexperience, for behaviour so inconsiderate: - May I, my Lord, hope that you will?" "May I," cried he, "hope that you will pardon the ill-grace with which I have submitted to my disappointment? And you will permit me," (kissing my hand) "thus to seal my peace?"... Just then, the door opened and I had only time to withdraw my hand ere the ladies came in. I have been, all day, the happiest of human beings!'

~ Libra ~

Late 1940s, England
Birth of **RICHARD GAYFORD**
(from <u>The Midwich Cuckoos</u> by John Wyndham)

He narrates the story and is a thoroughly nice man, a writer, happily married. As it was his birthday today, also because he wished to celebrate a contract he had just signed with a U.S. publisher, he and his wife went up to London for the day. 'Very pleasant too. A few satisfactory calls, lobster and Chablis at Wheelers, Ustinov's latest extravaganza, a little supper and so back to the hotel where Janet enjoyed the bathroom with that fascination which other peoples' plumbing always arouses in her.' Meanwhile, back in Midwich, at 10.17 p.m. precisely, an invisible barrier cut the place off from the rest of the world. When they tried to get back next day, they couldn't. Midwich lay entranced. Nine months later the Midwich Cuckoos were born, strange golden-eyed children who were going to cause untold trouble. Read it!

1965, 6.45 p.m., San Diego, Calif., adjusted for daylight saving
Birthday of **JANICE FREEMAN**
(from <u>Murder in Scorpio</u> by Martha C. Lawrence,
shortlisted for the Edgar & Agatha Awards)

The bookworm Astrologer rarely finds such a treasure trove and is not surprised to learn that Martha C. Lawrence is an astrologer and that her private investigator, Elizabeth Chase, is a psychic. Janice was murdered on June 9, 1992 at 2200 hours in California. She was a top drawer Libran, radiantly beautiful both physically and spiritually, highly intelligent and a genuinely good person. To track down the killer Elizabeth got a printout of Janice's birth and death charts. Her death chart was superimposed on to her natal chart to see the reaction, which is what you have to do. There was a cluster of planets in Scorpio in the natal chart (hence the title) in Janice's 8th house. "The 8th house sometimes represents death," explained Elizabeth to her companion. "Right in the middle of the cluster we find Neptune the mystery planet - placed here in the 8th house it indicates death under mysterious circumstances - and Mars, the planet named for the god of war and often associated with destructive energy." On the day

~ Libra ~

of Janice's death Mars was being approached by Pluto, the planet named for the god of the underworld and also associated with death so, "I was expecting a Mars/Pluto connection. You see it frequently in charts of accidents and crimes." But Venus was also involved which indicated the presence of a woman!

SEPTEMBER 28

1890s, near London
Christening of Baby Hose
(from The Jealous Governes or The Granted Wish
by Angela Ashford, sister of the better-known Daisy)

This astonishing tale was written when Angela was eight. Mr. and Mrs. Hose decided they would like a baby and the doctor duly arrived with a box under his arm. Mrs. Hose asked if it was a boy or girl. "Well, I don't know," said the Dr., "quite, but I'll leave you to find out." (It was a boy.) The baptism took place on 'a lovely day on the 28th of September.' After the slight contretemps of the baby being left in the carriage they entered the church - Mr. Hose taking off his hat very reverently - where they found the godmother and the priest but Mr. Johns the godfather arrived half-an-hour late. He was not at all put out, 'said a few prays and then went down to the bottom of the church and said in a rather loud wisper had not we better begin.' When it was all over they took their departure and went home in the carraige. "As we are passing the confectioners," said Mr. Hose to his wife, "we might tell them to send up a nice sugar cake in honour of baby's Xning." Better stop there with the icing on the Xning cake as the account loses its Libran gloss and gets somewhat harrowing later!

SEPTEMBER 29

Michaelmas
(from Sam's Three Wishes or Life's Little Whirligig
by Walter de la Mare)

"'I'm thinking and thinking," said old Sam Shore,
'"Twere somebody knocking I heard at the door.'"

It was a fairy, as you might expect from Mr. de la Mare, and she'd come to grant Sam three wishes for his kindness to the Little Folk and because he was old and lonely. Sam was amazed but, as it was Michaelmas, thought he fancied a nice fat goose. (Michaelmas was

~ Libra ~

traditionally celebrated with a roast goose.) The bird was immediately sizzling and sputtering and the kitchen became alive in the fire blaze. The next wish was a natural follow-on. His old mum back again to share it with him. And there she was! But so frail and old that the third wish was obvious. It was that they should all be young again. And they were. Even his old dog Shag came back as a puppy. The years went by. Old Shag lay asleep again under a stone, then mother was laid to rest leaving Sam all alone once more. But one Michaelmas Sam was fidgety with the thought that what was happening had happened before. As he sat with his frugal supper by candlelight he heard a faint tap-tapping at the door. If you want to read Sam's story to the end you must turn back to the beginning.

'For all sober records of life (come to write 'em),
Are bound to continue - well - ad infinitum!'

SEPTEMBER 30

1924, U.S.A.
Birth of 'FRED'
(from Breakfast at Tiffany's by Truman Capote)

Breakfast at Tiffany's is really Holly Golightly's story. Audrey Hepburn took the part of the sensational free-spirit in the film, the girl who wanted to find a real-life place to live like Tiffany's which would make her feel at home. 'Fred' is the name she gave the narrator, an aspiring writer who lived in the neighbouring Manhattan apartment. Because it is Holly's story, we don't learn much about him except that he was a very good friend indeed to Holly in the heady days of the early 1940s, especially remembering the bizarre situations she dragged him into. On one of his birthdays, she took him horseback riding in Central Park although he was a complete novice. He fell off the bolting horse in Fifth Avenue and caused havoc. It was in his bathroom that she fought a policewoman and was arrested on a narcotics charge while, in the mêlée, he stepped on a broken bottle and nearly severed two toes. Through it all, 'Fred' bore her no ill-will. Everybody needs a Libran friend. But wait! **TRUMAN CAPOTE** himself was born on September 30, 1924 and can be identified as 'Fred', so everything falls into place.

Capote could sit on either side of the Libran seesaw. He was equally adept with the Libran light romance of Breakfast at Tiffany's as he was with the dispassionate In Cold Blood, his famous reconstruction of a true-life brutal multi-murder from its beginning to its finale in the execution shed with Libran justice triumphant.

~ Libra ~

1967, London
Holiday Mood
(from <u>Vacation</u> by Alan Sheridan)

Birthdays are not happy times for everyone and suicide attempts are not uncommonly made then. Such a one is described in <u>Vacation.</u> Christopher Smith did not wish to continue living beyond his 40th year. He had been born October 8, 1927 and he spent his 39th year putting his affairs in order and planning how he would spend his last days. Today he began his vacation by checking into a boarding house and then filling every day with some task which he meticulously wrote up in a calm, logical way so the account would be found after his death. An air of contentment pervades the story of this pleasant, poetical, civilised man who apparently had nothing to live for. He recorded the weather and the permutations of the trains passing his window. He charted the inscriptions on the gravestones of the Brompton Cemetery. He joined a lecture tour at the British Museum of Ancient Egyptian Burial Customs and read the biography of the lady explorer **ISABELLA BIRD**, herself a Libran in birth and death (15/10/1831 - 7/10/1907). To his delight they had much in common. At 11.10 p.m. on October 8 he wrote his last words, at midnight he took 40 Seconal tablets, one for each year, washed down with champagne. 'Thus fortified by bread and wine, I shall set out to descend an immense flight of steps leading down a mountain side to the edge of a lake...'

1872, London
In a Calm and Contemplative Fashion
(from <u>Around the World in Eighty Days</u> by Jules Verne)

At 11.29 a.m. Phileas Fogg, as regular in his habits as a metronome, engaged a new servant, Passepartout. Then, as he did every day, he left his house in Savile Row at 11.30, paced 575 times with his left foot and 576 with his right to reach his club, the Reform in Pall Mall, where he spent the day dining, reading, playing whist and discussing the day's events with his friends. At 6.45 p.m. he bet £20,000 that he could encircle the world in eighty days. At 7.25 p.m. he returned to his house and informed Passepartout of his intention. They left the

~ Libra ~

house at 8.00 p.m. The Moon was so new that it wouldn't have been visible as they made their way to the railway station, but a New Moon is a good time to start a new venture. Phileas Fogg's birthday is nowhere mentioned but he sounds like a routine-ridden Virgo.

OCTOBER 3

1911, Little Fordham
Little People Lost, Stolen or Strayed
(from The Borrowers Avenged by Mary Norton)

Miss Menzies went to the village constable, Mr. Pomfret, and reported that the little people who lived in the model village were missing. It was an uneasy interview as Mr. Pomfret thought she meant the wooden people which populated the village whereas she was referring to the Clock family - Pod, Homily and Arrietty - who were as alive as he was but who were no longer there (although she <u>had</u> made one of the houses so cosy for them). It wasn't surprising that they had upped sticks and stolen away for the Clocks were 'Borrowers', little folk, five or six inches tall, who lived by 'borrowing' discarded bits and pieces from the 'human beans' under whose floors and in whose furniture they lived. To be discovered was death to a Borrower. The Clocks had, to some extent, trusted Miss Menzies but it was an uneasy trust and they became increasingly frightened. They knew the unscrupulous Platters were looking for them to put them on show. Besides, they were used to foraging for themselves, not having everything handed to them on a plate. They were dears, taking nothing that they weren't certain was no longer needed and in their way (Homily being a notable housewife and home-maker) lived in Libran style with thick blotting paper for carpets, cotton reels for furniture and candle stubs for warmth and light. Gracious living too, used postage stamps graced the walls as works of art.

OCTOBER 4

1837, England
Birth of **Mrs. MARY BRADDON**, author

She was a famous Victorian novelist who wrote the best-selling melodrama <u>Lady Audley's Secret.</u> She was credited with having introduced the blonde, innocent-looking <u>femme fatale</u> and killer into the <u>genre</u>. Up to then the bad girls were brunettes, the Libran type were the heroines. Her own life was a bit of a romance. Her mother

~ Libra ~

left her father, and before she was 20 Mary was writing non-stop to keep them both. She wrote some 74 novels and edited several magazines. She lived with a publisher, John Maxwell, which was scandalous then, until his wife, who was mad, died and they were able to marry. So there was a happy ending.

OCTOBER 5

1717, New Style, London
Birth of **HORACE WALPOLE**

He was the son of the Prime Minister Robert Walpole and led a charmed life. He wrote the popular romantic novel, <u>The Castle of Otranto</u>, which spawned many imitators. He was a wit, a virtuoso, a man of letters, a connoisseur of art and beauty. His letters were a joy, full of humour, gossip, descriptions and sheer fun. The great event of his pleasant life was his removal to Strawberry Hill in Twickenham which kept him happily occupied for years. 'I am going to build a little Gothic Castle at Strawberry Hill,' he wrote, and he did - battlements, arches, painted glass, round tower, picture gallery, cloister and all. He then filled it with miniatures, statues, books, enamels, old china, snuff boxes, gems, coins, seal rings, filigree and all manner of knick-knacks dear to every Libran heart. 'It is a little plaything house that I have got, the prettiest bauble you ever saw. It is set in enamelled meadows, with filigree hedges.'

OCTOBER 6

1911, Vienna
Tales of Old Vienna
(from <u>Madensky Square</u> by Eva Ibbotson)

Madensky Square was a fairy tale place. Susanna, a couturiére, created just the sort of <u>toilettes</u> which are to be expected in such a place at such a time...cream silk, georgette tiers of rough cream lace, pearl grey faille striped with rose, in her salon of yellow and white 'like the inside of a daisy'. Her best friend sang in the chorus of the Opera House and was a milliner of genius. Both had lovers whom they adored. A child prodigy practised all day and Mozart floated out over the fountain and the statue of General Madensky to mingle with the Cathedral bells and the smells of fresh bread and vanilla. Today was to have been a special occasion for everyone. Susanna was off to spend three days with her lover, the little pianist was to give his first concert, Herr Schnee the saddler's birthday was to be celebrated by his nephew, a cavalry officer, leading his troop into the Square in full regalia... It all went wrong. The Polish prodigy mistook the horseman for Cossacks who had killed his mother and went berserk, the resident dog joined in and was killed by the rearing horses. The chaos resulted in the prodigy being dragged away, shaking and sobbing and Susanna missing her train and her rendezvous. (But it was all the stuff of charming Viennese operetta and it all came right in the end!)

OCTOBER 7

1970s, London
Wedding March I
(from <u>Foul Matter</u> by Joan Aiken)

Not all Libran marriages are made in heaven. One that wasn't took place today at 11.45 a.m. between Tuesday and Dan Suter 'in a Registry Office like the inside of a shoe box.' They had the wedding lunch at a friend's Chelsea flat. It was slow at first but suddenly, in the flat below, an instrumental group began practising and they invited them up. After a few glasses of Bollinger they went berserk and smashed the place up. The police were called. At the bridegroom's suggestion, the bride and her friends went to the pictures while he and his friend went to Gravesend for a sail on his boat. Actually they filled themselves with brandy and phenobarb and opened the seacocks. Their bodies were found a week later. Tuesday spent her wedding night at a bed-and-breakfast where the bed felt and smelt like a sardine tin.

OCTOBER 8

Late 1930s, Oxford
Wedding March II
(from <u>Busman's Honeymoon</u> by Dorothy Sayers)

The marriage took place of Lord Peter Wimsey to Miss Harriet Vane. After a long courtship the knot was finally tied. Harriet wore gold lamé by Worth and carried chrysanthemums. She looked like a Renaissance portrait. Peter was white but charming to everyone. There was much hugging and kissing and congratulations. They were smuggled out to avoid the reporters and driven down to Talboys in Hertfordshire for the honeymoon. Peter had bought the house for the bride as a wedding present. All very romantic - so far. But nobody

~ Libra ~

was at the house to welcome them. Mr. Noakes, who should have been, wasn't, but his absence was explained later when he was found murdered in the cellar. Lord Peter, of course, solved the crime, justice was done and they had a lovely honeymoon which fits in with Libra in all its moods.

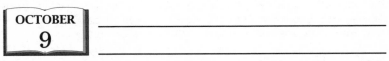

OCTOBER 9

1849, Yorkshire
Wedding March III
(from The Moonstone by Wilkie Collins)

Marriage of Mr. Franklin Blake to Miss Rachel Verinder. Gabriel Betteredge, house-steward to Lady Verinder, relates the greater part of the story. For today's happy event he had a new suit of clothes and - 'Family festivals having been rare enough at our home...I own to having taken a drop too much on the strength of it.' Having taken the drop too much, Betteredge sought an antidote and applied his infallible remedy for any situation - a quick slurp of Robinson Crusoe. 'Where I opened that unrivalled book, I can't say. Where the lines of print at last left off running into each other I know, however, perfectly well. It was at page 318. This concerned Robinson Crusoe's marriage, as follows: "With these Thoughts I considered my new-engagement, that I had a Wife" - (observe! So had Mr. Franklin!) - "one Child born" - (observe again! what might yet be Mr. Franklin's case too!)... I scored the bit about the child with my pencil and put a morsel of paper for a mark to keep the place: "Lie you there" I said...' And, of course, Robinson Crusoe came up trumps in due course. Robinson Crusoe was cast ashore on the desert island in 1659 on September 30 and kept the day as a solemn celebration ever after. If he was using the old Julian calendar then, by the New Style calendar, it would have been October 10. The coincidence would quite likely have sent Betteredge off for another quiet nip.

OCTOBER 10

1890s, New York
An Annual Birthday Spring Clean
(from The House of Mirth by Edith Wharton)

'In Mrs. Peniston's youth, fashion had returned to town in October,' (observe! Libra!) 'therefore on the tenth day of the month the blinds of her Third Avenue residence were drawn up and the eyes of the Dying

~ Libra ~

Gladiator in bronze who occupied the drawing room window resumed their survey of the deserted thoroughfare. The first two weeks after her return represented to Mrs. Peniston the domestic equivalent of a religious retreat. She went through the linen and blankets in the precise spirit of the penitent exploring the inner field of conscience; she sought for moths as the stricken soul seeks for lurking infirmities. The topmost shelf of every closet was made to yield up its secret, cellar and coal-bin were probed to their darkest depths and, as a final stage in the lustral rites, the entire house was swathed in penitential white and deluged with expiatory soapsuds.' This is Virgo's work not Libra's, but Edith Wharton is a greatly admired author excelling in her novels of high class New York Society which gives the requisite Libran tone to the day.

OCTOBER
11

1930s(?), New York
DASTINY!
(from The Education of H*Y*M*A*N K*A*P*L*A*N by Leo Rosten)

"What date is tomorrow?" asked Mr. Parkhill of his evening class of immigrants, to whom he was struggling to impart the rudiments of the English language. "Mine boitday!" an excited voice sang out. The voice belonged to Hyman Kaplan, Mr. Parkhill's most devoted and enthusiastic pupil, the most amiable soul alive and a love! Mr. Parkhill tried to ignore it. "October 12," he said firmly. "And on October 12, 1492..." "October twalf I'm born; October twalf I'm tsalee-brantink! All mine life I'm hevink boitdays October twalf. No axceptions!" Mr. Parkhill bowed to the inevitable, wished Mr. Kaplan many happy returns and said it was a great coincidence that he should have a birthday on the very day in 1492 that Columbus sailed the ocean blue and discovered America. "Columbiss?" Mr. Kaplan's rapture passed beyond containment. "Christover Columbiss?" Mr. Kaplan was in a world of dreams... "October twalf I'm arrivink in de voild, an' October twalf Columbiss picks ott for discoverink U.S. DASTINY!"

c.1860, U.S.A.
Birth of **ROSE CAMPBELL**
(from <u>Eight Cousins</u> by Louisa M. Alcott)

And now a real American born today and probably more entitled to the auspicious day than Hymie Kaplan. Rose was an orphan but doted upon by her relations, including her seven boy cousins all of whom wanted to marry her. The title of the sequel, <u>Rose in Bloom</u>, describes the sort of girl she was, very pretty and sweet-natured yet managing not to be too goody-goody or spoilt. A lucky Libran!

1862, Minneapolis
Birth of **EDGAR ELMORE**
(from <u>Happy to be Here</u> by Garrison Keillor
of <u>Lake Wobegon</u> fame)

Like Rose, this true-born nephew of Uncle Sam has more right to the day than the immigrant Hymie Kaplan! Edgar and his brother Roy ran Elmores' Court Restaurant famed for six delicious varieties of sandwich. Edgar, a fine old gentleman, a devout Presbyterian and a natty dresser, set out to improve the quality and tone of the clientele to accord with the delectable sandwiches. He invested in a string quartet to play at lunchtimes and wrote advertisements extolling the beauties of the Court, its music, architecture and civility. 'The establishment to which gentlemen repair with no fear of embarrassment.' Brother Roy grumbled that it made them sound like a French whorehouse and got thoroughly fed up with the sandwiches. He suggested they ran a local radio station so they could target possible patrons right in their homes. Edgar worried about the expense, the danger of electrocution and the influence of radio waves on the brain but, nevertheless, Station WLT (With Lettuce and Tomato) opened on April 6, 1925. Edgar, genteel Libran that he was, fretted until the day of his death in 1940 that a vulgar remark might be shouted by someone in the audience. A hand had to be kept on the Off switch at all times and the announcers were big sturdy fellows ready to bundle off anyone giving signs of telling an off-colour story or breaking into <u>filth</u> in a foreign language.

~ Libra ~

1961, U.S.A.
Birth of **FOX WILLIAM MULDER**, FBI Agent
(from TV's <u>The X Files</u> by Chris Carter)

He's very dishy and has many female admirers. His partner is the luscious Dana Scully (see November 21). And, of course, he's on the side of Libran justice, although the truth may well be 'Out There'. The violence in his life can be accounted for by the underside of the sign. Another birthday which has been floated around is October 11, but as his creator, Chris Carter, was born on October 13 (1956, 9.51 p.m., Compton, California) and as authors often have a fancy for giving their characters some of their own traits and their birthdays, October 13 gets the casting vote. 'Mulder' was Carter's mother's maiden name and 'Fox' the name of someone he grew up with. Carter was never into Sci-Fi, preferring <u>The Avengers</u> type of cult classic with its witty, verging-on-the-romantic interplay between the male/female leads. He says he is an equal part of both Mulder and Scully with a desire to believe in the supernatural, but an inability to do so. This dichotomy is very Libran.

c.1850, Cranford
Peace Restored
(from <u>Cranford</u> by Elizabeth Gaskell)

Mrs. Gaskell ended her famous novel with a luncheon party at the <u>George</u> with a magic show in the evening. All the characters were there from the Honourable Mrs. Jamieson to Miss Betsy Barker (she was the one who dressed her Alderney cow in a grey flannel waistcoat and drawers). Miss Matty's brother, Mr. Peter, returned from the East, did a little diplomatic manoeuvring behind the scenes and the coolness which had existed between some of the town's genteel Society was entirely smoothed away. 'Ever since that day there has been the old friendly sociability in Cranford society, which I am thankful for because of my dear Miss Matty's love of peace and kindliness. We all love Miss Matty, and I somehow think we are all of us better when she is near us.' Miss Matty's birthday is unknown but Mrs. Gaskell was a Libran, born September 29, 1810. She was a lovely person who charmed all her many friends. She was a serious Libran too in that she pressed the need for better understanding and reconciliation not only in Cranford but between employer and employed in both the industrial and farming communities in which she lived as a clergyman's wife.

OCTOBER 15

1896, Ambridge
Birth of **DAN ARCHER**, fictional farmer on The Archers (radio)

Dan was the patriarch of the Archers of Ambridge. His Sun was in Libra, the sign of justice and balance, and Dan, true to type, was an adept at seeing the other fellow's point of view. Ralph Bellamy had right on his side but so had Mike Tucker. The Vicar had a good case but the village bobby upheld the law. Everyone always asked Dan's opinion but it's hard to see why they bothered. To make matters worse, Dan had no planets in the Fire element, no planets strongly placed by sign, and an unaspected Jupiter. A negative sort of chart. Never mind, his marriage to Doris lasted them both out, which is more than can be said of the relationships of their descendants.

OCTOBER 16

1854, Dublin
Birth of **OSCAR WILDE**

Talented author and aesthete who placed the appreciation of art and beauty above everything. He wrote two books of beautiful, hauntingly sad fairy tales, The Happy Prince and A House of Pomegranates. His light social comedies like The Importance of Being Earnest still delight us. He married and had two sons but unhappily took his Libran need for beautiful relationships too far for the morals of the time, was imprisoned for homosexual offences and ruined. To think of the dandified, affected Oscar doing two years hard is - well, unthinkable. He was 'sent up' as the poet Bunthorne by W.S. Gilbert in the Savoy opera Patience, in such gems as 'If you're anxious for to shine in the high aesthetic line as a man of culture rare' and 'Conceive me if you can ....' 'A most intense young man,/A soulful-eyed young man,/An ultra-poetical, super-aesthetical,/Out-of-the-way young man!'.... 'A Japanese young man,/A blue-and-white young man,/Francesca di Rimini,/Miminy-piminy,/Je-ne-sais-quoi young man!' Never mind, he had the last laugh. Whoever can forget "Handbag!".

~ *Libra* ~

1900, Walworth
Birth of **MAGDA MALLING** aka MAGDA CRATER
(From <u>The Mind of Mr. J.G. Reeder</u> by Edgar Wallace)

She was the daughter of the night watchman of the London Scottish & Midland Bank. They had rigged up an elaborate plot to rob the bank and pin the blame on the branch manager. Unfortunately for them it went wrong and Malling fell victim to his own duplicity and died. Magda was able to hook it and not altogether empty handed either so her Libran luck held. It went wrong because the policeman on the beat had fallen for the charming Magda and had been picking flowers and writing poetry for her when he should have been, according to Malling's calculations, checking the bank. (They did in those days.) Mr. Reeder, of course, in his nervous, apologetic way solved the case. Magda was as pretty and bewitching as befits a lady Libran but her Mercury in Scorpio square Mars denotes a certain viciousness. Today, on her birthday in 1923, Saturn conjoined her Sun which foreshadowed the death of her dad.

1990, 8.00 p.m., Islington
Dinner Party
(from <u>Symposium</u> by Muriel Spark)

On the face of it it looked like a good time to have ten Yuppies to dinner. Sun, Moon, Mercury and Venus conjoined in Libra is all gracious living and high society, but they all took a battering from a strong Saturn. Then, Mars, right on the ascendant as the dinner started, square Pluto, was guaranteed to take the shine off the silver plate. Lord Suzy had recently been burgled and went on about it. Another guest, an assistant TV producer, had a theory that we are all psychologically of a certain era - Ancient Greek, Regency, Victorian etc., and cannot cope with the present century - something to think about. Lord Suzy said his burglars must have been Neanderthals. "They pee'd all over the place." Meanwhile, yet another guest, who was to have come in after dinner, was being murdered in Hampstead for the Monet she had just bought as a wedding present. The butler and his assistant were informers to a gang of thieves and tipped them off when likely houses were going to be unoccupied for the evening.

~ Libra ~

No, the salmon mousse, pheasant, small sausages wrapped in bacon and the sauté potatoes were destined to turn to ashes.

OCTOBER 19

1784, Middlesex
Birth of **LEIGH HUNT**, poet and essayist

With Leigh Hunt it's impossible to get away from Libran charm. He fairly dripped with the stuff and had the sunniest, most optimistic temperament, yet he was also a political writer who was jailed for two years for seditious libel on the Prince Regent. But no dank dungeon for Leigh! He papered the walls with a trellis of roses and had the ceiling coloured with clouds and sky. 'The barred windows I screened with Venetian blinds and when my bookcases were set up with their busts, and flowers and a pianoforte made their appearance...' - you get the idea. His wife moved in. His many friends, including Charles Lamb and Lord Byron visited, and Charles Dickens based the dilettante, beauty-loving Harold Skimpole in <u>Bleak House</u> on him. ('"I only ask to be free; the butterflies are free," said Mr. Skimpole.') His most famous poem is the charming - charm again - <u>Jenny Kissed Me</u>:

> Jenny kissed me when we met,
> Jumping from the chair she sat in;
> Time, you thief, who loves to get
> Sweets into your list, put that in...
> Jenny kissed me!

OCTOBER 20

1981, Dorset
Too Many Girls
(from <u>Queen of Stones</u> by Emma Tennant)

A group of girls on a sponsored walk got lost in the fog and disappeared on the 17th. They were a strange mixture as revealed by their psychological case histories while searchers looked for them. One was obsessed with fairies, another was a poltergeist and had been exorcised, all were under strange stresses. They couldn't describe what happened when they were eventually found today, minus one of their number. Fantasy, fairy tales, puberty and sexual awakening are all mixed up inside a sugar coating of beautiful poetic writing which, however, leaves us really none the wiser. A strange mixture of planets

~ Libra ~

too extended over the 3-4 days of their disappearance. Five were in Libra: Saturn at 14°, Jupiter at 22°, Sun and Mercury at 26°/23°, Pluto at 24°. The conjunction of Jupiter exaggerates the Sun/Mercury/Pluto complex to denote a suggestive, psychic power at work.

OCTOBER 21

1960s/1970s, Pennsylvania
Explanation (?)
(from House of Many Shadows by Barbara Michaels)

At a house called Trail's End, the hero and heroine got involved in a time slip. They saw three murderers waiting on the lawn. Three burly bearded men dressed in black with broad brimmed black hats pulled down low. In the moonlight. Waiting. The mystery was, why should they be seen on the night of the 21st when the murder had been committed on October 11th? The hero found out that by 1752 the Old Style calendar was more than a week out and the crime took place in 1740. The trained astrologer isn't altogether sure that he had all his facts right. For example: "So they fixed it by adding ten days." (Eleven surely?) "Every date (?) before 1752 is ten days (?) off according to our reckoning. Modern historians automatically correct for that. Apparently my source didn't and the newspaper account naturally had the old date. The old October 11 is our October 21." The Three Murderers weren't much good at calculations either. Pity. If they had come on October 22 the Sun might well have been in Scorpio which would have been much more fitting. Anyway, it's a jolly good read like all the prolific Barbara Michaels'.

OCTOBER 22

1483, Germany
Birth of **MARTIN LUTHER**, leader of the Protestant Reformation
(from Tristram Shandy by Laurence Sterne)

According to The Life and Opinions of Tristram Shandy Gentleman, the two Universities of Strasburg fell out over the point of Martin Luther's damnation. 'The Popish doctors had undertaken to demonstrate á priori, that from the necessary influence of the planets on the twenty-second day of October 1483 - when the moon was in the twelfth house, Jupiter, Mars and Venus in the third, the Sun, Saturn and Mercury, all got together in the fourth - that he must in course, and unavoidably, be a damned man - and that his doctrines, by a direct corollary, must be damned doctrines too. By inspection into his horoscope, where five planets were in coition all at once with Scorpio (in reading this my father would always shake his head) in the ninth house, which the Arabians allotted to religion - it appeared that Martin Luther did not care one stiver about the matter...' The Lutheran doctors held that it was another man born that day who was damned and that the true Martin Luther was born on November 10 1484 on the Eve of Martinmas, hence his name. Astrologers have been bedevilled by this sort of thing since horoscopes began, but in any event, whichever of the two Luthers is right, he was a Scorpio, as was Tristram (November 5, 1718). Even with the Sun still just in Libra you may be more of a Scorpion than a Libran if born today.

OCTOBER 23

c.80 B.C., Rome (?)
Birth of **CASSIUS LONGINUS**, Roman General
(from <u>Julius Caesar</u> by William Shakespeare)

Cassius formed the conspiracy to assassinate Julius Caesar on the notorious Ides of March (see March 15). According to Shakespeare he was born on October 23. He certainly died on it - at the Battle of Philippi in 42 B.C. He and his fellow Republican, Marcus Brutus, were fighting Mark Antony and Octavius Caesar, Julius Caesar's heir. Brutus and Cassius lost and fell upon their swords in time-honoured Roman fashion. All of which marks our man down as a Scorpion. He wasn't <u>nice</u>. Julius Caesar had pardoned him once before for insurrection but Cassius continued to hate him and was obsessively jealous of him. On the credit side he was brave. He was, of course, a real person who was fictionalised by Shakespeare but one feels that Shakespeare got it right when he made Caesar say, "Yond Cassius has a lean and hungry look; He thinks too much, such men are dangerous...Seldom he smiles; and smiles in such a sort / As if he mock'd himself and scorn'd his spirit / That could be mov'd to smile at any thing. Such men as he be never at heart's ease whiles they behold a greater than themselves; And therefore are they very dangerous." While Cassius has the immortal lines,

> "The fault, dear Brutus, is not in our stars,
> But in ourselves, that we are underlings."

~ Libra ~ Scorpio ~

OCTOBER 24

Early 1960s, Green Town, Illinois
The Circus Comes to Town
(from <u>Something Wicked This Way Comes</u> by Ray Bradbury)

Will Halloway was born one minute before midnight on October 30, his friend Jim Nightshade (and what Scorpion Hallowe'en-y names they are!) was born one minute after on October 31. They did everything together. Will lit the birthday candles at one minute before midnight, Jim blew them out at one minute past. Today, Cooger & Dark's Pandemonium Shadow Show & Marionette Circus came to town. As the boys' birthdays bracketed the ghostly time of Hallowe'en they were, perhaps, unusually sensitive to this spookiest of circuses. They heard the train chuff past their respective windows at 3 a.m. and immediately slid down their drainpipes and ran towards Rolfe's meadow where the cortège had drawn up. The train dated back to the Civil War and it was all so <u>quiet</u>. Setting up a circus should produce a cacophony of noise. This one was all shadows and gestures. The canvases were ripped off passing clouds. "I don't like it," whispered Will. And as for the sideshows! MR. ELECTRIC! MEPHISTOPHELES, THE LAVA DRINKER! THE MONSTER MONTGOLFIER! THE DANGLING MAN! MADEMOISELLE TAROT! THE DEMON GUILLOTINE! THE ILLUSTRATED MAN! EGYPTIAN MIRROR MAZE! SAINT ANTHONY'S TEMPLE OF TEMPTATION! and - most dangerous of all and don't you get on it if Cooger & Dark's Circus comes to your town - <u>the merry-go-round</u>!

OCTOBER 25

3018 of the Third Age, Rivendell, Middle-earth
The Council of Elrond
(from <u>The Lord of the Rings</u> by J.R.R. Tolkien)

Frodo Baggins the hobbit, carrying the evil One Ring, has passed through many perils to get to Rivendell home of Elrond the Elf-Lord, where a Grand Council of all the Great Ones of Middle-earth was held today. It was conducted in true Scorpio-epic high-flown style - all 'Aragorn son of Arathorn'. The Tale of the Ring was told from its forging by Sauron in the Second Age to its loss after Sauron's defeat by the Last Alliance of Elves and Men, and later its finding by the hobbits. After many fine speeches and a pooling of knowledge

~ Libra ~ Scorpio ~

concerning Sauron's determination to regain the Ring, it was agreed that Frodo should continue as Ring-bearer and a Company of the Ring was formed to accompany him to Mordor, the heart of Sauron country, to destroy it at the place of its forging. The Company consisted of 3 hobbits, Gandalf the Wizard, Aragorn and Boromir representing Men, Legolas the Elf and Gimli the Dwarf. Middle-earth elves and dwarves in those days didn't swing on foxgloves or sing <u>Heigh-ho</u>. They were terrifying. Elves were creatures of Air and Starlight who never slept or aged, the highest vibration of Gemini, just as dwarves were the highest vibration of Capricorn, strong dour fighters with axes, and workers in metal and stone. They were going to need all the strength and talent they possessed.

OCTOBER 26

1890s, the Baltic
Espionage
(from <u>The Riddle of the Sands</u> by Erskine Childers)

Today was the climax of this famous spy-thriller which set the pattern for a wave of imitators. Carruthers from the Foreign Office joined his friend, the scruffy Davies, for what he thought was to be a yachting holiday along the Baltic coast with some duck-shooting as an added attraction. It turned out that Davies had become suspicious of German activity in the area and wanted Carruthers, who spoke fluent German and was far more a man-of-the-world than he, to help him. The cold Scorpion sea itself plays as big a part as the characters. The book was published in 1903 to great acclaim and actually opened the Admiralty's eyes to weaknesses in its naval defences, resulting in a number of measures being taken to counteract these. In a postscript to the book Childers asked, 'Is it not becoming patent the time has come for training all Englishmen systematically either for the sea or for the rifle?' The irony is that, although born an upper-class Englishman, **ERSKINE CHILDERS** became a fervent supporter of Irish Home Rule. Caught in possession of a small souvenir pistol he was tried as a traitor and executed by firing squad in 1922. He had been decorated for outstanding bravery in the Boer War. He was born June 25, 1870 and, unless Scorpio was rising, didn't have a drop of that sign in him. Sailing was his passion.

~ Scorpio ~

1942, Ranpur
The Scorpion's Sting
(from <u>Jewel in the Crown</u> by Paul Scott)

At 4 p.m., Miss Edwina Crane, Superintendent of the district's Protestant Mission Schools, who was attacked by a mob during the August riots and the Indian school teacher with her clubbed to death, committed suicide. She wore a white sari like a widow. This is reminiscent of the old tradition of a scorpion, surrounded by a ring of fire, stinging itself to death. She had prepared her garden shed for her act of <u>suttee</u> by soaking the walls with paraffin on a scorching, windless day, and setting it alight. White is for widowhood and mourning.

St. Jude, Patron Saint of Lost Causes

This might be the birthday of **ANNIE**! Born 1921 in the States and left on the doorstep of an orphanage. Alternatively, as with all these showbiz birthdays, there is another possibility - October 18, 1922 - which would make her a Libran. But Annie was a red-haired spunky little thing, surviving all her trials and tribulations and today seems a better fit.

In <u>Mennyms Under Siege</u> by Sylvia Waugh, two of the life-sized rag dolls took this as their birthday. They were the twins Pilbeam and Soobie who decided it should be their 17th and that would be the year they stayed at. The significance of the day was not lost on Soobie. "Ours is a lost cause," he said. "People are becoming more and more inquisitive. There is no privacy any more. Computers are taking over the world. We may not be able to confuse them for much longer." So they were Scorpios. Pilbeam was the family beauty with her fairy-tale princess looks and her long back silky hair. She loved the theatre and, muffled up, went when she could. Soobie was a solitary, jogging through the deserted streets at night. His eyes were bright shining intelligent silver buttons and he was <u>blue</u>, which made him even more different. He was deeply sensitive, pessimistic and cynical. He had some nasty experiences; once he fell on the gas fire and another time was abducted and put on top of a Guy Fawkes bonfire. They had left their marks.

~ Scorpio ~

Year Unknown, The Observatory, Stellmere Park, England
Another Eclipse
(from <u>Venus Observed</u> by Christopher Fry)

This poetic drama takes place today when the Duke of Altair, a keen astronomer, invites guests to see a total eclipse of the Sun through his giant telescope. There were two solar eclipses on October 29 in the 19th century but the action here is later. So - why October 29? Because, according to Mr. Fry, it's Hallowe'en. But Hallowe'en, when magic is abroad, is October 31. Bookworm astrologers quickly learn that even the best authors are careless with dates. It's called poetic licence. Never mind. This is a dazzling Christopher Fry coruscation of words celebrating astronomy and astrology. For example, the Duke's agent, speaking of his daughter Perpetua says:

> "She really makes me
> Respectful of astrology: it must
> Have been the arrangement of stars she was born under.
> It couldn't have been all me and her mother. Why,
> I couldn't ever dream so beautifully
> Let alone propagate."

The enchanting Perpetua is the <u>Venus Observed</u> and surely a Libran. She was born in the autumn. The Duke was Sagittarius, we are told. His love of archery and astronomy, his easy-going nature and his oath 'By the groin of Jupiter!' all confirm it. His son Edgar must have inherited it as he practically lived in the stables and was an excellent archer too. But we must return to Scorpion country.

1920s/1930s, Chipping Cleghorn
Murder!
(from <u>A Murder is Announced</u> by Agatha Christie)

A notice appeared in the local newspaper that a murder would take place today at Little Paddocks at 6.30 p.m. Friends were to accept the notice as the only intimation. By 6.30 the elite of the neighbourhood had gathered at the residence of Miss Blacklock and her companion Miss Bunner. Sherry was served and - on the dot - the lights went out. Gasps and squeals were heard in the darkness. "It's beginning!", "I don't like it!", "How terribly, terribly frightening!", "Archie, where are you?" Then the door crashed open, a flashlight played around the

~ Scorpio ~

room and a hoarse voice commanded "Stick 'em up!" The guests delightedly did so but two shots rang out and terror set in. This wasn't a game!

OCTOBER
30

1940s(?), U.S.A.
The Night before All Hallow's Eve
(from The Homecoming by Ray Bradbury)

In the evening Timothy went out into the October meadows collecting toadstools and spiders. How many relations were coming? Seventy? A hundred? 'At midnight a storm hammered the house. Lightning struck outside in amazing snow-white bolts. There was a sound of an approaching, probing, sucking tornado, funnelling and nuzzling the moist night earth. Then the front door, blasted half off its hinges, hung stiff and discarded, and in trooped Grandmama and Grandpapa, all the way from the old country!' All the relations were vampires arriving at Timothy's parents' house for the Hallowe'en party, and vampires are serious Scorpio/Pluto/8th house business. They had all brought their polished mahogany coffins with them and were ushered into the cellar where they would sleep in rows until the following night when they would explode into revelry.

OCTOBER
31

1829, England
Birth of **LUCAS BELL**
(from Midnight is a Place by Joan Aiken)

Lucas, an orphan, lived at cold, miserable Midnight Court just outside the industrial city of Blastburn, with his awful, swindling guardian Sir Randolph. The day before his 13th birthday a relation of Sir Randolph's arrived, another orphan, a little French girl called Anna-Maria. They became friends. His birthday today marked a turning point as Midnight Court was burnt down, Sir Randolph with it, and Lucas and Anna-Maria were cast out into an unfriendly world and had no alternative but to beg or to accept the most degrading work. Enterprising Anna-Maria picked up cigar stubs and recycled them. The man who brought them from her (as new cigars) hired Lucas to find bric-a-brac for his secondhand stall. He admitted that it was mucky work and Lucas wouldn't end the day smelling like a rose garden but there were decent pickings to be made. It turned out to be

~ Scorpio ~

'toshing' in the sewers. It was a horrible trade. The last boy had drowned down there in the Muckle Sump, and the <u>rats</u> and the <u>hogs</u>...! Needs must when the devil drives and Lucas stuck to his Scorpion work until their fortunes changed but it was a close thing as Lucas's mate had the amiable habit of drowning his young assistants and keeping their finds for himself. Luckily, Lucas was a Scorpion born and so able to survive where weaker signs would have crumbled.

NOVEMBER 1

Year Unknown
Birthday of **MARY POPPINS**
(from <u>Mary Poppins in the Park</u> by P.L. Travers)

Under 'job description' it would have to be simply 'Nanny' to the Banks children of Cherry Tree Lane, but Mary Poppins is a magical, mystical Scorpio. The fact that she's uppish, insufferably perfect and extremely tart and that she's usually in a state of outrage or haughty disdain, does not lessen her charm. Marvellous adventures await her little charges when she is with them. There are things about the prim, trim, ramrod stiff Miss P which can never be explained. Where she comes from nobody knows, and where she's going no one can guess, but she's unforgettable.

1755, U.S.A.
Birth of **ONE-HOSS SHAY**
(from <u>The Wonderful One-Hoss Shay</u> by Oliver Wendell Holmes)

What a birthday! Another indestructible!

'It was on the terrible earthquake day
That the Deacon finish'd the one-hoss shay.'

The Lisbon earthquake occurred today and verifies the birthday of this remarkable carriage. The Deacon knew that <u>somewhere</u> in everything is a weakest spot which is why things break down but don't wear out (same goes for us too). A principle which held good for chaises. So he built one which didn't have a weakest part. The strongest oak, ash from the straightest trees, whitewood that cut like cheese but lasts like iron, steel of the finest, bright and blue, tough old hide found in the pit when the tanner died... It was a masterpiece.

'Colts grew horses, beards turned grey,
Deacon and deaconess dropp'd away,

~ Scorpio ~

Children and grandchildren - where were they?
But there stood the stout old one-hoss shay
As fresh as on Lisbon earthquake day.'

Then came its centenary and the parson went for a drive. It was half-past nine by the meet'n'-house clock, just the hour of the earthquake shock, when all at once the horse stood still and the parson found himself sitting on the ground in a heap of dust. The chaise had disintegrated all over, all at once. Logic! Although inanimate it was Scorpion, and Scorpios are as tough as old boots.

NOVEMBER 2

Late 1930s, 9.30 p.m., London
Poison!
(from Sparkling Cyanide by Agatha Christie)

Yesterday was All Saints Day for remembering the mighty Dead, today is All Souls for remembering the mere people, the humble Dead. Tonight a dinner party was held at the Luxembourg. A macabre dinner for six at a table laid for seven. In front of the empty place was a sprig of rosemary in memory of Rosemary Barton who had died there from cyanide poison exactly a year before. Her husband George had laid a trap but the tables were turned on him when he asked them to drink to Rosemary for remembrance. George it was whose face turned purple, George whose hands clawed at his neck... Scorpio poison again! Agatha Christie even gave the true murderer a Scorpionic name.

NOVEMBER 3

1856, Ireland
Birth of **MARY CARSON**
(from The Thorn Birds by Colleen McCullough)

"Do ye mark that! November the t'urrd herself was born," whispered Minnie, one of the hired helps. "Why, and to be sure it means herself is a Scorpio woman. The wurrst sign a woman can find herself born into. Ooh, they're children of the Devil, so they are!" Which all goes to show that Colleen McCullough chose her characters' birthdays with every care. Mrs. Carson was the wealthy owner of the Drogheda homestead in Australia and is referred to as the old spider in her wing chair at the exact centre of her web, issuing a never-ending stream of

~ Scorpio ~

orders and dealing out her brand of imperial malevolence. She knew every detail of the running of the station, had a sharp wit, was cynical, demanding, jealous and - she left a Will in keeping with her Scorpio nature, bound to cause trouble!

1913, Edinburgh
First House on Monday Night
(from <u>Lost Empires</u> by J.B. Priestley)

Richard Herncastle had just joined his Uncle Nick in his magical act touring the music halls. Not a happy time and this was the worst night and worst house of the week. A thin, gloomy house and, although Uncle Nick was a good illusionist (Ganga Dun), he wasn't a <u>nice</u> man. In fact, at times he sounds the very worst type of Scorpio. We don't know his birthday, so can speculate. He criticised everything and everyone including Richard's new friend Julie. 'I felt vaguely there was in him a dark and wicked envy of anybody and anything of finer quality, a hatred, half-contemptuous, half-envious, of any kind of life more generous and therefore more vulnerable than his own. He was like that Sunday-newspaper public which enjoy nothing better than seeing a reputation clawed down.' Well, that's the downside of Scorpio but Uncle Nick had the pleasure of being regarded with superstitious awe by his fellow performers who felt he really <u>could</u> do magic and it wasn't altogether an illusion. That's Scorpio too.

NOVEMBER 4

1805, New Style, Balkans
First Whiff of Grapeshot!
(from <u>War and Peace</u> by Leo Tolstoy)

The Russian huzzars crossed the bridge over the River Enns and were fired on by the French. Nicholas Rostov was on the bridge with the soldiers who were to burn it. Two were wounded. He gazed into the distance at the waters of the Danube, at the sky, and at the sun... There was peace and happiness.

> "In myself alone and in that sunshine there is so much happiness; but here... groans, suffering, fear, and this uncertainty and hurry... There - they are shouting again, and again are all running back somewhere, and I shall run with them, and it, death, is here above me and around... Another instant and I shall never again see the sun, this water, that gorge!"

~ Scorpio ~

At that instant the sun began to hide behind the clouds and other stretchers came in view before Rostóv. And the fear of death and of the clouds and other stretchers, and love of the sun and of life, all merged into one feeling of sickening agitation.

> "O Lord God! Thou who art in that heaven, save, forgive, and protect me!"

He felt that he was a coward but he was congratulated for his coolness. "Well, it seems that no one has noticed," he thought. 'And this was true. No one had taken any notice, for, every one knew the sensation which the cadet under fire for the first time had experienced.'

NOVEMBER 5
_____

_____

17__, Shandy Hall, County of _____
Birth of **TRISTRAM SHANDY**, Gent.
(from <u>Tristram Shandy</u> by Lawrence Sterne)

Today Tristram Shandy was brought forth 'into this scurvy and disastrous world' - a Scorpion. 'I wish I had been born in the Moon, or in any of the planets (except Jupiter or Saturn, because I never could bear cold weather) for it could not have fared worse with me in any of them (though I will not answer for Venus) than it has in this vile, dirty planet of ours - which, o' my conscience with reverence be it spoken, I take to be made up of the shreds and clippings of the rest... for I can truly say, that from the first hour I drew my breath in it to this - I have been the continual sport of what the world calls Fortune... I affirm it of her, that in every stage of my life, and at ever turn and corner where she could get fairly at me, the ungracious duchess has pelted me with a set of as pitiful misadventures and cross accidents as every small Hero sustained.' This was written after that troublesome revision of the calendar in 1752. If he hadn't altered his birthday to accord with the new reckoning then his birthday was November 16 and we should have stuck to firework anecdotes! In either case he was a Scorpio.

1930s, England
Birth of **CHARLES PARIS**, actor
(from <u>An Amateur Corpse</u> by Simon Brett

A seedy actor, usually 'resting', deserted by his wife and with a drink problem. He's dogged by murder and dark deeds but, as a Scorpio, is a competent sleuth able to untangle the goriest clues.

~ *Scorpio* ~

1980s?, England
Birth of **FRANCESCA FANTORA**
(from <u>The Fantora Family Files</u> by Adèle Geras)

Scorpionically contrariwise on this auspicious Guy Fawkes day, Francesca decided, on one particular birthday, that she didn't want fireworks. She wanted a tobogganing and ski-ing party instead. Being a magic-working Scorpio, she was able to control the weather and, quite soon, storm clouds massed and snow fell, settling 'like sugar being sifted on strawberries', and a lovely time was had by all in the park. The Fantoras were not ordinary. Grandmother predicted the future, aunt was a veggy-vampire and even the cat, Ozymandias, was extraordinarily literate - for a cat.

NOVEMBER
6

Early 1920s, Kennington Oval
Sidesman Hypnotised by Brass Eagle!
(from <u>Augustus Carp</u> by Himself)

Augustus Carp's father, senior sidesman at St.James-the-Least-of-All, had a rival for the position of vicar's churchwarden in a retired fishmonger named Carleek, who impudently presented the church with a lectern in the image of an eagle. Today, the first Sunday of the bird's installation, the Carp family turned up to denounce the brazen image. They entered the church, and to quote Augustus '... we were facing an image that, for malignant effrontery was surely unparalleled in Church history.' As they drew nearer to it up the central aisle, he became aware of an unforeseen and infinitely sinister significance. Approaching their pew, the first one on the right '... it was perfectly clear that its eyes had been so fashioned as to be capable of regarding us, either separately, or in unison, with an almost unbelievable degree of venom. But they could do more, for what was my horror, just as we were about to turn into our pew, to perceive that my father was still holding on towards the chancel - towards the very image that he had come to condemn, with his eyes fixed and slowly converging upon the baleful eyeball of the bird itself!' As the pew rocked beneath his feet, Augustus realised that his poor father had been foully (!) and deliberately hypnotised. The eagle being a Scorpion symbol is increased in its dire potency at this time.

~ Scorpio ~

Late 1800s, 8.00 p.m., Queen's Hall, Regent Street, London
Panic!
(from <u>The Lost World</u> by Arthur Conan Doyle)

'The much-discussed meeting of the Zoological Institute, convened to hear the report of the Committee of Investigation sent out last year to South America to test the assertions made by Professor Challenger as to the continued existence of prehistoric life upon that continent, was held... it was likely to be a red-letter-day in the history of Science, for the proceedings were of so remarkable and sensational a character that no one present is ever likely to forget them' (<u>Daily Gazette</u>). Too true. Professor Challenger had brought back living proof of his claim - a pterodactyl which created uproar in the Hall among the learned. To make matters worse it escaped and was last seen heading south-west over the Atlantic. The whole central traffic of London was disrupted. 'And so ended one of the most remarkable evenings London has seen for a considerable time,' commented the reporter with commendable restraint. Bats come under Scorpio so pterodactyls, a sort of flying reptile, must surely be classified as Scorpionic too.

1920, U.K.
First Appearance/Birth of **RUPERT BEAR** in the Daily Express

Wrong, wrong, wrong! Not at all the right sign for that nice little Rupert Bear to be born under. All that can be said is that he has endured wars, strikes and changing fashions so is a survivor. His horoscope is excellent which has helped. The Sun is at the mid-point of a Mars/Jupiter trine and is in good aspect to both. Happiness and success. Rupert has seen off his early rivals Teddy Tail and Pip, Squeak and Wilfred. He has a fan club and his early Annuals can realise two thousand pounds. Rupert was indeed born under a lucky star.

Dogpatch, U.S.A.
Sadie Hawkins' Day
(from <u>Li'l Abner</u> cartoon by Al Capp)

A custom, apparently introduced in 1938, whereby spinsters may lawfully pursue bachelors and, if they catch them, drag them to the altar! No true Scorpio lady would baulk at this either! One who not have had to resort to such methods was **IRENE FORSYTE** (from <u>The Forsyte Saga</u> by John Galsworthy) who was born today in 1862 or 1863. (Secrets and mysteries accompany Scorpios). Scorpio women are the ones anxious mothers warn their sons against, with good reason and no success. Male Scorpios are bad enough, female Scorpios are lethal! Irene was beautiful but, like everything brushed by Scorpio, enigmatic and dangerous. She had a seductive power beyond her own control, an alluring strangeness. All men were attracted to her but it was Soames Forsyte who got her. Financial circumstances forced her to marry him but she loathed him from beginning to end. "But what have I done?" cried Soames, ignorant, poor soul, of the spiteful, unreasoning resentment of an aroused Scorpio. Scorpio's other face, its passionate devotion, is shown by Irene's love for Philip Bosinney (who, let's face it, she purloined from June Forsyte) and her single-minded devotion to his memory for the twelve years after his death until she married young Jolyon Forsyte. Their son was to get entangled with Soames' daughter by his second marriage - Fleur, another Scorpio woman.

1960, Where? - dunno. He denies it was the London sewers
Birth of **NEIL GAIMAN**,
award-winning author of graphic literature (comics)

Not just any old comics with Urghhs and Splatts padding out the minimal story line. <u>The Sandman</u> is a comics series, dovetailing writer and artists and ushering its devotees into an adult fantasy world which expects them to recognise the cultural references to Shakespeare, Marlowe, folklore, Greek mythology and Alice. 'A comic strip for intellectuals,' said Norman Mailer. The same characters recur. For instance, the Endless or Immortals - Dream (aka The Sandman), Desire, Despair, Destiny, Delirium, Destruction and Death

~ Scorpio ~

who is an adorable sort of spiritual punk whom nobody could possibly mind going off with when the time comes. As a child Gaiman's favourite game was to find somewhere inaccessible and go and read there for hours. Now he lives in an odd, rambling house of uncertain location, where he writes in a basement (what else?) room filled with books and old armchairs. He says he rarely writes anything interesting before the sun sets and rarely stays up much after sunrise. He certainly has all the dark imaginings of a fully paid up Scorpio.

NOVEMBER 11

1918, 11 a.m.
Armistice Day

Many authors have used this date in their books. The eleventh hour of the eleventh day of the eleventh month. Wild jubilation but a sombre Scorpion mood underneath. Lolly Willowes, in a novel of the same name by Sylvia Townsend Warner was doing up parcels in a London depot as her war work when she heard the cheering and hooters. She packed up and went home. The house was empty. She felt cold and sick and shook uncontrollably. The hooters rose over the noise of rejoicing with sarcastic emphasis making, she thought, the walls of the room shake. She fainted. She had 'flu. The terrible 1918 Spanish 'flu which killed as many people world-wide as the hostilities had. A Scorpio day in more ways than one.

NOVEMBER 12

1918, Winston, England
Minefield!
(from Dodo Wonders by E.F. Benson)

Dodo had a great time in London yesterday and went home today to have a second celebration. A gardener recalled a cache of fireworks purchased pre-war in the toolhouse and a display was arranged on the lawn under the direction of a convalescent gunner. Unhappily they had got damp and there was nothing but a few half-hearted sparks in clouds of dense smoke. The half-asphyxiated gunner emerged with steaming eyes, beaten, but as a last gesture, had lit the last remaining rockets and a fuse attached to a square box called a mine of which he knew nothing whatever and hoped less. He had hardly explained this when the mine went off with an explosion which rattled the windows and the rockets shot skywards and burst into showers of stars.

~ Scorpio ~

1850, 1.30 p.m., Edinburgh, Scotland
Birth of **ROBERT LOUIS STEVENSON**

Before turning to literature he practised in two Scorpion pursuits, engineering and the law. Chronic bronchitis sent him travelling in search of a better climate. He wrote for many periodicals but his first full-length work, <u>Treasure Island</u>, brought him fame. This was followed by the frightening Scorpio tale of <u>Dr. Jekyll and Mr. Hyde</u>. He also wrote poetry including the classic <u>Child's Garden of Verses</u>. Underlying even the lightest of his work is a dark skein of suffering. He had an adventurous life, a vibrant personality and many friends. Not surprising remembering his lovely gift to a little girl aggrieved at having been born on Christmas Day - a signed and sealed document handing over his own birthday to her.

> 'In consideration that Miss Annie H. Ide...was born out of all reason upon Christmas Day, and is therefore out of all justice denied the consolation and profit of a proper birthday: And considering that I have attained an age when, O, we never mention it and that I have no further use for a birthday of any description... Have transferred... to the said Annie H. Ide, all and whole my rights and privileges in the thirteenth day of November, formerly my birthday, now hereby, and henceforth; the birthday of the said Annie H. Ide, to have, hold, exercise and enjoy...'

Soon after, he died suddenly at the age of 44 in Samoa, so think on before you part with your birthday. The stars may not like it and it may be unlucky.

1888, London
High Words
(from <u>Diary of a Nobody</u> by George and Weddon Grossmith)

The Pooters prepared to give a party to celebrate their son Lupin's engagement to Daisy Mutlar. Lupin disapproved of all the arrangements and the other guests and Mr. Pooter lost his temper and said, "Lupin, allow me to tell you Miss Daisy Mutlar is not the Queen of England. I gave you credit for more wisdom than to allow yourself to be inveigled into an engagement with a woman considerably older than yourself. I advise you to think of earning your living before entangling yourself with a wife whom you will have to support and, in all probability, her brother also who appeared to be nothing but a loafer." Instead of receiving this advice in a sensible manner, Lupin jumped up and said, "If you insult the lady I am engaged to, you insult me. I will leave the house and never darken your doors again." He went out, slamming the hall door but came back for his supper and a game of Bézique.

Lucky for him **ENA SHARPLES**, harridan of Coronation Street, wasn't there. She was born today in 1899 with Sun and Jupiter in very close conjunction, which no doubt explains her success. Unless it refers to the Glad Tidings Mission of which she was the caretaker.

NOVEMBER 15

1970s, Lakeland, England
Plague!
(from Plague Dogs by Richard Adams)

The local newspaper carried an exclusive shock-horror story, revealing that although the authorities were maintaining a conspiracy of silence, two dogs had escaped from the Animal Research Station at Lawson Park near Coniston. The animals which had been playing cops-and-robbers among the local farmers' sheep and hens, escaped from the experimental pens. The reporter had discovered that at the time of the escape investigations were taking place in the laboratories into Bubonic Plague. 'This terrible killer-disease, which once decimated the London of Merry Monarch Charles II 300 years ago, has now been unknown in this country for many years past, being carried by fleas-parasites of the common rat.' Had the escaped dogs come into contact with the deadly, infected fleas? (And were their readers now in a state of sickening fright?) The whole story reeks of Scorpio on its darker side.

~ Scorpio ~

Early 1900s, U.S.A.
Cremation and Regeneration
(from <u>Daddy Long-Legs</u> by Jean Webster)

A very popular book which was made into a musical comedy. A collection of letters written by a young girl to her unknown benefactor who was paying for her college education. Today a blight fell over the literary career of Judy Abbott. She received her novel back from the publisher (30 cents due) to whom she had sent it with his reader's opinion included. 'Plot highly improbable. Characterization exaggerated. Conversation unnatural. A good deal of humour but not always in the best of taste.' "And I thought I was making a notable addition to American literature." She took it walking with her in the afternoon, "and when I came to the gas house I went in and asked the engineer if I might borrow his furnace. He politely opened the door, and with my own hands I chucked it in. I felt as though I had cremated my only child! I went to bed last night utterly dejected... but what do you think? I woke up this morning with a beautiful new plot in my head and I've been going about all day planning my characters, just as happy as I could be."

1952, England
Birth of **THEODORE FINN**
(from <u>The Lake of Darkness</u> by Ruth Rendell)

'Scorpio is metaphysics, putrefaction and death, regeneration, passion, lust and violence... <u>Scorpians</u> are magicians, astrologers, alchemists, surgeons, bondsmen and undertakers... and its card in the Tarot is Death.' How much better a <u>proper</u> writer puts it than a bumbling astrologer. Sends shivers up the spine! Finn, a central character in the book, is the Scorpio referred to and was born on the same day as the Emperor Tiberius, who wasn't the nicest of characters either. Finn was a murdering psychopath who graduated from child poltergeist to hired assassin. To him death was just a transition from one cycle of being to the next - he was doing his victims a favour by dispatching them so promptly. Miss Rendell has, as usual, chosen the right birthday. Both Sun <u>and</u> Moon were in Scorpio, poorly aspected by Pluto, which rules it. Finn got the full force of the darker side of the configuration by being born into a spooky occult hothouse. His mother was a schizophrenic and her circle was 'into' planchettes and pendulums. Finn had piercing silvery eyes, ate sparingly and lived

~ Scorpio ~

austerely - no curtains, no cooker, no furniture. He meditated daily and, apparently, levitated. He was studying to become a magus under the tutelage of Crowley, Gurdjieff and Blavatsky. He craved silence and solitude, everyone was scared of him and the Tarot card of Death came up for him at the end.

NOVEMBER 17

1915, Ohio
Ghosties and Ghoulies
(from <u>My Life and Hard Times</u> by James Thurber)

'The ghost that got into our house on the night of 17 November 1915 raised such a hullabaloo of misunderstanding that I am sorry I didn't just let it keep on walking, and go to bed.' The entire Thurber family was barking - at least, so the American humorist would have us believe. The footsteps began in the early hours and walked round the dining room table. James Thurber woke his brother Herman who had always suspected something would 'get him' in the night and could only cry "Awp" in a low hopeless tone. The footsteps stopped circling the table and started up the stairs two at a time. The brothers slammed the door shut at the top of the stairs and held it tight. The footsteps ceased and were never heard again, but Mother was awake by this time and made one of her lightning decisions. She threw a shoe through the neighbour's window and screamed for the police. Bodwell, the neighbour, had one of his attacks. ('Most everyone we knew or lived near had <u>some</u> kind of attacks.') The police came and woke up Grandpa who got the idea they were army deserters, grabbed one of their guns and let fly yelling, "Back t' the lines, ye goddam lily-livered cattle." A reporter came. Mars was in the ascendant at the time and Mars and Uranus were in opposition, both square the Sun denoting severe tension.

NOVEMBER 18

Year Unknown, England
Birthday of **HILDA RUMPOLE** nee Wystan
- She Who Must Be Obeyed (from the <u>Rumpole of the Bailey</u> series)

Daughter of C.H. Wystan a barrister. The unfortunate Horace Rumpole entered his chambers and was immediately earmarked by Hilda as a future husband. She is an ambitious lady who had hopes of grooming him to be Lord Chancellor but this came to nothing. She

~ Scorpio ~

proposed to him and the matter was concluded without him saying a word. A formidable Scorpion. Rumpole's name for her comes from Rider Haggard's novel <u>She</u>. The original was kept alive in a cave for about a thousand years and may have been Cleopatra, and <u>she</u> could very well have been a Scorpion.

1928, U.S.A.
Birth of **MICKEY MOUSE**

Today marks his first appearance on screen in the title role of <u>Steamboat Willie</u>, an experimental sound cartoon, brain-child of Walt Disney. A regular guy and survivor, not only to our own day but beyond if the author **J.G. BALLARD** (himself a Scorpio born November 15, 1930) is to be believed. <u>Hello America</u> is set in 2114 A.D. and today finds the narrator Wayne and his party at <u>The Desert Inn</u> in Las Vegas which has reverted to the wild and is populated by exotic escapees from the Californian zoos. A special film show is put on for them. As they sit on the terrace a sudden flare of light streams across the lake, an intense beam as wide as a runway. 'A dozen rainbows shimmered in the night air then came together to form an immense 3-dimensional figure as high as a skyscraper. We all stared at the creature, a sprightly animal from an old nursery wallpaper with a round smiling face, ears sticking up like black fans and a button nose.' MICKEY MOUSE!

NOVEMBER
19

1890/1900, Sussex
More Vampires!
(from <u>The Adventure of the Sussex Vampires</u> by Arthur Conan Doyle)

Today Sherlock Holmes became involved in a case of vampirism. It's a famous tale, not least because of Holmes's throwaway line concerning the giant rat of Sumatra: "<u>a story for which the world is not yet prepared!</u>" "But what do we know about vampires?" Holmes asked, intrigued. "Anything is better than stagnation, but really we seem to have been switched on to a Grimm's fairy tale." Watson took down the great index volume and Holmes read aloud, slowly and lovingly, the record of old cases, mixed with the accumulated information of a lifetime. "Voyage of the <u>Gloria Scott.</u> That was a bad business. I have some recollection that you made a record of it Watson, I was unable to congratulate you upon the result. Victor Lynch, forger. Venamous lizard or gila. Remarkable case that! Vittoria, the circus belle. Vanderbilt and the Yeggman. Vipers, Vogir, the Hammersmith

Wonder. Hullo! Hullo! Good old index. You can't beat it. Listen to this, Watson. Vampirism in Hungary. And again, Vampires in Transylvania." He turned over the pages with eagerness, but after a short intent perusal he threw down the book with a snarl of disappointment. "Rubbish, Watson, rubbish! What have we to do with walking corpses who can only be held in their graves by stakes driven through their hearts? It's pure lunacy." But there was more to the matter than met the eye.

NOVEMBER 20

1901, 7.15 p.m., Mapledurham
Birth of **FLEUR FORSYTE**
(from The Forsyte Saga by John Galsworthy)

Another Scorpion beauty but not a terribly nice girl. She went for what she wanted, always, and got everything she wanted except the man. Moreover, she was to be, literally, the death of her father, Soames Forsyte. She had to be centre of the stage, she had to know every celebrity. She was publicly called a snob which led to slander proceedings and her ostracism from Society. She was a schemer, an intriguer, a sensation-seeker and pursuer of clandestine affaires and entanglements. She brought trouble and tragedy wherever she went. In a Scorpion tantrum of blinding jealousy she accidentally set Soames's house on fire but was saved by him at the cost of his own life when she deliberately tried to commit suicide in the flames. Final glimpses show she had learned to conceal her turbulent emotions under a cynical Jazz Age mask. Scorpio is good at that.

NOVEMBER 21

1964, U.S.A.
Birth of **DANA KATHERINE SCULLY**, FBI Agent
(from TV's The X-Files by Chris Carter)

Dana's birthday has also been given as February 23, 1964, the same as fellow agent Jack Willis, with whom she has had a relationship, but Scorpio fits the beautiful, intelligent Dana better. Her investigative powers, degree in physics and forensic expertise are a credit to the sign. Her experiences, professional and private, have been hair-raising. Her sister was shot dead, perhaps in mistake for her. She has, unknown to herself, had an electrode implant and was also impregnated without her knowledge or consent. Her relationship

~ Scorpio ~

with fellow agent Fox Mulder (see October 13) is intriguing. They were assigned to work together because she was the one with the conventional scientific approach and he was the way-outer. She was supposed to keep tabs on him but she became more and more open-minded and interested in his theories.

1965, Martha's Vineyard
Birth of **SAMANTHA ANN MULDER**
(from TV's <u>The X-Files</u> by Chris Carter)

Apparently abducted by aliens when eight and not seen since, which is Scorpionic enough for anyone, her disappearance (see November 27) led her brother into his investigations into the Great Unknown. Strange that two characters in a series should have the same birthday? Yes, and a warning to Bookworm Astrologers. Chris Carter's wife was born on November 21, and he uses the date frequently - 11/21 as the Americans put it - not only for birthdays but as the time phone calls are recorded, autopsies begun etc. Still, they're all Scorpio in character, so perhaps there <u>is</u> something Out There directing all this!

NOVEMBER
22

1938(?), Germany
Nazi Thugs!
(from <u>The Adventures of Hiram Holliday</u> by Paul Gallico)

For the thousandth time Hiram Holliday walked the narrow stone cell and racked his tired brain for a thought, a glimmer, a hope of escape. It was the night of November 22. On the morning of November 23, less than 12 hours away, Hermann Weide, Communist, German citizen, convicted of high treason, was to be executed. And HE was Hermann Weide. His identity as Hiram Holliday had been taken from him. He didn't know for certain what had become of it but he half suspected the truth. There was not the slightest chance of regaining it. Once, he had tried to remove the bandages from his head and he had been beaten with sections of rubber hose. Since then the bandages, which completely covered his features, had remained in place. It was obvious why. On no account was anyone to recognise him. They would still be on his head when it rolled on to the ground in the prison yard in the morning. A chilling end to Scorpio.

~ Scorpio ~ Sagittarius ~

1819, Warwickshire
Birth of **GEORGE ELIOT**, author

Mary Ann Evans was handicapped in the Glamourpuss Stakes by actually looking like a horse! But it proved she was a Sagittarian. We can't all be beautiful and brainy, and Mary Ann chose the brains. She was more or less obliged to adopt a masculine pen-name to become one of the greats of Eng. Lit. <u>Middlemarch</u> is one of the few English novels written for grown-up people according to Virginia Woolf. Other classics are <u>The Mill on the Floss</u>, <u>Adam Bede</u> and <u>Scenes of Clerical Life</u>. Early in life she held strict religious views and became a convert to Evangelicalism. She then questioned this and joined an intellectual circle of free-thinkers but was always strongly influenced by religious concepts. Like many women of her time whose lives were circumscribed it was the men in her life who were as indicative of her Sun sign as she was, perhaps more so. Clergymen, editors and publishers comprised many of her male friends and acquaintances. Nevertheless, she had an unusual degree of freedom and travelled widely. German was her second language. She translated books and was assistant editor of the <u>Westminster Review</u>. She also defied convention for 24 years by living with a married man although, somehow, in an aura of the utmost priggishness and without affecting Queen Victoria's high opinion of her!

NOVEMBER
23

1638 and 1988, Windsor
Dr. Who and the Golden Arrow
(from <u>Silver Nemesis</u> by Kevin Clarke)

This adventure concerns a statue of a man carrying a bow and arrow - Sagittarius' own symbol - made of a living metal called vallidium by the evil 17th century sorceress Lady Peinforte. She was thwarted by the doctor who sent the statue, but not the bow and arrow, into space in an asteroid. The statue had to be complete before it could be activated. Since 1638 the asteroid had been approaching the earth at 25 year intervals, leaving disaster in its wake. Today, in 1988, it crashlanded in the grounds of Windsor Castle exact to the moment of its launching (although this makes no allowance for the eleven day discrepancy when the Julian calendar was updated in 1752 but, under the aegis of Sagittarius, sign of space and travel, what does that matter?) Then it's a rather confused mishmash of the doctor, Lady Peinforte, Nazis, Cybermen and H.M. the Queen in the distance plus corgis. The first episode of Dr. Who was also aired today in 1963, with the Sun in Sagittarius and Moon in eccentric Aquarius.

~ Scorpio ~ Sagittarius ~

1849, England
Birth of **FRANCES HODGSON BURNETT**, author

She had a free-and-easy, adventurous life. She came from a poor but
once wealthy family who emigrated to the United States and lived in
a log cabin. A happy child and a happy successful adult despite two
broken marriages. She wrote Little Lord Fauntleroy, he of the velvet
suits, which was rapturously received and, probably dearer to the
hearts of most of us, The Secret Garden. But they were only the top
two of her many children's book. She adored being in Society and was
an awful snob but did publishing a great service when she got the
copyright laws amended following the pirating of Fauntleroy on the
London stage. She had many interests ranging from gardens to
spiritualism and is altogether a jolly good catch for Sagittarius.

1805, New Style, Russia
Royal Review
(from War and Peace by Leo Tolstoy)

Today there was a ceremonial march past of the Russian and Austrian
troops before their respective Emperors. Rostov on his horse Bedouin
rode at the rear of his squadron, alone. Before reaching his Emperor,
Rostov, a splendid horseman, spurred Bedouin and put him to the
showy trot which the animal indulged in when excited. 'Bending his
foaming muzzle to his chest, his tail extended, Bedouin, as if also
conscious of the Emperor's eye upon him, passed splendidly, lifting his
feet with a high and graceful action as if flying through the air
without touching the ground.' (And if that isn't Sagittarius, what is?)
'Rostov himself, his legs well back and his stomach drawn in and
feeling himself one with his horse, rode past the Emperor with a
frowning but blissful face, "like a vewy devil", as Denisov expressed it.
"Fine fellows, the Pavlograds!" remarked the Emperor. "My God, how
happy I should be if her ordered me to leap into the fire this instant!"
thought Rostov.

~ Sagittarius ~

NOVEMBER 26

All in the 1800s, England
A Sagittarian Miscellany

In the Court & Social Register, Elizabeth Bennet danced with the high-and-mighty Fitzwilliam Darcy at the ball at Netherfield Park (Pride and Prejudice by Jane Austen). The Church is represented by the curate who preached the very good sermon heard today by Mr. Pooter 'although his appearance is not so impressive as the dear old Vicar's' (The Diary of a Nobody by George and Weedon Grossmith). On the legal scene Mr. Gilmore, the Fairlie family lawyer, had to draw up the altered marriage settlement which disinherited the very persons whom Laura Fairlie had informed him she was most anxious to benefit in the event of her dying before her husband-to-be, Sir Percival Glyde. 'I had no choice. Another lawyer would have drawn up the deed if I had refused to undertake it (but) no daughter of mine should have married any man alive under such a settlement as I was compelled to make for Laura Fairlie.' All the same, he had just drawn up her death warrant (The Woman in White by Wilkie Collins).

NOVEMBER 27

1973, Martha's Vineyard
The Lady Vanishes
(from TV's The X-Files by Chris Carter)

FBI Agent Fox Mulder's sister, Samantha Ann (see November 21), simply and inexplicably disappeared in a flash of blinding light from the family home. She was eight and Fox was twelve. He was paralysed temporarily and unable to do anything to help her. It was this apparent alien abduction which led Mulder to start searching for explanations of UFOs and strange happenings. Hypnotic regression revealed that he heard a voice telling him that his sister would not be harmed and she would be returned some day, but that day hasn't come yet. Alien abductions must be the ultimate in Sagittarian long-distance travel.

~ Sagittarius ~

1757, London
Birth of **WILLIAM BLAKE**, poet, painter and visionary

At 8 years of age he saw a treeful of angels on Peckham Rye. Had no schooling because he could not stand discipline, so taught himself reading and drawing and was apprenticed to an engraver. Married a poor girl and taught her to read, write and draw. They were devoted, her only complaint being - "I have very little of Mr. Blake's company. He is always in Paradise." An intellectual cult has grown up around his Prophetic Books and scriptural drawings which are crammed with mysticism and symbolism. Just before he died he burst out singing of the things he saw in heaven. Amongst them must have been that Tiger! Tiger! Burning bright! Jerusalem is pure Sagittariana:

> Bring me my bow of burning gold!
> Bring me my arrows of desire!

1774, Keswick
Birth of **JUDITH PARIS** (nee HERRIES)
(from The Herries Chronicles by Hugh Walpole)

She was the daughter of two vagabonds - old 'Rogue' Herries himself, the patriarch of the family, and his second wife, a gypsy/actress. Judith considered herself half a vagrant, the finer, truer, more happy and fortunate half. It had been her dearest wish to get away from the proper, managing, materialist Herries family and go and live in the hills as her mother had, but it stayed a dream. She had lovely auburn hair and seemed to grow younger with age. Sagittarians should be tall but she was rather small, however, she was active, didn't know fatigue and 'rode a horse like a commander'. And she was sociable, attending all the balls, parties and hunts in the neighbourhood. She loved bright colours. Could be tempestuous and was rather dominating and too fond of ruling the roost but she was greatly loved. Today in 1874 she was 100 years old. There was a family lunch, a presentation, speeches and cheers. She had a lovely day and was full of vigour and enthusiasm but she died that night in her sleep while the family was dancing down below. Just as she would have wanted.

~ Sagittarius ~

NOVEMBER 29

1661, Old Style/December 9 New Style, Somerset
Birth of **JOHN RIDD**
(from Lorna Doone by R.D. Blackmore)

A giant of a man, a renowned wrestler, an Exmoor legend. A real, old-time hero of simple faith and sheer goodness. Today in 1673 on his twelfth birthday he was sent for at his school in Tiverton to come home. His father had been murdered by the outlawed Doones. On the way he saw, although he didn't know it, his future wife, Lorna Doone '...a little girl, dark-haired and very wonderful.' She was really Lady Lorna Dugal but she was due to see her family killed by the Doones and to be adopted by them as a future bride for the ghastly Carver. Years later John Ridd rescued her, restored her to her estates and put paid to the Doones once and for all and, of course, married her. His character was said to have been based upon a real person.

NOVEMBER 30

1835, U.S.A.
Birth of **MARK TWAIN**, author

His real name was Samuel Clemens. He wrote the famous Tom Sawyer and The Adventures of Huckleberry Finn, and was the original Sagittarian homespun philosopher and humorist. ('Cauliflower is nothing but cabbage with a college education'.) He was a printer's apprentice and reporter before becoming a river boat pilot on the Mississippi. That was where he got his pen-name, from the linesman's call when taking soundings. The Celebrated Jumping Frog of Calveras City established him as a writer. He was an unwearied gambler and, although his last years were clouded by financial worries, he was a jolly cove with a huge appetite for living. It was he who said that the reports of his death were greatly exaggerated and recommended that we live in such a manner that, when we come to die, even the undertaker will be sorry.

Today's boys are more likely to read the English **GEOFFREY HOUSEHOLD** born today in 1900, author of Rogue Male.

~ Sagittarius ~

1911, 8.00 p.m., Chicago
Birth of **TARZAN** (Lord Graystoke)
(from <u>Tarzan of the Apes</u> by Edgar Rice Burroughs)

Tarzan was the creation of Edgar Rice Burroughs and we have it on
the authority of Burrough's biography that this was Tarzan's actual
'birthday'. Tarzan was, in fact, the aristocratic Lord Graystoke no less
but he got mislaid as a baby in Africa and was raised by giant apes
which closed the Court of St. James to him, temporarily. However, he
quickly adapted to another facet of Sagittarius and can safely be
catalogued as the outdoor type, swinging from trees and bonding with
animals.

c.1910, England
A Successful Ball
(from <u>Dodo II</u> by E.F. Benson)

A fine time for jollity when Sagittarius holds sway. As a grand finale
to Dodo's enjoyable ball, all the guests danced though the house from
cellar to garret, led by a section of the band.

> 'They waltzed though the drawing-rooms and dining-
> room, and up the stairs, and through Dodo's bedroom...
> into cul-de-sacs, and impenetrable servants' rooms. And
> somehow it was Dodo all the time who inspired these
> childish orgies, those near her saw her, those behind
> danced wildly after her to catch sight of her. There was
> no accounting for it, except in the fact that while she was
> enjoying herself so enormously, it was impossible not to
> enjoy too.'

They went twice round the huge kitchen where Dodo ordered the chef
to join in, which he did, bringing up the rear with the first kitchen
maid.

1801, Germany
Birth of **KARL BAEDEKER**, publisher

He published famous guide books which crop up again and again in novels of the 19th and early 20th century. In fact 'Baedeker' became a synonym for guide book and it's only fitting that the gentleman should have been born under much-travelled Sagittarius. He started the starring system marking with one or more stars places of interest. (He can't be blamed for the disappointment often caused by this often misused system today!) To be fair to Scorpio (for a change!), he did have five planets in that pre-eminent sign of research.

1857, Russian Ukraine
Birth of **JOSEPH CONRAD**

Another far-flung Sagittarian author. Whether the date is Old or New Style, he was an Archer with his sights set on far horizons. He went to sea as a sailor and his experiences provided much of the material for his later, successful novels. English was his third language but he is regarded as one of the greatest English novelists of modern times.

1835, England
Birth of **SAMUEL BUTLER**, author

He was the son of a clergyman and the grandson of a Bishop and was intended for the Church himself. So he had the right Sagittarian background. However, religious doubts estranged him from his father and he emigrated as far away as possible - New Zealand - where he sheep farmed for five years before returning. His best known book is Erewhon (Nowhere spelt backwards), a mythical land cut off from the outside world by mountains. Its inhabitants were of great beauty and treated ugliness, disease and poverty as enemies - which we could accept today - but went on to destroy all machinery because they saw it as getting too powerful which we couldn't. He also wrote The Way of All Flesh which contains the couplet, 'Tis better to have loved and lost, Than never to have lost at all - a cheering motto for the heartbroken.

~ Sagittarius ~

Late 1860s, Space
Cosmic Exploration
(from <u>Journey to the Moon</u> by Jules Verne)

On December 1 at 13 minutes and 20 seconds before 11 p.m., a projectile was launched at the Moon from Florida (a forerunner of things to come). It was an aluminium shell, 108" diameter with sides a foot thick, weighing 19,250 lbs. The cannon which launched it was cast iron 900 feet long, the charge was 400,000 lbs of guncotton. The journey was calculated to take four days. On board were two dogs and three men. Early today they saw 'the Queen of the Night' through the portholes and greeted her with a confident and joyous Hurrah! The Moon was advancing majestically across the starry firmament and in a few more degrees would reach the exact point where the projectile was to meet her. Then they realised they would not be able to land on the Moon. The meteor they had encountered on the way had deflected them from their course. Never mind! They went around it and back again, which wasn't bad (see December 12).

1807, 7.30 p.m., Keswick
Birth of **JOHN HERRIES**
(from <u>The Herries Chronicles</u> by Hugh Walpole)

He was the son of Francis and Jennifer Herries, and another Sagittarian gent. He was fair, slim, handsome, courteous and an aristocrat in the best sense of the word. The following words describe perfectly his Leo ascendant and Piscean Moon:

'He walked with his head up as though he were made to
rule the earth. But he was too gentle and unselfish to
wish to rule anyone.'

He had 'beautiful natural manners and was over-aware of the feelings of others. He loved to be liked, hated to be disapproved of... was eager to heal a quarrel, wretched in an atmosphere of unfriendliness.' He wasn't a dandy but always wore fine, exquisitely clean and well-fitting clothes. Even the man who shot him dead saw his air of high breeding.

~ Sagittarius ~

1913, Leeds
Votes for Women!
(from Lost Empires by J.B. Priestley)

Mrs. Foster-Jones, the suffragette leader, known to be wanted by the police everywhere, made a triumphant appearance from behind a screen on a public platform in Leeds, made a short speech and then - vanished into thin air. At five minutes to nine p.m. there she was, emerging from behind the screen and coming down the central steps with the whole place in an uproar, at five minutes past nine she said farewell, went behind the screen and disappeared, leaving the hastily-summoned police baffled. It wasn't magic, it was a trick pulled by the master illusionist, Nick Ollanton (Ganga Dun) at the Leeds Empire. And why has this episode made the Sagittarius slot? Because it got young Richard Herncastle, Ollanton's nephew and assistant, thinking for the first time about women's rights. He was greatly impressed by Mrs. Foster-Jones and came to the conclusion that 'given equal opportunities, women <u>are better than ordinary men</u>, only extraordinary men can rise to their level.' It's one of the nicest things about Sagittarian men. They look on women as comrades, best mates, Good Companions (to quote Priestley again) and treat them accordingly.

1911, New Zealand
Birth of **MEGHANN CLEARY**
(from The Thorn Birds by Colleen McCullough)

This created a furore when first published and televised. Meghann was stunningly beautiful with red-gold hair and eyes like jewels. She rode well, side saddle or astride. Australasia 'comes under' Sagittarius and the sign certainly fits that sports-mad gambling country of the wide open spaces, but Meghann's life was also bound to the Church, another manifestation of the sign. She was brought up as a Catholic, attended a convent school and fell in love, when she was ten, with Father Ralph de Bricassart. Of course they couldn't marry but she had a child by him who was passed off as her husband's. This son, out of the blue and not knowing his parentage, told her he was determined to become a priest and did. So we can't escape our destiny or genes (same thing really).

~ *Sagittarius* ~

DECEMBER 9

1873, England
Birth of **LAURA** ('Lolly') **WILLOWES**
(from <u>Lolly Willowes</u> by Sylvia Townsend Warner)

Her father was in love with her from the first moment he set eyes on her. "Oh, the fine little lady!" he cried out when she was shown to him. She grew up to be of middle height with a rather thin and pointed face. 'Her skin was brown, inclining to sallowness; it seemed browner still by contrast with her eyes, which were large, set wide apart, and of that shade of grey which inclines neither to blue nor green, but seems a much diluted black. Such eyes are rare in any face, and rarer still in conjunction with a brown colouring. In Laura's case the effect was too startling to be agreeable.' Sylvia Townsend Warner got her birthday right. She was a true Sagittarian country girl, roving the countryside looking for herbs and simples 'and many were the washes and decoctions that she made from sweet-gale, water purslane, cowslips and the roots of succory.' She wrote a little book called <u>Health by the Wayside</u> extolling the use of the old simples and herbs. **SYLVIA TOWNSEND WARNER**'s own birthday was December 6.

DECEMBER 10

1911, England
Birth of **DICK BARTON**, Special Agent

Radio programme hero of yore, a forerunner of all those Supermen. Jupiter entered Sagittarius, its own sign, where it is exceptionally happy and successful, during the early hours of the day, a fine augury.

1830, Amherst, Massachusetts
Birth of **EMILY DICKINSON**

The antithesis of Dick Barton, she was a reclusive poet, whose travel and adventures were cerebral not physical and that's Sagittarian too. She lived in a world of her own imagination, yet that world contained enough excitements to satisfy even Dick. She wrote of volcanoes, shipwrecks, storms and, always, death and immortality:

~ Sagittarius ~

Because I could not stop for Death,
He kindly stopped for me;
The carriage held but just ourselves
And Immortality...

DECEMBER 11

17??, Russia
Arctic Exploration
(from <u>Frankenstein</u> by Mary Shelley)

This is a picture of exploring Sagittarius in snow boats and ear muffs! The explorer, Captain Walton, had planned his Arctic exploration since boyhood. It had been his dream to get to the North Pacific Ocean through the seas which surround the North Pole. He had read everything he could lay hands on and commenced his apprenticeship 'by inuring my body to hardship. I accompanied the whale-fishers on several expeditions to the North Sea. I voluntarily endured cold, famine, thirst and want of sleep. I often worked harder than the common sailors during the day and devoted my nights to the study of mathematics, the theory of medicine and those branches of physical science from which a naval adventurer might derive the greatest practical advantage...' but none of this had prepared him on his hazardous journey for the sight of Frankenstein's monster on a dog sledge on the ice floes and then for rescuing Frankenstein himself who was in pursuit of his evil creation from a similar sledge and hearing his incredible tale. His sole purpose, he told Captain Walton, was to follow and kill 'the daemon'.

DECEMBER 12

Late 1860s, 1.17 a.m., Pacific Ocean, 27°7'N 41°37'W
Return of the Wanderers
(from <u>Journey to the Moon</u> by Jules Verne)

The <u>Susquehanna</u> of the U.S. Navy was taking soundings here when the crew members on deck heard an unfamiliar whistling sound in the distance. They thought at first this was caused by some steam escaping but when they looked up realised the noise was coming from the highest regions of the air. The whistling reached a frightening intensity and there suddenly appeared a huge meteor, heated to incandescence by the speed of its fall and by atmosphere friction. This fiery mass grew larger before their eyes and fell with a thunderous

~ Sagittarius ~

roar on the corvette's bowsprit, breaking it off close to the stem, and plunging into the sea with a deafening splash. A few feet nearer and the <u>Susquehanna</u> would have foundered with all hands. The Captain appeared, half dressed, in the little forecastle where all his officers had hurriedly assembled, demanding to know what had happened. 'And the midshipman, appointing himself, as it were, the spokesman of the ship, cried; "Captain, it's <u>them</u>! They've come back!" <u>Them</u> and <u>they</u> were, of course, the intrepid astronauts for whom the civilised world had been watching out for days. We met them setting out on December 5.

DECEMBER 13

1906, 2.00 a.m., Philippolis, South Africa
Birth of **SIR LAURENS VAN DER POST**

Usually referred to as the Prince of Wales' guru. Well, the original Archer, the Centaur Chiron, was a wise teacher, philosopher, healer and friend, which gives Sagittarians their enviable and noble reputations. Certainly Sir Laurens was a Sagittarian writer, notching up many works of travel, anthropology and adventure such as <u>The Lost World of the Kalahari</u>, <u>Flamingo Feather</u>, <u>The Heart of the Hunter</u> and <u>A Far-Off Place</u> - all Sagittarian titles. He believed in the therapy of wilderness and solitude and that our survival depends on going back to Nature. He had strange mystical experiences when in deserts. He was the 13th of 15 children, his parents were VIPs and he was brought up by a pure African nurse who taught him her (now extinct) tribe's legends. His Jupiter was conjunct Neptune in Cancer, not unique to him alone, but they were together on his mid-heaven, indicative of a dreamer, mystic and idealist - given half a chance.

1915, California
Birth of **ROSS MACDONALD**

He had several pen-names but his real name was Kenneth Millar, and he was married to popular fellow crime writer Margaret Millar. His private detective hero was Lew Archer (note the Archer!), whom he modelled on himself. He wasn't Archer exactly, but Archer was him, he said. The hardboiled Archer matured throughout his career (1949 - mid 1970s), developing a conscience and solving complex puzzles with a kick at the end. Critics rate Macdonald a better novelist than Chandler or Dashiell Hammett.

~ Sagittarius ~

1861, Windsor
Death of Prince Albert
(from <u>The Houses in Between</u> by Howard Spring)

The death was recorded in her diary by Sarah Rainborough who had been present at the age of three at the Great Exhibition in the Crystal Palace which was the brain child of the Consort. She had just returned from a walk in the woods today when a caller told her the news. It shook her deeply because he had been a key figure in that splendid memory in May when she held her father's hand and saw the flags flying and the flowers and the flashing crystal of the Palace. 'It was only of the moment that I had been conscious then and that I was conscious of now as it recreated itself in my memory: the Prince walking amid all this splendour, holding a little girl by the hand, and the Queen holding a little boy. She was in pink and silver, and now she would be in black.' She stayed in black for the rest of her long life and never quite forgave the future George VI for being born on this day in 1895. The Queen would have been gratified to know that the stars were in sympathy with her. The Sun on that fatal day in 1861 was opposed by Uranus and squared by Jupiter, Saturn and Neptune - shock, hysteria, loss, grief, despair, tears...

1891, Guildford
Birth of **JONATHAN** (JONAH) **MANSEL**
(from <u>Jonah & Co</u> by Dornford Yates)

Jonah features strongly in the humorous 'Berry' books by Dornford Yates and also that author's straight thriller yarns like <u>Perishable Goods</u> (once recommended 'unreservedly' by Dashiell Hammett). Captain Mansel had served in World War I and was left with a DSO and a slight limp. He was a sportsman, an officer and a gentleman. Even the irreverent Berry (Bertram Pleydell) didn't bait him much. Indeed, he obviously admired him for his intelligence work in the murky world of espionage and his bravery under fire. "When Jonah takes his coat off, it's time to go home," he said. They were cousins. The Pleydell clan was very inter-related, very wealthy, very grand, very sure of itself and very Sagittarian. It is this snobbish, England-for-the-English attitude (enthusiastically shared by its creator) which

~ Sagittarius ~

alienates many people but fans are able to swallow this and have a stunningly good read in consequence. Jonah is a superb driver, never far from his Rolls-Royce and the edge-of-the-seat car chases, a feature of Dornford Yates's books, impressed no less a person than Ian Fleming. So that's a taste of Jonah, Sagittarian, "King by name and nature," said the gypsy, wisely.

DECEMBER 16

1775, 11.45 p.m., Steventon, Hampshire
Birth of **JANE AUSTEN**, author

Whatever we've said about Miss Austen's ignorance of the zodiac and her confusion over dates, she was and is unsurpassable. She was a sprightly brunette, a clergyman's daughter and the ornament of a large, happy, devoted family. And what tit-bit does she offer for today, her birthday? It has to be from <u>Pride and Prejudice</u> which she must have thoroughly enjoyed writing and it has to feature the appalling Reverend Mr. Collins who was under the patronage of the equally appalling Lady Catherine de Bourgh. On his first visit to Longbourn on November 18, Mr. Collins had proposed to Elizabeth Bennet and been rejected, then to Elizabeth's friend Charlotte Lucas who had accepted. He had reported back to Lady Catherine for permission to proceed and it was probably today that he returned to make the nuptial arrangements. Elizabeth could only wonder at Charlotte's decision but Charlotte herself was tolerably composed. Mr. Collins, to be sure, was neither sensible nor agreeable and his society was irksome, but without thinking highly of either men or matrimony, marriage had always been Charlotte's object. It was the only honourable provision for well-educated young women of small fortune and, however uncertain of giving happiness, must be their pleasantest preservative from want. This was presumably Jane's philosophy for the majority of females. She herself never married although she had her chances and on one occasion had, apparently, 'cut and run for it'.

DECEMBER 17

1843, London
Publication of <u>A Christmas Carol</u> by Charles Dickens

A heart-warming tale issued just in time for Christmas. Among the set pieces is the Fezziwigs' Christmas Eve dance recalled by the Ghost of Christmas Past. This was a jolly, thumpingly high-spirited, Jovian

~ Sagittarius ~

knees-up, held at the office of the youthful Scrooge's employer with cold roast, boiled cod, mincepies, negus and beer, forfeits and dancing. Such dancing too, accompanied by a fiddler with a pot of porter especially provided. Twenty couples at once; hands half round and back again all the other way; down the middle and up again; round and round. Mrs Fezziwig - one vast substantial smile - the three lovely Miss Fezziwigs and, of course, the apprentice Ebenezer Scrooge, before he became a solitary old miser.

It's the season for parties, and another fictitious dance was held in England today in 1920 (from <u>Invitation to the Waltz</u> by Rosamond Lehmann). This was a very grand, coming-out ball for Marigold, daughter of Sir John and Lady Spencer, and shows Jupiter at its most formal and aristocratic. The parquet floor stretched out like yellow ice, huge white chrysanthemums were massed around the green marble pillars, footmen in green with gilt buttons and upper-crust young men in hunting coats (Jupiter!) graced the scene. As for Marigold, her frock of cream spotted net with a sash of water-green satin made other frocks look 'insipid, commonplace, unenterprising'.

DECEMBER
18

1929, London
Birth of **NICHOLAS WILLOW**
(from <u>Carrie's War</u> by Nina Bawden)

In 1939 Nick and his sister Carrie were evacuated to Wales and this story is about what happened to them. Nina Bawden, a well-known children's author, was herself evacuated to the Principality so had first-hand experience. Nick doesn't do too well as a Sagittarian - he got sick when travelling but that was probably because he ate too much first (greed is also linked with Sagittarius). Apart from that, he had a gift for being happy, bounced back after setbacks and was very affectionate. He knew how to deal with grown-ups and they liked him very much. Well, so did Carrie, although she called him a greedy pig!

~ Sagittarius ~

Early 1920s, London
Who Wants to be a Millionaire?
(from <u>The Amazing Quest of Mr. Ernest Bliss</u>
by E. Phillips Oppenheim)

E. Phillips Oppenheim was a tremendously popular author in his day. He specialised in sophisticated novels of high life, lightweight but entertaining. Ernest Bliss was a young, dissipated millionaire who today went to see a doctor because of general under-the-weather-ness. The doctor brusquely told him that what he wanted was a spell of hard work and they made a bet that Bliss could not cut adrift from this life of pleasure and idleness and, starting out with only five pounds in his pocket and accepting help from no one, earn his living for a year. (Sagittarians need a quest to keep them optimistic.) He won and in so doing got an entirely new perspective on life, did a lot of good, regained his health and acquired a charming wife.

1935, England
The Box is Opened
(from <u>The Box of Delights</u> by John Masefield)

Today Kay Harker opened the Box of Delights which had been given to him yesterday by the old Punch & Judy man. It was magical of course. Inside was an open book, the leaves all beautifully illuminated; it gave the effect of staring into a wood. It was full of life, light and sound... birdsong and bells and riding towards him was an antlered man - Herne the Hunter! Before he knew it, Kay was in Windsor Great Park with the mighty Herne. Traditionally Herne is the ghost of a royal huntsman but he was known and worshipped long before kings came to Windsor as a Celtic god. He has a stag's antlers growing from his brow, rides a black horse and is attended by a pack of baying hounds. A Sagittarian as near as dammit! There follows thrills a-plenty in this exciting classic adventure story for children which ends happily on Christmas Eve with evil defeated and goodness triumphant. Not only was the Sun in that Box of Delights sign, Sagittarius, but Jupiter was as well. To Jupiter, this is like being at home and it positively radiates expansiveness and geniality.

~ Sagittarius ~

1872, 8.59 p.m., London
A Wager Won
(from <u>Around the World in Eighty Days</u> by Jules Verne)

This is the day that Phileas Fogg's wager would be lost or won. He won with a mere second to spare and only because he had gained a day by travelling constantly eastwards. Had he undertaken to encircle the globe in a westerly direction he would have lost a day. He won £20,000 but had spent £19,000 so didn't make a fortune. He gave his man, Passepartout, a present of £500 less the price of the gas which he had forgotten to turn off. 'Phileas Fogg had won his wager and had made his journey round the world in eighty days. To do this he had employed every means of conveyance - steamers, railways, carriages, yachts, trading vessels, sledges, elephant...' At noon in London the Sun had moved into Capricorn (in harmonious aspect to Jupiter for a successful conclusion) and the dashing about in all directions of Sagittarius had come to an end. Tony Hancock once set out to emulate the exploit of Mr. Fogg. With modern transport he confidently expected to do it in a day, but eighty days on still hadn't managed to get out of Grimsby!

c. 1960, Berkshire
Birth of **WILL STANTON**
(from <u>The Dark is Rising</u> by Susan Cooper)

Will had learnt that he was the last-born of the 'Old Ones', so to have his birthday at the mysterious Winter Solstice when the Sun crosses into Capricorn, sign of maturity and ancient myth, was most appropriate. On the morning of his 11th birthday he awoke to snow and the sound of delicate, rippling music. But when he looked out of the window the familiar landscape had gone. Instead there was a forest of massive trees. Yet it was the same because he could still see the River Thames in the distance. He went out into the whiteness of the new, centuries-old world where he had some frightening adventures and more of the picture was filled in for him. He experienced some of the power which he had inherited and learned what a burden it was. He found that he had to devote himself to the conflict between Light and Dark and that his birth had completed a circle which had been growing for 4000 years in every oldest part of the land, the Circle of the Old Ones. Will is the youthful Capricorn hero figure ladened with responsibilities beyond his years and having to learn hard lessons through trials and error before winning through. Susan Cooper weaves together ancient Celtic and English traditions and legends for this award-winning dramatic fantasy sequence.

DECEMBER 23

1980, Westbourne Park, London
Birth of **KATHERINE MacDOUGALL** ('Goddess')
(from <u>Kate's House</u> by Harriet Waugh)

Kate's house was, in fact, a very grand dolls' house which the 4-year old was given as a Christmas present. Instead of furnishing it slowly and carefully with little antiques as her mother had wished, Kate insisted that it was a Pakistani house lived in by several families and furnished it with dolls and furniture from Woolworth. As she played with it strange things happened in a run-down lodging house in Westbourne Park which mirrored what Kate was doing. One of the more startling was a virgin birth with a Mrs. MacDougall cast, willy-nilly, in the role of Mary. She thought she would have a boy born on the 25th but it was a girl born today. She had high hopes for this special child and prayed a lot, supposing that in future this day would be celebrated as Katherinemas. Unfortunately, Katherine's life was short. Left alone while the family went to see the Royal Wedding, she disappeared. She <u>was</u> a small baby and over in Wimbledon Kate <u>would</u> keep singing 'Your baby has gone down the plughole, your baby has gone down the plug...' Poor Katherine was a Capricorn, a sign not recommended for a good start in life. Capricorns get better as they go on. But don't take it to heart! Today, Mercury conjoined Neptune which means <u>fantasy fiction</u>.

DECEMBER 24

c. 1800, England
Birth of **BELL**
(from <u>Early Lessons</u> by Maria Edgeworth)

Generations of 19th century children were brought up on Edgeworth's <u>Early Lessons</u> and <u>Moral Tales</u>. Very Capricorn, Maria was an interesting character, herself born in the sign (January 1, 1767). Her father was an educator and she was very much under his stern

~ Capricorn ~

guidance. They wrote books like <u>The Parents' Assistant</u> and <u>Practical Education</u>, and were bulwarks of the Victorian principals of industry, honesty and thrift. Recommended toys were educational, dolls and fairy tales were out. Maria's books were in every nursery and despite their insistence on wickedness being punished and good, very meagrely, rewarded, have a strange compelling hold on the reader. She was way out though in making Bell a Capricorn. Bell was a thoroughly spoiled brat. She was idle, fretful and selfish so that nothing could make her happy not even on her birthday. Everybody in the house tried to please her and they succeeded so well that between breakfast and dinner she had only six fits of crying. She behaved so disgracefully at her party that she had to be carried off by her maid in her eighth fit of crying, excused by her mother as having "too much sensibility". Her mother was to blame. She had taught her not to value things for being pretty or useful but for being such as nobody else could procure. (There could be a smidgen of truth in the last but the rest - No!)

| DECEMBER |
| 25 |

1870s, London
Birth of **CAROL BIRD**
(from <u>The Birds' Christmas Carol</u> by Kate Douglas Wiggins)

It was also the day she was going to die, in America, after a long illness etc. She was born when the choirboys were singing, hence her name, and looked like a rose dipped in milk, a pink cherub. She was lovely in all ways and those born on Christmas Day are held to be better than the rest of us. 'People say there is everything in a good beginning.' She arranged a grand Christmas/birthday party for today and invited the poor Ruggles children. They were sent a proper printed invitation which Mrs. Ruggles framed and hung under the kitchen clock. She then proceeded to drill her brood in company manners so the name of Ruggles shouldn't be disgraced.

> "'Yes, I know it's bothersome but yer can't go int' s'ciety 'thout takin' some trouble... Miss Peory, do you speak for white or dark meat?"
>
> "I ain't perticler as ter color, anything that nobody else wants will suit me," answered Peory with her best air.'

The party turned out to be an enjoyable shambles.

~ Capricorn ~

1870, Wessex
Enduring Love
(from <u>Far from the Madding Crowd</u> by Thomas Hardy)

In the morning Bathsheba Everdene received a letter from Gabriel Oak terminating his employment with her as a bailiff. Through all her vicissitudes he had loved her devotedly. In the evening she went to his cottage. 'She put on her bonnet and cloak and went down to Oak's house just after sunset, guided on her way by the pale primrose rays of a crescent Moon a few days old.' A little later he accompanied her back up the hill. 'They spoke very little of their mutual feelings; pretty phrases and warm expressions being probably unnecessary between such tried friends. Theirs was that substantial affection which arises (if any arises at all) when the two who are thrown together begin first by knowing the rougher sides of each other's character; and not the best till further on, the romance growing up in the interstices of a mass of hard prosaic reality.' Well, that's Capricorn. No giddy, ephemeral springtime romance, but mature, long-lasting respect and devotion.

1870s, U.S.A.
More Unpretentious Capricorn Romance
(from <u>Rose in Bloom</u> by Louisa M. Alcott)

Rose's cousin Archie had proposed to her former maid, Phebe. Phebe thought his love wouldn't last and went away, telling him he must wait for a year before asking her again. Today the year was up and Archie went in search of her. '"Phebe?" Only a word but it wrought a marvellous change, for the devout expression vanished in the drawing of a breath, and the quiet face blossomed suddenly with colour, warmth and 'the light that never was on land or sea', as she turned to meet her lover, with an answering word as eloquent as his - "Archie!" Archie led her into what other eyes would describe as a dismal square with a boarded-up fountain in the middle, but to them as they walked in the pale sunshine with dead leaves dancing in the wintry wind, it was a summery Paradise.

Thinking of dead leaves, the ash is the birthday tree for today. It

~ Capricorn ~

signifies grandeur and prudence and in the language of flowers says 'With me you are safe'. An appropriate Capricornian sentiment and a good day for 'poppin' and answering the question.

DECEMBER 28

Year Unknown, North of England
Birthday of **WENDOLENE RAMSBOTHAM**
(Creator Nick Park)

Data, such as it is, gleaned from a Cheese Lovers magazine. Wendolene is a sort of girl friend of Wallace of Wallace and Gromit fame. The romance hardly qualifies as passionate or - as Wendolene dislikes cheese - to have much future, but there has been some interest shown on both sides. Wendolene is not a beauty but is a plain, no-nonsense businesswoman with her own shop, so she may very well be a Capricorn and this is indeed her correct birthday.

DECEMBER 29

1910, Shallowford, West Country
Birth of **MARY CRADDOCK**
(from <u>A Horseman Riding By</u> by R.F. Delderfield)

Paul Craddock recorded in his journal: 'About 2 p.m. on December 29th, my wife presented me with a daughter weighing 6 pounds 15 ounces; she has dark hair and blue eyes.' He then fell to considering names suitable for a girl with a tranquil and contented temperament, which was what his wife prophesied for the infant, and which proved to be true. He thought of all the Biblical names and finally hit on Mary, which had a simplicity which pleased him. Yes, Capricorns aren't the <u>frilly</u> sort. He added, 'Everyone about here describes her as a rare pretty li'l maid, and so she be!' Capricorns range from extreme plainness to great beauty, the beauty being in the bone structure, which the sign rules. In the less fortunate, the bones are exaggerated and they become what used to be called 'lantern-jawed'. Mary, in due course, married and had children of her own, becoming part of the family tree of the popular Craddock family saga.

~ Capricorn ~

1865, India
Birth of **RUDYARD KIPLING**

Sent to an English boarding school when he was six, his childhood was desperately unhappy. He bore the mental and physical scars of a feeling of abandonment and near blindness all his life. However, things looked up later when he became a journalist in India and then a celebrated novelist and poet. He drew widely on his Indian experiences in his <u>Tales of the Raj</u>. India, with its rigid caste system, is ruled by Capricorn, which also likes to see everyone in his/her proper place. Despite his great success, he was lonely and reserved and didn't have a happy life. His only son was killed in World War I. <u>Kim</u> is considered his masterpiece but <u>The Jungle Book</u>, <u>The Just So Stories</u>, and <u>Stalky & Co</u> must run it close. His standards were rigorous; flabby intellectuals he could not stand. He coined the phrase 'the White Man's Burden', and his creed was beneficent imperialism. His stirring <u>If</u>:

> If you can keep your head while all about you
> Are losing theirs and blaming it on you

was recently voted the most popular English poem, and would certainly top any Capricorn selection. But Kipling can be quoted from forever: <u>You're a better man than I am, Gunga Din</u>! <u>On the road to Mandalay</u>. <u>He travels the fastest who travels alone</u>...

1993, late at night, Yorkshire
The Great Emmerdale Disaster

An Eastern European airliner crashed on to the village killing several characters in this greatly loved 'soap'. The stars were not happily disposed. The Sun and five planets were all in Capricorn and the rest were huddled close at hand either in Scorpio or Aquarius. The only one apart was the sad waning Moon rising over the eastern horizon looking down on the destruction below.

~ Capricorn ~

1930/1931, Fenchurch St. Paul, East Anglia
Ring Out the Old
(from <u>The Nine Tailors</u> by Dorothy L. Sayers)

It was nearly midnight. The Rector gave a simple and moving little address in which he spoke of praising God not only upon strings and pipes but upon the bells of their beautiful church. The organ played the opening bars of a hymn and Hezekiah Lavender muttered, "Now lads," and the bell ringers shuffled up the belfry stair. They intended to ring in the New Year with 15,840 Kent Treble Bob Majors which would take nine hours to get through all the changes. If they succeeded it would equal the record of the College Youths in 1886. Lord Peter Wimsey, who had been co-opted as a member of the team, saw with pleasure that the landlord of the <u>Red Cow</u> had provided the 'usual' refreshments in the shape of an enormous brown jug and nine pewter tankards. The ringers advanced to their stations. Hezekiah spat on his hands, grasped the Sallie of Tailor Paul and swung the great bell over the balance. Toll-toll-toll; toll-toll-toll; toll-toll-toll... the Nine Tailors, the teller strokes that mark the passing of a man and the passing of a year. Twelve strokes more, one for each month, then silence until the clock overhead chimed midnight. "Go!" commanded Hezekiah...... and <u>you</u> can go back to the beginning on January 1 and start all over again!

~ Capricorn ~

DATA SOURCES

Unless stated, all the references to fictitious events and characters have originated from the book in question. The following are the sources for timed data of authors in The Sun Sign Reader:

Jeffrey Archer	*From him to Penny Thornton*
Jane Austen	*Isabelle Pagan q. a letter from Austen's father "born before midnight"*
Charles Baudelaire	*From birth certificate (Gauquelin, vol.6)*
Simone de Beauvoir	*From autobiography, Memories of a Dutiful Daughter (1959)*
Ray Bradbury	*Edwin Steinbrecher q. birth certificate, CST time zone confirmed*
Bertolt Brecht	*Arno Muller q. birth certificate*
Rupert Brooke	*Modern Astrology (1919) q. Brooke's mother, "between 6.30 and 7.30 p.m."*
W.S. Burroughs	*Filipe Ferreira q. birth certificate*
Chris Carter	*Sally Davis q. birth certificate*
Colette	*From birth certificate (Gauquelin, vol.6)*
Robert Graves	*From Robert Graves: His Life and Work by Martin Seymour-Smith, an astrologer and personal friend of Graves*
William Randolph Hearst	*Marion Meyer Drew pictures a chart "from him to two of my associates" (5.58 a.m.)*
Ernest Hemingway	*From Ruth Hale Oliver q. his "mother's unpublished papers"*
James Herbert	*From him to David Fisher*
Karl Marx	*Maurice Wemyss q. recorded information*
Dorothy Parker	*From The Late Mrs. Dorothy Parker by Leslie Frewin (1987), p. 5, "shortly before 10.00 p.m."*
Marcel Proust	*From birth certificate (Gauquelin, vol.6)*
Ruth Rendell	*From her to David Fisher*
Bertrand Russell	*From Passionate Skeptic by Alan Wood (1957), p. 15*
William Shatner	*From him to L. Boggs*
Robert Louis Stevenson	*From family records*
Laurens van der Post	*From him to David Fisher*
Jules Verne	*From birth certificate (Gauquelin, vol.6)*
Queen Victoria	*From official palace records*
Virginia Woolf	*Frances McEvoy q. Woolf to a colleague*
William Wordsworth	*From Memoirs of Wordsworth*

SUN SIGN TABLES (OVERLEAF)

The tables overleaf are designed to help the reader ascertain their Sun Sign. For those born 'on the cusp' (ie. around the period when the Sun changed sign), you may need to know your birth time to calculate your true Sun Sign. All the times are in Greenwich Mean Time (GMT), so if you were born during daylight saving time (roughly from late March / April to early October each year), please subtract one hour from your birth time. Those born in Great Britain between the following dates will need to subtract two hours from their birth time (Greenwich War Time):

> *4 May - 10 August 1941*
> *5 April - 9 August 1942*
> *4 April - 15 August 1943*
> *2 April - 17 September 1944*
> *2 April - 15 July 1945*

In addition, <u>all</u> those born in Great Britain between 18 February 1968 and 31 October 1971 will need to subtract one hour from their birth time to obtain GMT.

Time changes before 1981 were made at 02:00 GMT. Time changes after 1981, and changes from one hour of Daylight Saving Time to two hours (during War Time - see above), were made at 01:00 GMT.

With thanks to David Fisher and his leaflet, Time Changes in Great Britain (AA, 1991).

Sun Sign Tables (GMT)   1920-1969

	Aquarius begins JAN	Pisces begins FEB	Aries begins MAR	Taurus begins APR	Gemini begins MAY	Cancer begins JUN
1920	21 (08:04)	19 (22:29)	20 (22:00)	20 (09:39)	21 (09:20)	21 (17:38)
1921	20 (13:53)	19 (04:19)	21 (03:51)	20 (15:32)	21 (15:16)	21 (23:34)
1922	20 (19:47)	19 (10:15)	21 (09:48)	20 (21:29)	21 (21:10)	22 (05:26)
1923	21 (01:37)	19 (16:01)	21 (15:30)	21 (03:08)	22 (02:48)	22 (11:05)
1924	21 (07:32)	19 (21:55)	20 (21:23)	20 (09:01)	21 (08:43)	21 (17:02)
1925	20 (13:21)	19 (03:45)	21 (03:14)	20 (14:53)	21 (14:34)	21 (22:52)
1926	20 (19:12)	19 (09:36)	21 (09:03)	20 (20:39)	21 (20:18)	22 (04:33)
1927	21 (01:11)	19 (15:34)	21 (15:01)	21 (02:35)	22 (02:11)	22 (10:26)
1928	21 (06:56)	19 (21:18)	20 (20:43)	20 (08:16)	21 (07:54)	21 (16:09)
1929	20 (12:43)	19 (03:06)	21 (02:32)	20 (14:07)	21 (13:45)	21 (22:00)
1930	20 (18:34)	19 (09:00)	21 (08:29)	20 (20:04)	21 (19:40)	22 (03:51)
1931	21 (00:19)	19 (14:43)	21 (14:08)	21 (01:41)	22 (01:15)	22 (09:27)
1932	21 (06:07)	19 (20:29)	20 (19:55)	20 (07:29)	21 (07:07)	21 (15:22)
1933	20 (11:50)	19 (02:14)	21 (01:42)	20 (13:18)	21 (12:57)	21 (21:11)
1934	20 (17:35)	19 (07:59)	21 (07:26)	20 (18:59)	21 (18:35)	22 (02:49)
1935	20 (23:30)	19 (13:52)	21 (13:17)	21 (00:50)	22 (00:26)	22 (08:40)
1936	21 (05:15)	19 (19:35)	20 (18:59)	20 (06:31)	21 (06:07)	21 (14:22)
1937	20 (11:03)	19 (01:23)	21 (00:47)	20 (12:19)	21 (11:56)	21 (20:11)
1938	20 (16:59)	19 (07:21)	21 (06:46)	20 (18:17)	21 (17:51)	22 (02:03)
1939	20 (22:51)	19 (13:10)	21 (12:31)	20 (23:59)	21 (23:30)	22 (07:41)
1940	21 (04:43)	19 (19:02)	20 (18:23)	20 (05:52)	21 (05:26)	21 (13:38)
1941	20 (10:33)	19 (00:55)	21 (00:19)	20 (11:50)	21 (11:23)	21 (19:35)
1942	20 (16:23)	19 (06:46)	21 (06:09)	20 (17:37)	21 (17:08)	22 (01:17)
1943	20 (22:19)	19 (12:41)	21 (12:04)	20 (23:33)	21 (23:04)	22 (07:14)
1944	21 (04:06)	19 (18:27)	20 (17:49)	20 (05:18)	21 (04:51)	21 (13:03)
1945	20 (09:52)	19 (00:13)	20 (23:36)	20 (11:06)	21 (10:40)	21 (18:52)
1946	20 (15:44)	19 (06:07)	21 (05:31)	20 (17:02)	21 (16:34)	22 (00:45)
1947	20 (21:34)	19 (11:54)	21 (11:13)	20 (22:40)	21 (22:10)	22 (06:20)
1948	21 (03:22)	19 (17:40)	20 (16:58)	20 (04:25)	21 (03:58)	21 (12:11)
1949	20 (09:10)	18 (23:29)	20 (22:49)	20 (10:17)	21 (09:50)	21 (18:01)
1950	20 (14:59)	19 (05:18)	21 (04:36)	20 (16:00)	21 (15:27)	21 (23:35)
1951	20 (20:51)	19 (11:09)	21 (10:26)	20 (21:50)	21 (21:17)	22 (05:26)
1952	21 (02:38)	19 (16:55)	20 (16:11)	20 (03:35)	21 (03:03)	21 (11:12)
1953	20 (08:22)	18 (22:40)	20 (21:58)	20 (09:22)	21 (08:50)	21 (16:57)
1954	20 (14:12)	19 (04:33)	21 (03:53)	20 (15:18)	21 (14:45)	21 (22:52)
1955	20 (20:02)	19 (10:21)	21 (09:38)	20 (21:00)	21 (20:25)	22 (04:31)
1956	21 (01:48)	19 (16:06)	20 (15:23)	20 (02:47)	21 (02:15)	21 (10:25)
1957	20 (07:36)	18 (21:55)	20 (21:16)	20 (08:42)	21 (08:12)	21 (16:22)
1958	20 (13:27)	19 (03:46)	21 (03:04)	20 (14:28)	21 (13:54)	21 (22:00)
1959	20 (19:21)	19 (09:39)	21 (08:55)	20 (20:17)	21 (19:44)	22 (03:54)
1960	21 (01:13)	19 (15:29)	20 (14:44)	20 (02:06)	21 (01:34)	21 (09:44)
1961	20 (07:03)	18 (21:19)	20 (20:34)	20 (07:56)	21 (07:22)	21 (15:30)
1962	20 (12:58)	19 (03:16)	21 (02:32)	20 (13:53)	21 (13:18)	21 (21:24)
1963	20 (18:54)	19 (09:09)	21 (08:21)	20 (19:38)	21 (19:00)	22 (03:05)
1964	21 (00:41)	19 (14:56)	20 (14:08)	20 (01:26)	21 (00:50)	21 (08:56)
1965	20 (06:29)	18 (20:46)	20 (20:02)	20 (07:23)	21 (06:47)	21 (14:53)
1966	20 (12:19)	19 (02:37)	21 (01:51)	20 (13:09)	21 (12:29)	21 (20:31)
1967	20 (18:07)	19 (08:24)	21 (07:37)	20 (18:55)	21 (18:17)	22 (02:22)
1968	20 (23:52)	19 (14:08)	20 (13:22)	20 (00:41)	21 (00:05)	21 (08:12)
1969	20 (05:36)	18 (19:52)	20 (19:07)	20 (06:26)	21 (05:49)	21 (13:54)

	Leo begins JUL	Virgo begins AUG	Libra begins SEP	Scorpio begins OCT	Sagittarius begins NOV	Capricorn begins DEC
1920	23 (04:33)	23 (11:21)	23 (08:28)	23 (17:13)	22 (14:15)	22 (03:16)
1921	23 (10:28)	23 (17:13)	23 (14:19)	23 (23:02)	22 (20:05)	22 (09:08)
1922	23 (16:18)	23 (23:02)	23 (20:09)	24 (04:54)	23 (01:57)	22 (14:59)
1923	23 (22:02)	24 (04:52)	24 (02:03)	24 (10:51)	23 (07:55)	22 (20:56)
1924	23 (03:59)	23 (10:49)	23 (07:57)	23 (16:43)	22 (13:45)	22 (02:45)
1925	23 (09:47)	23 (16:34)	23 (13:43)	23 (22:29)	22 (19:33)	22 (08:35)
1926	23 (15:28)	23 (22:18)	23 (19:30)	24 (04:21)	23 (01:28)	22 (14:33)
1927	23 (21:20)	24 (04:09)	24 (01:21)	24 (10:11)	23 (07:17)	22 (20:20)
1928	23 (03:04)	23 (09:55)	23 (07:07)	23 (15:57)	22 (13:03)	22 (02:06)
1929	23 (08:53)	23 (15:41)	23 (12:52)	23 (21:41)	22 (18:48)	22 (07:54)
1930	23 (14:41)	23 (21:27)	23 (18:36)	24 (03:26)	23 (00:34)	22 (13:40)
1931	23 (20:21)	24 (03:10)	24 (00:24)	24 (09:16)	23 (06:24)	22 (19:29)
1932	23 (02:16)	23 (09:05)	23 (06:15)	23 (15:03)	22 (12:09)	22 (01:12)
1933	23 (08:04)	23 (14:50)	23 (11:59)	23 (20:47)	22 (17:53)	22 (06:57)
1934	23 (13:42)	23 (20:32)	23 (17:45)	24 (02:37)	22 (23:46)	22 (12:51)
1935	23 (19:35)	24 (02:25)	23 (23:39)	24 (08:30)	23 (05:37)	22 (18:40)
1936	23 (01:19)	23 (08:12)	23 (05:26)	23 (14:18)	22 (11:25)	22 (00:27)
1937	23 (07:07)	23 (13:58)	23 (11:13)	23 (20:05)	22 (17:15)	22 (06:20)
1938	23 (12:57)	23 (19:47)	23 (17:02)	24 (01:56)	22 (23:07)	22 (12:13)
1939	23 (18:37)	24 (01:31)	23 (22:50)	24 (07:47)	23 (05:00)	22 (18:06)
1940	23 (00:34)	23 (07:27)	23 (04:44)	23 (13:38)	22 (10:49)	21 (23:55)
1941	23 (06:27)	23 (13:16)	23 (10:30)	23 (19:24)	22 (16:36)	22 (05:43)
1942	23 (12:09)	23 (19:00)	23 (16:17)	24 (01:14)	22 (22:29)	22 (11:38)
1943	23 (18:07)	24 (00:58)	23 (22:14)	24 (07:10)	23 (04:21)	22 (17:28)
1944	22 (23:57)	23 (06:49)	23 (04:04)	23 (12:58)	22 (10:08)	21 (23:14)
1945	23 (05:46)	23 (12:36)	23 (09:51)	23 (18:46)	22 (15:57)	22 (05:05)
1946	23 (11:38)	23 (18:28)	23 (15:43)	24 (00:38)	22 (21:50)	22 (10:57)
1947	23 (17:16)	24 (00:10)	23 (21:30)	24 (06:28)	23 (03:41)	22 (16:46)
1948	22 (23:08)	23 (06:03)	23 (03:21)	23 (12:17)	22 (09:28)	21 (22:34)
1949	23 (04:56)	23 (11:48)	23 (09:05)	23 (18:02)	22 (15:14)	22 (04:21)
1950	23 (10:29)	23 (17:23)	23 (14:45)	23 (23:46)	22 (21:03)	22 (10:13)
1951	23 (16:21)	23 (23:16)	23 (20:37)	24 (05:38)	23 (02:53)	22 (16:01)
1952	22 (22:06)	23 (05:01)	23 (02:21)	23 (11:21)	22 (08:36)	21 (21:44)
1953	23 (03:50)	23 (10:43)	23 (08:03)	23 (17:03)	22 (14:20)	22 (03:31)
1954	23 (09:43)	23 (16:34)	23 (13:54)	23 (22:54)	22 (20:12)	22 (09:23)
1955	23 (15:24)	23 (22:19)	23 (19:41)	24 (04:42)	23 (02:00)	22 (15:09)
1956	22 (21:20)	23 (04:14)	23 (01:34)	23 (10:34)	22 (07:48)	21 (20:57)
1957	23 (03:15)	23 (10:07)	23 (07:25)	23 (16:24)	22 (13:39)	22 (02:48)
1958	23 (08:53)	23 (15:48)	23 (13:10)	23 (22:13)	22 (19:32)	22 (08:43)
1959	23 (14:50)	23 (21:47)	23 (19:11)	24 (04:13)	23 (01:29)	22 (14:37)
1960	22 (20:41)	23 (03:38)	23 (01:01)	23 (10:03)	22 (07:19)	21 (20:27)
1961	23 (02:25)	23 (09:21)	23 (06:45)	23 (15:49)	22 (13:08)	22 (02:19)
1962	23 (08:18)	23 (15:15)	23 (12:39)	23 (21:44)	22 (19:04)	22 (08:16)
1963	23 (13:59)	23 (20:58)	23 (18:25)	24 (03:31)	23 (00:52)	22 (14:04)
1964	22 (19:51)	23 (02:49)	23 (00:14)	23 (09:19)	22 (06:38)	21 (19:50)
1965	23 (01:46)	23 (08:40)	23 (06:02)	23 (15:06)	22 (12:26)	22 (01:39)
1966	23 (07:22)	23 (14:16)	23 (11:42)	23 (20:49)	22 (18:12)	22 (07:26)
1967	23 (13:15)	23 (20:12)	23 (17:37)	24 (02:43)	23 (00:03)	22 (13:14)
1968	22 (19:06)	23 (02:02)	22 (23:26)	23 (08:29)	22 (05:48)	21 (18:58)
1969	23 (00:46)	23 (07:41)	23 (05:05)	23 (14:10)	22 (11:31)	22 (00:44)

~ Sun Sign Tables ~

Sun Sign Tables (GMT)   1970-2019

	Aquarius begins JAN	Pisces begins FEB	Aries begins MAR	Taurus begins APR	Gemini begins MAY	Cancer begins JUN
1970	20 (11:24)	19 (01:41)	21 (00:56)	20 (12:15)	21 (11:38)	21 (19:44)
1971	20 (17:16)	19 (07:30)	21 (06:41)	20 (17:56)	21 (17:17)	22 (01:22)
1972	20 (23:01)	19 (13:14)	20 (12:24)	19 (23:39)	20 (23:01)	21 (07:08)
1973	20 (04:48)	18 (19:03)	20 (18:15)	20 (05:33)	21 (04:56)	21 (13:02)
1974	20 (10:44)	19 (00:58)	21 (00:07)	20 (11:21)	21 (10:38)	21 (18:39)
1975	20 (16:34)	19 (06:48)	21 (05:56)	20 (17:08)	21 (16:26)	22 (00:29)
1976	20 (22:25)	19 (12:37)	20 (11:46)	19 (23:00)	20 (22:20)	21 (06:25)
1977	20 (04:14)	18 (18:29)	20 (17:39)	20 (04:53)	21 (04:10)	21 (12:11)
1978	20 (10:04)	19 (00:21)	20 (23:33)	20 (10:48)	21 (10:06)	21 (18:07)
1979	20 (16:00)	19 (06:15)	21 (05:24)	20 (16:36)	21 (15:53)	21 (23:55)
1980	20 (21:47)	19 (12:01)	20 (11:10)	19 (22:23)	20 (21:42)	21 (05:45)
1981	20 (03:33)	18 (17:49)	20 (17:01)	20 (04:17)	21 (03:39)	21 (11:43)
1982	20 (09:30)	18 (23:44)	20 (22:53)	20 (10:06)	21 (09:22)	21 (17:23)
1983	20 (15:19)	19 (05:32)	21 (04:39)	20 (15:49)	21 (15:06)	21 (23:09)
1984	20 (21:08)	19 (11:18)	20 (10:25)	19 (21:37)	20 (20:56)	21 (05:01)
1985	20 (02:58)	18 (17:09)	20 (16:15)	20 (03:26)	21 (02:41)	21 (10:42)
1986	20 (08:46)	18 (22:58)	20 (22:05)	20 (09:15)	21 (08:29)	21 (16:30)
1987	20 (14:39)	19 (04:50)	21 (03:53)	20 (15:00)	21 (14:13)	21 (22:13)
1988	20 (20:25)	19 (10:35)	20 (09:38)	19 (20:46)	20 (19:58)	21 (03:58)
1989	20 (02:06)	18 (16:19)	20 (15:26)	20 (02:37)	21 (01:52)	21 (09:52)
1990	20 (08:00)	18 (22:13)	20 (21:19)	20 (08:26)	21 (07:37)	21 (15:33)
1991	20 (13:46)	19 (03:58)	21 (03:03)	20 (14:09)	21 (13:21)	21 (21:20)
1992	20 (19:30)	19 (09:41)	20 (08:47)	19 (19:57)	20 (19:12)	21 (03:14)
1993	20 (01:21)	18 (15:32)	20 (14:38)	20 (01:47)	21 (01:01)	21 (08:59)
1994	20 (07:08)	18 (21:21)	20 (20:27)	20 (07:35)	21 (06:48)	21 (14:48)
1995	20 (13:04)	19 (03:14)	21 (02:16)	20 (13:22)	21 (12:34)	21 (20:35)
1996	20 (18:56)	19 (09:04)	20 (08:05)	19 (19:11)	20 (18:23)	21 (02:23)
1997	20 (00:42)	18 (14:53)	20 (13:56)	20 (01:04)	21 (00:17)	21 (08:18)
1998	20 (06:44)	18 (20:53)	20 (19:55)	20 (06:58)	21 (06:06)	21 (14:02)
1999	20 (12:35)	19 (02:44)	21 (01:44)	20 (12:46)	21 (11:53)	21 (19:50)
2000	20 (18:22)	19 (08:31)	20 (07:32)	19 (18:36)	20 (17:47)	21 (01:46)
2001	20 (00:16)	18 (14:26)	20 (13:28)	20 (00:31)	20 (23:40)	21 (07:34)
2002	20 (06:01)	18 (20:14)	20 (19:16)	20 (06:20)	21 (05:27)	21 (13:22)
2003	20 (11:53)	19 (02:02)	21 (01:03)	20 (12:05)	21 (11:14)	21 (19:10)
2004	20 (17:40)	19 (07:48)	20 (06:49)	19 (17:52)	20 (17:00)	21 (00:57)
2005	19 (23:19)	18 (13:29)	20 (12:32)	19 (23:38)	20 (22:49)	21 (06:47)
2006	20 (05:14)	18 (19:24)	20 (18:24)	20 (05:25)	21 (04:33)	21 (12:28)
2007	20 (11:02)	19 (01:10)	21 (00:07)	20 (11:07)	21 (10:13)	21 (18:09)
2008	20 (16:45)	19 (06:51)	20 (05:48)	19 (16:50)	20 (16:00)	20 (23:59)
2009	19 (22:39)	18 (12:46)	20 (11:43)	19 (22:43)	20 (21:49)	21 (05:43)
2010	20 (04:25)	18 (18:33)	20 (17:30)	20 (04:29)	21 (03:32)	21 (11:26)
2011	20 (10:17)	19 (00:23)	20 (23:18)	20 (10:15)	21 (09:19)	21 (17:14)
2012	20 (16:09)	19 (06:15)	20 (05:11)	19 (16:08)	20 (15:11)	20 (23:04)
2013	19 (21:50)	18 (11:59)	20 (10:58)	19 (21:58)	20 (21:04)	21 (04:58)
2014	20 (03:48)	18 (17:57)	20 (16:55)	20 (03:53)	21 (02:55)	21 (10:47)
2015	20 (09:40)	18 (23:48)	20 (22:44)	20 (09:41)	21 (08:43)	21 (16:35)
2016	20 (15:23)	19 (05:30)	20 (04:27)	19 (15:27)	20 (14:34)	20 (22:31)
2017	19 (21:19)	18 (11:27)	20 (10:24)	19 (21:24)	20 (20:28)	21 (04:22)
2018	20 (03:08)	18 (17:17)	20 (16:13)	20 (03:11)	21 (02:14)	21 (10:07)
2019	20 (09:01)	18 (23:05)	20 (21:59)	20 (08:55)	21 (07:59)	21 (15:54)

~ Sun Sign Tables ~

	Leo begins JUL	Virgo begins AUG	Libra begins SEP	Scorpio begins OCT	Sagittarius begins NOV	Capricorn begins DEC
1970	23 (06:37)	23 (13:34)	23 (10:59)	23 (20:05)	22 (17:26)	22 (06:38)
1971	23 (12:17)	23 (19:16)	23 (16:45)	24 (01:53)	22 (23:14)	22 (12:25)
1972	22 (18:04)	23 (01:04)	22 (22:33)	23 (07:40)	22 (05:00)	21 (18:11)
1973	22 (23:57)	23 (06:55)	23 (04:22)	23 (13:30)	22 (10:52)	22 (00:05)
1974	23 (05:32)	23 (12:31)	23 (10:02)	23 (19:13)	22 (16:40)	22 (05:55)
1975	23 (11:24)	23 (18:26)	23 (15:57)	24 (01:09)	22 (22:33)	22 (11:47)
1976	22 (17:19)	23 (00:19)	22 (21:48)	23 (06:58)	22 (04:22)	21 (17:36)
1977	22 (23:03)	23 (06:00)	23 (03:28)	23 (12:39)	22 (10:06)	21 (23:23)
1978	23 (04:59)	23 (11:57)	23 (09:26)	23 (18:37)	22 (16:04)	22 (05:20)
1979	23 (10:47)	23 (17:46)	23 (15:17)	24 (00:28)	22 (21:54)	22 (11:09)
1980	22 (16:39)	22 (23:38)	22 (21:07)	23 (06:17)	22 (03:41)	21 (16:55)
1981	22 (22:37)	23 (05:35)	23 (03:03)	23 (12:12)	22 (09:36)	21 (22:51)
1982	23 (04:15)	23 (11:14)	23 (08:45)	23 (17:58)	22 (15:25)	22 (04:40)
1983	23 (10:05)	23 (17:08)	23 (14:41)	23 (23:53)	22 (21:19)	22 (10:32)
1984	22 (15:58)	22 (23:00)	22 (20:32)	23 (05:43)	22 (03:08)	21 (16:22)
1985	22 (21:35)	23 (04:35)	23 (02:07)	23 (11:21)	22 (08:49)	21 (22:06)
1986	23 (03:23)	23 (10:25)	23 (08:00)	23 (17:15)	22 (14:45)	22 (04:01)
1987	23 (09:06)	23 (16:09)	23 (13:45)	23 (23:01)	22 (20:31)	22 (09:47)
1988	22 (14:51)	22 (21:52)	22 (19:26)	23 (04:41)	22 (02:10)	21 (15:27)
1989	22 (20:45)	23 (03:45)	23 (01:17)	23 (10:31)	22 (08:01)	21 (21:19)
1990	23 (02:23)	23 (09:22)	23 (06:56)	23 (16:13)	22 (13:45)	22 (03:05)
1991	23 (08:13)	23 (15:15)	23 (12:50)	23 (22:06)	22 (19:35)	22 (08:52)
1992	22 (14:09)	22 (21:11)	22 (18:44)	23 (03:58)	22 (01:26)	21 (14:42)
1993	22 (19:51)	23 (02:50)	23 (00:23)	23 (09:39)	22 (07:09)	21 (20:28)
1994	23 (01:42)	23 (08:45)	23 (06:21)	23 (15:38)	22 (13:09)	22 (02:26)
1995	23 (07:31)	23 (14:36)	23 (12:14)	23 (21:32)	22 (19:03)	22 (08:19)
1996	22 (13:18)	22 (20:23)	22 (17:59)	23 (03:17)	22 (00:47)	21 (14:05)
1997	22 (19:13)	23 (02:18)	22 (23:55)	23 (09:13)	22 (06:46)	21 (20:05)
1998	23 (00:54)	23 (07:58)	23 (05:37)	23 (15:00)	22 (12:35)	22 (01:56)
1999	23 (06:44)	23 (13:49)	23 (11:30)	23 (20:52)	22 (18:25)	22 (07:44)
2000	22 (12:41)	22 (19:46)	22 (17:24)	23 (02:44)	22 (00:17)	21 (13:37)
2001	22 (18:24)	23 (01:24)	22 (23:01)	23 (08:21)	22 (05:57)	21 (19:19)
2002	23 (00:13)	23 (07:16)	23 (04:55)	23 (14:17)	22 (11:52)	22 (01:13)
2003	23 (06:04)	23 (13:08)	23 (10:47)	23 (20:08)	22 (17:42)	22 (07:01)
2004	22 (11:49)	22 (18:52)	22 (16:29)	23 (01:48)	21 (23:20)	21 (12:40)
2005	22 (17:41)	23 (00:44)	22 (22:22)	23 (07:42)	22 (05:15)	21 (18:35)
2006	22 (23:20)	23 (06:24)	23 (04:04)	23 (13:27)	22 (11:03)	22 (00:24)
2007	23 (05:04)	23 (12:11)	23 (09:53)	23 (19:16)	22 (16:50)	22 (06:09)
2008	22 (10:56)	22 (18:05)	22 (15:46)	23 (01:08)	21 (22:43)	21 (12:02)
2009	22 (16:35)	22 (23:40)	22 (21:21)	23 (06:45)	22 (04:23)	21 (17:46)
2010	22 (22:19)	23 (05:26)	23 (03:10)	23 (12:37)	22 (10:16)	21 (23:39)
2011	23 (04:09)	23 (11:18)	23 (09:03)	23 (18:30)	22 (16:09)	22 (05:31)
2012	22 (09:56)	22 (17:02)	22 (14:44)	23 (00:09)	21 (21:47)	21 (11:10)
2013	22 (15:50)	22 (22:55)	22 (20:38)	23 (06:03)	22 (03:43)	21 (17:07)
2014	22 (21:37)	23 (04:42)	23 (02:25)	23 (11:53)	22 (09:34)	21 (22:59)
2015	23 (03:27)	23 (10:34)	23 (08:17)	23 (17:44)	22 (15:22)	22 (04:44)
2016	22 (09:27)	23 (16:34)	22 (14:17)	22 (23:42)	21 (21:19)	21 (10:40)
2017	22 (15:13)	22 (22:17)	22 (19:59)	23 (05:24)	22 (03:03)	21 (16:27)
2018	22 (21:00)	23 (04:07)	23 (01:52)	23 (11:21)	22 (09:01)	21 (22:23)
2019	23 (02:51)	23 (10:02)	23 (07:49)	23 (17:18)	22 (14:57)	22 (04:19)

~ Sun Sign Tables ~

Other Titles Published by Flare
(with their current UK prices)

Bookstores and internet bookshops stock most Flare titles,
but if you wish to keep informed of new books as they become available,
please write to us at:
Flare Publications, 29 Dolben Street, London SE1 0UQ, England
(or fill in the order form at the back of this book),
or call: 0207 922 1123
or contact us at flareUK.com

The Draconic Chart - Rev. Pamela Crane   £16.99. Flare Pioneers Series
The fruit of 22 years' study and experience, Pamela Crane's important work is
now available in a new, enlarged and revised edition. This trail-blazing volume
unravels the history of Draconic and its meaning in the natal chart, synastry,
forecasting, in rectification and even horary with a host of examples. All this as
well as revealing Pamela Crane's own impassioned journey of discovery. Acquire
deeper insights into your life meaning, your driving principles, your spiritual
purpose, your karma and your vocation.

Shorthand of the Soul - David Hayward   £12.99. Flare Astro-Links Series
The first book to bridge the gap between the symbolic worlds of literature and
astrology, this inspirational collection of quotations with astrological references
provides an invaluable tool for both astrologers and students. A unique anthology
embracing every aspect of life, from professional thoughts to personal reflections,
you'll find David Hayward's collection amusing, provocative and enlightening.

British Entertainers - Frank C. Clifford
            Special Price: £5.99 (RRP: £9.99) Flare Astro-Profiles Series
This popular reference work combines astrology with concise biographies of
over 700 prominent personalities from the worlds of film, theatre, television,
comedy and music. It also uncovers the prime indicators of performing talent
in birth charts. All data are meticulously researched and classified.

Teachers and Group Study Organisers: please enquire about our special discounts
for purchases of six or more copies of each title.

In 2000, **Flare** will be publishing titles in astrology, palmistry, and other Mind
Body & Spirit disciplines (as well as publishing the first in a series of
entertainment books) from a number of writers, including: Christeen Skinner,
Richard J. Swatton, Frank C. Clifford, Peter Upton, and Jenni Dean.

For books, popular discounted titles, consultations, and giveaways,
check out our new website at:
www.flareUK.com